Predestined for Heaven?
Yes!

Examining Wrong Views of
The Doctrines of Grace

Jeffrey W. Alexander

Isa 30:18

Jeffrey W. Alexander

Predestined for Heaven? Yes!

*Examining Wrong Views of
The Doctrines of Grace*

Jeffrey W. Alexander

Published by Cause of God and Truth Publications
A ministry of Calvary Baptist Church of Lamar
907 South Third Street, Lamar, Colorado 81052-3415

All Scripture quotations are from the King James Version
unless otherwise noted.

PRINTED BY:
BRENTWOOD CHRISTIAN PRESS
4000 BEALLWOOD AVENUE
COLUMBUS, GEORGIA 31904

DEDICATION

This book is dedicated to the people of the Calvary Baptist Church of Lamar, Colorado, whose steadfast love and loyalty to God and His truth have been the inspiration for me to pursue this work.

PREFACE

There are many good books that have been published on the doctrine of sovereign-grace salvation. My purpose in adding this book is not to provide any new information or insight but rather to examine some current concepts of the gospel that deny God's sovereign grace in support of "free-will." Sometimes we accept an idea without considering the lurking difficulties because we have not asked the appropriate questions.

The subject of sovereign grace is closely linked to what has been called "Calvinism." I wish to make it clear at the onset that I would prefer to avoid the use of that term. *Calvinism* conjures up all sorts of images. Problems with the term abound. First, very few who reject the doctrine of sovereign-grace salvation understand the term *Calvinism* correctly. So, in approaching the subject, I would rather discuss issues than struggle over misunderstood terms. My first experience with *Calvinism* was a little book by Dr. John R. Rice, late evangelist and publisher of the *Sword of the Lord*, a weekly evangelistic periodical of interdenominational fundamentalism. In my uninformed beginnings, I considered Dr. Rice's examination of the position to be true and trustworthy. I have since discovered that Dr. Rice was woefully biased in his opinion, which bias seriously flawed his scholarship in approaching the subject.

Second, the term *Calvinism* is almost inseparably linked to covenant theology. Many find it impossible to divorce Calvinism from covenant doctrine—a marriage I do not support since I reject pedobaptism and amillennialism. Also, many covenant Calvinists (Puritans), arguing that the covenant made at Sinai was a covenant of grace, have erred in applying the Law of Moses to Christianity as a way of life. Those who take the New Testament position that believers are not under the Mosaic system often find themselves being falsely labeled antinomians even though they may believe in a sovereign-grace salvation.

Third, *Calvinism* is often falsely attributed to John Calvin, giving Calvinism's critics excuse to call it a "man-made" system that has no biblical support. No one "invented" the position that has come to bear Calvin's name, least of all John Calvin. Also, sovereign-grace salvation is biblical doctrine, not a system *per se*. It is the modern gospel of free will that is a man-made system.

4

Last, even as reformed covenant theologians hold, the doctrine of sovereign-grace salvation has been taught since the days of the apostles. It is not new. *Calvinism* as a label dates from 1618, but the doctrine itself is New Testament.

Even after saying all this, it is nearly impossible to avoid the label *Calvinism* because there is a certain convenience in labels. For this reason, I implore the reader to think past the term and focus on the facts, weighing them in light of Scripture. Since consistent Scriptural interpretation divides the issue into only two camps, free-will salvation (Arminianism) and sovereign grace (Calvinism), I encourage all readers who think themselves to be neither Calvinists (or less than five-point Calvinists) nor Arminians to compare their beliefs with Arminian doctrines. Such readers may be surprised to find that they are in greater agreement with Arminianism than with Calvinism, even though they may hold to eternal security (the reason most evangelicals reject the term *Arminian*).

The whole controversy can be reduced to this: which view focuses upon human "free will" while limiting God's will? On the other hand, which view exalts and magnifies the Lord by promoting His free will? It is my desire that the reader who may be having difficulty sorting out the issues may find this volume helpful. Since much of the misunderstanding on the topics covered in this volume arise from varying definitions, I have included a glossary.

CONTENTS

INTRODUCTION

"John answered and said, A man can receive nothing, except it be given him from heaven."

–John 3:27

The past century has witnessed changing attitudes and actions in many Christians. There seems to be a subtle but very real general rebellion against and a pulling away from the old standards of purity and holiness in the churches. Some of this resistance is perhaps a justifiable reaction to the false proposition that mere conformity to rules is a means of acceptance and a proof of spirituality. However, a significant part of this reluctance is evidence of a more serious problem: a lack of spiritual power—power that ought to produce personal holiness and unconditional submission to God's standards.

On the other hand, according to reliable information, "Christianity" claims a larger segment of the world's population than ever before. In an effort to show an optimistic view of the spiritual climate of the times, author Jim Peterson shows us that "forty-two percent of all adults in America attend religious services at least once a week"; that "nearly one in every three Americans now claim[s] to have been 'born again'"; that today "1300 radio stations—one out of every seven in America—is Christian owned and operated"; and that evangelical publishers now account for a third of the total domestic commercial book sales.[1]

While this news appears to be hopeful, the fact is today's culture of secularization (the "new heathenism") is overrunning the culture of the Reformation.[2] In spite of Christianity's growing prominence, its influence on society is actually diminishing. At the very least, many professed believers show little outwardly perceivable distinction from unbelievers. Sadly, much of the modern gospel-related experience compares little to that which Paul describes of the Thessalonian church:

> *For our gospel came not unto you in word only, but also in power, and in the Holy Ghost, and in much assurance . . . having received the word in much affliction, with joy of the Holy Ghost: So that ye were ensamples to all that believe in Macedonia and Achaia . . . how ye turned to God from idols to serve the living and true God* (I Thessalonians 1:5-10).

7

WHY NO THESSALONIAN RESULTS TODAY?

Why is it that modern gospel work does not produce Thessalonian results? Perhaps we have been guilty of "altering" the true gospel message so that it depends more on appeal and persuasion than on the power of God. Perhaps the skill of salesmanship has been substituted for the work of the Holy Spirit. If so, are we then failing to look at the evidence and to see that *"the working of his mighty power"* (Ephesians 1:19) is missing? Of the supposed thirty-three percent of the population who claim to be "born again," how many truly evidence a genuine spiritual regeneration with spiritual fruit? Jesus said, *"By their fruits ye shall know them"* (Matthew 7:20).

These serious questions demand that we reexamine the theology and application of our gospel message. But even to suggest such an idea creates controversy. In spite of Scriptural admonitions (II Corinthians 13:5; II Peter 1:10), many Christians are not interested in probing the genuineness of their spiritual experience in the light of biblically definable standards. There are reasons for this reluctance. First, Christianity is dominated by subjective empiricism that teaches us to evaluate our encounters by how we feel they should be. Second, we pride ourselves in "being right"; thus, questioning one's beliefs and practices can be too threatening, especially if there are already nagging doubts.[3] Third, the dogmatic spirit of traditional evangelicalism[4] conditions one to believe that, in spite of glaring inconsistencies, one must never question an adopted position. Of course, one ought to be suspicious of "new" or "different" doctrine. Suspicion is natural and healthy, but closed minds are not now nor ever have been good for the church.

A "New" Gospel of Christian Humanism?

Tragically, this climate has allowed "the humanist theology of Erasmus of Rome"[5] to capture fundamental[6] and evangelical pulpits. Although many preach salvation by grace, their "new gospel" insists that spiritually dead sinners can act like living beings and cooperate with God without first having a spiritual resurrection (regeneration). Noted author J. I. Packer writes:

> Without realizing it, we have during the past century bartered that [old] gospel for a substitute product which, though it looks similar enough in points of detail, is as a whole a decidedly different thing. Hence our troubles; for the substitute product does not answer the ends for which the authentic gospel has in past days proved itself so mighty. Why?

8

We would suggest that the reason lies in its own character and content. It fails to make men God-centered in their thoughts and God-fearing in their hearts because this is not primarily what it is trying to do. One way of stating the difference between it and the old gospel is to say that it is too exclusively concerned to be "helpful" to man—to bring peace, comfort, happiness, satisfaction— and too little concerned to glorify God.[7]

This "new" helpful gospel, based on man's supposed inherent ability to choose for Christ in salvation, has gradually gained popularity since the Reformation. In modern times it has become the major evangelical position on salvation due in no small part to the popular philosophical and theological underpinnings of John Wesley's modified Arminianism with its "prevenient grace," Charles Finney's self-generated revivalism with its "new methods," and D. L. Moody's gospel of "sudden conversion" with its manipulative music, "feeling" faith, and "experience" assurance.[8] These men held doctrines rooted in the error of Pelagianism (fifth century), fostered in the philosophy of humanism (fifteenth and sixteenth centuries), and defined in the theology of Jacobus Arminius (seventeenth century).

A Christianity of Hodgepodge Doctrine

This trend in modern evangelical thinking has produced an age of "hodgepodge Christianity" in which many Christians hold a shallow blend of diverse and conflicting theological opinions based on what they pick up from various doctrinally divergent popular Christian personalities. The confusion that results can be blamed on lack of discernment, and lack of discernment can be blamed on negligence to investigate the biblical accuracy of what Christians receive through books, radio, TV, or even the pulpit (Acts 17:10, 11). We may charge this negligence of Christians to be discerning and this reluctance to clearly define beliefs to three failures:

First, many *professed Christians* are strangely reluctant to study the doctrines of God's Word on their own.[9] Of course, the time and discipline of study discourage many, but that is no excuse. Satan does produce counterfeit Christianity, and "when he is at work, as 'an angel of light,' he does his best work when men blindly accept, instead of wisely testing, [sic] the results."[10] A discerning believer needs an understanding of God's Word for authentic spiritual development (Hebrews 5:11-14).

Second, many *practical Christians* view the science of theology with suspicion as the domain of "the scholarly intellect, the self-sufficient and proud-minded."[11] They see it as the playing field of those who delight in philosophical but impractical mental gymnastics. They

9

also see it as promoting divisiveness with theological shibboleths. Sadly, there is some justification for this charge, but theology is, nevertheless, a necessary and worthy science.

Third, many *precipitate Christians* want to abandon doctrine altogether because of a misdirected zeal for "Christian unity." However, only truth can produce true unity. False unity is based on so-called love. I say "so-called" love because genuine love *"rejoices in the truth"* (I Corinthians 13:6) while the usual nebulous concept called *love* is intolerant of doctrine. Sectarianism is the anathema of transdenominationalism. Christians who stand on doctrinal issues are labeled as intolerant and divisive. Seeking to avoid this censure, many Christians simply dodge any reference to doctrine in order to find acceptance with the broadest base of Christianity. They fail to understand that true Biblical unity can be achieved only on doctrinal grounds.

A WORD OF CAUTION

Before we investigate the faulty views of the gospel current in evangelical philosophy, we wish to issue a caution. Obviously, among those who recognize a "problem," all will not agree with our interpretation of that problem. Christian charity is needed for discussion, and the dispute must center on doctrine and philosophy, not on the character of persons holding the differing opinions. Thus, in citing names, we are not contending with the persons but with their opinions.

Of course, we will have disagreement. Among those who disagree, there are at least three kinds: (1) Those who definitely disagree but disagree agreeably. These are usually mature individuals, well grounded, though perhaps in error as to what they believe. (2) Those who are not sure of their position but disagree agreeably. Most of these are open to discuss their differences. They attempt to use the opportunity of disagreement to grow in their understanding of what to believe. (3) Those who disagree disagreeably. These people will not even tolerate a position with which they do not agree. Perhaps they feel somehow threatened by an opposing position, or they are simply unwilling to search out the question in order to understand an opinion that differs from their own.

No matter what philosophy of Christianity we hold, God's Word requires us to *"love one another"* (John 13:34). This does not preclude debate. The Apostle Paul's approach to dealing with those who differed with his gospel was to debate them. *"And Paul, as his manner was . . . reasoned [dialegomai, 'to dispute'] with them out of the Scriptures"* (Acts 17:2). Therefore, in the interest of defining the truth, let us debate! If we are wrong, let us be correctable by Scripture.

10

1

DOESN'T THE BIBLE SETTLE IT?

Theology,[12] unfortunately, is receiving bad billing in these days. It is a tedious and boring class in Bible colleges and seminaries; just ask the students. The reason for this attitude lies in the philosophical nature of the science. Theology requires thinking, and this generation does not like to think. We have been conditioned by television and Hollywood to be entertained. This is, no doubt, one reason why the sovereign-grace gospel has fallen into such disfavor. It does not suit the "entertain-me-so-that-I-feel-good" mentality of modern churchgoers. Our day needs a revival of the spirit of the Reformation with its battle cry, "*Sola Scriptura*" (Scripture only).

Theology is necessary to organize and define truths gleaned from Scripture. In the debates that have arisen throughout church history, theology has served to clarify and answer issues. The creeds of Christendom are the products of these debates. For example, the Nicene Creed was the answer to the fourth-century debate with the Arians over the nature of Christ.[13] It stands today as the orthodox position on Christ's deity. Although it still has its detractors (the modernists and Jehovah's Witnesses), all orthodox Christians accept the Nicene Creed as the statement of the Scriptures on the nature of Christ. However, all orthodox Christians do not accept the Canons of Dort (or Dordt) as the declaration of the Scriptures on the gospel of salvation. Let us clarify what we mean by the sovereign-grace (Calvinistic) view of the gospel of salvation.

FLOWERS AND SUCH

Tulips

The sovereign-grace gospel in this book refers to those Scriptural truths summarized in the acrostic *TULIP*. These truths constitute the old gospel of sovereign grace in salvation. Even in this, we are careful to note that we find problems with the terminology traditionally expressed in the acrostic. The Presbyterian theologian R. C. Sproul has expressed our view on this:

> Unfortunately, [the acrostic *TULIP*] has also caused
> great confusion and much misunderstanding. The

11

problem with acrostics is that the best terms we have for ideas don't always start with letters that will spell neat little words. The acrostic serves well as a memory device, but that is about all.[14]

We also wish to make it clear that the "five points" merely assist us in explaining *one point*—the Bible teaches us that *God saves sinners.* The "five points" form an unbreakable unity and merely detail the facets of that one fact—God alone saves sinners.

Total Depravity

"*T*" stands for "total depravity," which describes the condition of mankind in sin—that a sinner, by nature, is both *unwilling* and spiritually *unable* to respond on his own in repentance and faith to God. Inability does not mean that the sinner has no natural faculties (understanding and will) to respond to the gospel. Nor does it mean that a sinner is as bad as he could be. The sinner's inability is due to the fact that he has a moral nature that is corrupted by sin (Romans 7:5, 10, 11; Jeremiah 13:23; Romans 8:6-8). Because of this, an unregenerate sinner will never *will* to be saved. His nature is like a magnet that is naturally attracted to the world and sin while conversely repelled by the things of God and righteousness. Until the sinner's "polarity" is changed, he *cannot* and *will not* be attracted to Christ for salvation. It is this inability to believe the gospel that makes all the other "points" essential. If it were left to the sinner to respond out of his rebellious nature to receive his own salvation, *no one would be saved* (Psalm 51:5; 58:3; Genesis 6:5; Ecclesiastes 9:3; Jeremiah 17:9; I Corinthians 2:14; John 6:44).

Unconditional Election

Therefore, if anyone is going to be saved, God must do the saving. In His sovereign grace, He has chosen to save a great host of sinners, elected by Him *"according to His own purpose and grace"* (II Timothy 1:9) wholly apart from anything which He foresees in them, such as whether they will believe or how they will live. Grace, by definition, makes salvation the free and *unconditional* choice of God—the "*U*" in TULIP (II Thessalonians 2:13, 14; Titus 1:1; Romans 11:5; I Peter 1:1, 2; Ephesians 1:4; Acts 13:48; I Thessalonians 1:4).

Limited Atonement

In order to save these elect sinners, God provided for them a Savior who (1) demonstrably lived up to their responsibility to God's holy law and (2) suffered the judgment due to them under the wrath of God because of their sin and failure. The satisfaction of judgment,

12

which the Savior made to God through His sacrifice on the cross with its accompanying intercession, actually secures the salvation of those for whom He was given as a Savior. Thus, redemption is for these elect only. Rather than "limited atonement" (the *"L"* in *TULIP*), the term "particular redemption"—the redemption of His sheep (John 10:11)—would better describe this concept (Matthew 1:21; 20:28; Acts 20:28; Ephesians 5:25; Hebrews 2:17; 9:15, 28; Revelation 5:9).

Irresistible Grace

The *"I"* of *TULIP* stands for "irresistible grace"—the work of God's Spirit whereby the elect are effectually and inwardly called to participate in the salvation which God offers through the gospel. *Irresistible grace* might be better termed *effectual inward calling*. This point is the second most-resisted point (after particular redemption) because people somehow see irresistible grace as God's coercing sinners against their wills. This interpretation misconstrues the doctrine, for it assumes that some sinners, who are not elect, would wish to be saved while others, who are saved, may not have wanted to be saved. This just is not so. To propose that God coerces sinners against their will would be to accuse God of unrighteousness—an absurd presumption in any theology. Rather, in changing the "polarity" of the sinner's desire by regeneration, God makes it possible for sinners to choose Christ. Those thus "called" are given all the gifts of grace and faith needed for them to respond freely to the gospel. Through the work of the Word of God and the Spirit of God (gospel work), the elect yield to Christ and salvation willingly, happily, and gratefully. Those not "called" have already freely made their choice for sin and are left to the consequences of it. *Irresistible grace* does not mean that sinners cannot, for a time, resist and fight against God. Scripture and experience show otherwise. But God's purpose ultimately prevails (John 3:8; Acts 16:14; Ephesians 2:8; Colossians 2:12; II Timothy 1:9; Romans 1:6, 7; Ephesians 4:4).

Perseverance of the Saints

Salvation results in the elect sinner's becoming a new creature in Christ. The evidence for this work of grace is submissive obedience to the will of God and growing conformity of the child of God to Christ and holiness. Unlike the evangelical modification of *perseverance of the saints* to *eternal security*, which is more of a personal benefit than an evidence of grace, the *perseverance of the saints* stresses the responsibility of the believer to live a holy and godly life by the grace and power of God. This is the *"P"* of *TULIP* (John 10:27-30; 17:11; I Peter 1:5).

Some have argued that *perseverance of the saints* sounds as if our final salvation rests on our ability to persevere. *"[H]e that endureth to the end shall be saved"* (Matthew 10:22). Interpreting such verses may take two paths.[15] Free-willers teach that salvation depends upon one's holding out to the end. The sovereign-grace gospel argues that one's holding out to the end is the result of God's grace enabling the believer to persevere.[16] Steadfastness is the evidence of election, not the cause of it.

The whole work of salvation is thus powerfully and clearly summed up in the "golden chain" of Romans 8:30:

Moreover whom he did predestinate [to be chosen in Christ by His elective love to be like Christ], *them he also called* [by His effectual inward call through the gospel]: *and whom he called, them he also justified* [declared righteous by the substitutionary redemptive work of Christ]: *and whom he justified, them he also glorified* [securing their everlasting acceptance in holiness and righteousness by the sanctifying work of the Holy Spirit and the priestly work of Christ's intercession before the Father's throne].

improper definition

God did not predestinate us to be saved. He predestinated the result of our decision — heaven or hell.

What? No Flowers to Smell?

The free-will gospel has no acrostic to spell a flower name like *TULIP.*[17] In fact, the whole issue of "five points" arises out of a controversy in the Church of Holland in the early seventeenth century when the followers of James Arminius sued for the right to be recognized as orthodox in the church. They are the ones who set forth their "five points."

Partial Ability

Free-will gospel advocates reject "total depravity" in favor of "moral ability"—that sinners *can* be persuaded to choose salvation in their natural sinful state without God's first changing the polarity of the soul. They believe that *the sinner's will*, though damaged by sin, can choose good with the help of enlightenment and wooing from God. This moral ability, as we shall see, is due either to the fact that (1) Adam's fall was only a bad example to his posterity (Pelagianism); or that (2) Adam's fall did not totally corrupt the race (semi-Pelagianism); or that (3) Adam's fall did totally corrupt the race, but moral ability was restored to all the race by Christ's death in order to enable lost sinners to freely chose or reject salvation (John Wesley's prevenient grace).

When the sin can understand what and why it was necessary for God to become Christ in Jesus — then man will make the

14

the proper choice. But when man decides that's to easy I must have to "do" something he will not be saved

All Foreseen Faith Elected

Therefore, election is seen as "conditional" (dependent on the sinner's being persuaded to take the gospel offer) rather than "unconditional" (the free and sovereign election of God). Some modern evangelicals teach that election has nothing to do with salvation. However, Arminians have historically believed that election is God's choosing for salvation those whom He *foresees* will respond in faith to Christ. _incorrect/wrong_

Non-Discriminatory Atonement

Free-will advocates argue that fairness, which they confuse with God's justice, requires that God make salvation available to all; therefore, Christ's death was an atonement for the sins of every person who has lived in the world since Adam. God wants all sinners to be saved if they will only "make a decision" for Christ. Sinners will be punished, not because they are sinners but because they have rejected Christ. Christ's dying for everyone leaves them without excuse.

Saving Grace Resisted

Grace is redefined as God's freely providing an opportunity for salvation to anyone who will believe and receive Christ. Since it requires the sinner's response, grace can be rejected. Therefore, the "calling" of sinners to salvation is only an outward gospel announcement and is not "irresistible" or "effectual" in itself.

You Can Lose It

Finally, since God's saving work is contingent upon the response of the sinner, *salvation is conditional*. The saved sinner is not only responsible to be saved but to "keep saved." (not a) Negligence and sin may cost the believer his salvation, which he may or may not recover.[18]

It is interesting that many evangelicals will, with modification, reject the fifth point of Arminianism in favor of "eternal security." It would be more consistent with the whole scheme of Arminianism to believe in a conditional salvation, but eternal security is a more desirable benefit to believers. It is reassuring to be "secure" even if one is living a deliberately sinful and disobedient life. However, if it is within the power of the individual to receive salvation, would it not also logically follow that it is within his power to change his mind about being saved? Eternal security cannot therefore be a logical result of a conditional salvation.

It is the conditional nature of free-will salvation that makes it so popular. This gospel stresses the freedom of will to the point of limiting God to only "wishing" to fulfill what He purposes. People love

Man can claim (a emotional)15 salvation and not be saved. He still thinks he did something. If there's no change in the life there's no salvation!

their "free will"—the "Arminian idol," as the Puritan John Owen (1616-1683) called it.[19] Everyone likes to make his own choices even if he is reluctant to own up to the responsibility and consequences that go with them.[20]

SEARCHING FOR TREASURE

If, as is proposed here, the clash between the free-will and sovereign-grace gospels is philosophical in nature, then would it not be easy to settle the issue by simply appealing to the Scriptures? Without question, each position sees its view as the position of Scripture. Both cite Scripture references with remarks such as, "The verse plainly shows . . ." or "Exegesis clearly supports . . ." as if the passage obviously settles the issue. This practice is called "proof texting," however, and focuses on "proving points" rather than on expounding the Scripture.

One can throw verses back and forth all day without either side budging in the least. This leads one to ask, "Why did God not write these truths more plainly in Scripture? Is a required special gift of discernment given to a select few in order to discover the 'hidden truth'?" One would suppose that the whole controversy over the gospel could have been avoided entirely if God had arranged the Bible in a more doctrinally systematic order. One could then turn to the doctrine of salvation and find a clear and precise statement on the subject. But the Bible is not so arranged.

The fact is Scripture does not quickly or easily yield its truths. On the other hand, neither does understanding of Scripture require a degree from seminary. However, in order to come to the truth of Scripture, it is absolutely necessary to move past "proof texting." A correct interpretation of Scripture does require the special gift of spiritual enlightenment by the Holy Spirit (I Corinthians 2:7-16; Psalm 19:8; 119:30, 105; Isaiah 8:20; II Peter 1:19). Therefore, understanding revealed truth requires both the illumination of God's Spirit and diligent study (John 8:47; II Timothy 2:15). This process of discovering truth is not unlike prospecting for gold. It requires the same tenacity of the old prospector pursuing the elusive lode (Proverbs 2:1-5). God, in His great wisdom, has chosen that truth must be extracted from the whole fabric of the Word of God by a process consisting of comparing Scripture with Scripture and praying fervently with a seeking heart and an attitude of meekness and humility for God's revelation and enlightenment (Ephesians 1:17, 18).

If one supposes that he has "struck the vein" of truth, he must have the "ore" assayed in the crucible of controversy and debate in

[handwritten margin note: that alone will not save—It can strengthen the true belief]

order to prove the ore's genuineness. Therefore, debate must be welcomed. The goal is to become personally knowledgeable and Scripturally accurate in one's interpretation of the Word of God. One may think he has arrived at the truth, but in the controversy of debate the weaknesses in his arguments are revealed and the strengths of his arguments are fortified. This search is far more serious than that for temporal wealth; its finding has *eternal* consequences.

This controversy brings the stubbornness (if I may use this word in a good sense) of strong faith to those who are convinced of the truth (Hebrews 10:32-39). It is the stuff by which martyrs are prepared. Strong faith made the Polycarps remain unflinching as they faced the flames; the John Bunyans triumph under the rigors of Bedford jails; the Martin Luthers take their uncompromising stands in the face of great opposition and danger.

In a letter discussing a point of disagreement over these very doctrines, the letter writer challenged the recipient: "We want this to be a serious investigation of the Scriptures, not a debate nor an investigation of men's opinions." The challenge is great advice; however, the two opposing points of view set forth in this chapter have already received long and careful attention. The debate is not likely to end with my contribution either. Paul made an interesting statement in I Corinthians 11:19: *"For there must also be heresies* [parties or sects] *among you that they which are approved may be made manifest among you."* It is God who will make the approval clear, perhaps not fully until the judgment seat of Christ. Nevertheless, believers need to devote themselves to studying the issues and considering all the arguments for the sake of the love of the truth. This is how God makes *"manifest"* those *"which are approved among you."* Let us study to show ourselves approved! The Bible does settle it.

— if that is so —why would it seem so inconsistent to believe that salvation is of God yet requires belief from the sinner

17

In it's narrowest sense it would mean one who believes in the Bible as defined from the original definitions, translation not interpretation

2

LET'S WATCH THOSE LABELS

Nobody likes labels, especially when a label provokes controversy. Labels, however, are useful for identification. Some people might prefer to say that they are "Biblicists," but *Biblicist* does not identify what one believes. Both sovereign-grace (Calvinist) and free-will (non-Calvinist) gospels claim to be "Bible-only" gospels; thus, a precise doctrinal statement is a must to identify what one really believes. When one defines his beliefs succinctly, he gets a label. Charles Spurgeon observed:

> In the controversy [between sovereign-grace and free-will gospels] which has raged—a controversy which, I again say, I believe to have been rather healthy, and which has done us all a vast amount of good—mistakes have arisen from two reasons. Some brethren have altogether forgotten one order of truths, and then, in the next place, they have gone too far with others. We all have one blind eye, and too often we are like Nelson in the battle. We put the telescope to that blind eye, and then protest that we cannot see. . . . We do not want to see a truth, and therefore we say that we cannot see it.[21]

Spurgeon's evaluation remains true today. Many have a "blind eye," tending to overreact or go to extremes. The extremes in this controversy are actually *hyper*-Calvinism and Arminianism. As Spurgeon aptly pointed out, people tend to err in two directions. The sovereign-grace position (Calvinism), properly understood, is the middle ground of these two extremes *because it accepts both God's absolute sovereignty and man's moral responsibility,* though not on an equal footing.

People who react negatively to the truths that emphasize God's sovereignty in salvation do not understand how one can relate sovereign election to human responsibility and power of choice. Their failure is based on wrong assumptions. Clearing up these difficulties requires an attitude of humility and openness to examine one's presumptions.

A brother in Christ once explained to me that his former pastor had been accused of being a "Calvinist." My friend became curious.

He knew that the issue was the subject of a long and unresolved debate and that he was in no position to settle the dispute. He was determined, at least, to understand the issues. He told me, "I did not care which side was right; I just wanted to understand the question." The only thing that matters is the truth. If we are content to defend merely a *position*, we may find that in the end, we have lost everything. On the other hand, if it is the truth we must know, no matter how repugnant it may seem to us or how unpopular it is, we shall know the truth if God is pleased to reveal the truth (John 8:31, 32).

HOW DO THEY DEFINE IT?

A sovereign-grace gospel is obnoxious to sinful humans. Whatever people hate, they distort in order to make it more repulsive. This hatred makes people stubbornly refuse to be corrected in their contortions. Thus, their opposition to God's freedom to predestinate certain sinners to salvation proceeds from error. Then, the doctrine of election and predestination (sovereign-grace salvation) is defined something like this: "the dogma of a tyrant God who forces His will on poor helpless humans, deciding eternal destinies with neither human consultation nor consent." They argue that election condemns the non-elect to a horrible fate. One critic promoted this inaccuracy: "Four of the points [of the "five points"] named are expressly worded to teach that some are ordained to be damned."[22]

Just What Did He Mean by That?

This same faulty conception is expressed in another place, "Does God really predestinate some people to be saved and predestinate others to go to Hell, so that they have no free choice?"[23] In order to answer the question and to show the complexity of the issue, we must ask what the writer meant by "predestinate some people to be saved." Obviously, he believes that *every* fallen sinner *deserves* the opportunity to be saved. This is not so. No sinner is entitled to salvation. God, in His mercy, chose to save some undeserving sinners while allowing the rest to suffer the punishment their guilt warrants.

We must also ask what is meant by "predestinate others to go to Hell." The implication is that God is unrighteous if He condemns multitudes of sinners to perdition without first providing them an opportunity to escape that condemnation. On the contrary, God's justice requires Him to punish sinners. He is under no obligation to intervene in mercy, nor is He unrighteous for not intervening.

What is meant by "free choice"? Did the sinners who are sentenced to hell "freely" chose to do the evil for which they are judged

19

and condemned? If so, we agree. Sinners choose what they naturally desire—to sin; God does not make them sin.

Does "free choice" mean that sinners in their natural condition could "freely" choose an offer of salvation to escape their condemnation? If so, we disagree because sinners do not see themselves as offending God. The idea of salvation is repugnant to those who love their sin.

Supposed human "free will" is the point at issue. Sovereign-grace teachers do not deny that a sinner has the power of volition but that a sinner simply will not choose against his natural inclination. That is why God must do the saving. The sovereign-grace gospel says that when the sinner chooses to repent and trust Christ, it is because God has wrought a supernatural work in him to change his nature (Philippians 2:13). But the majority of evangelicals today believe that God cannot save sinners "*except* as he [the sinner] chooses, *of his own free will*, to repent of sin and trust Christ for salvation."[24]

Free-will theology gives "choice" the most powerful place in the universe. While free-willers would never say that their "free will" is *actually* greater than God's omnipotence (we refrain from argument for the purpose of discussion), they do consider it so important that they expect God to restrain Himself in dealing with humans. When God declares, *"I have purposed it, I will also do it"* (Isaiah 46:11), the free-willer arrogantly answers, "Not without the sinner's nod!" He believes that God, who *"is not willing that any should perish,"* will be frustrated by the perishing of multitudes of sinners who "of their own free will" refuse salvation! God *"purposed it,"* but He cannot *"do it."* What a gross denial of God's Word and power! Herein lies the crux of the argument.

Hate It? Call It "Hyper."

Because the sovereign-grace gospel is orthodox, being established in history and theology, it is difficult to impugn. Therefore, free-will gospel advocates not only distort the doctrine of election to salvation, but also cloak their attack, using labels such as "extreme Calvinism," "excessive Calvinism," and "hyper-Calvinism." However, on careful examination one discovers that what they attack as "hyper-Calvinism" is not hyper-Calvinism at all but simply sovereign-grace doctrine. Several examples of both distortion and subterfuge should be obvious as the reader proceeds.

Hyper-Calvinism Defined

In my study I have found four definitions of *hyper-Calvinism.* (1) The correct definition is a belief that in the preaching of the gospel an offer of salvation should not be made in the general hearing of any audience which may contain a mix of elect and non-elect. The offer of salvation is only for those who manifest signs of election, such as a definite interest or a deep conviction of sin.[25] The Gospel Standard Baptists of England maintain hyper-Calvinism in their confession of faith. Article 33 reads:

> Therefore, that for ministers in the present day to address unconverted persons, or indiscriminately all in a mixed congregation, calling upon them savingly to repent, believe, and receive Christ, or perform any other acts dependent upon the new creative power of the Holy Spirit, is, on the one hand, to imply creature power, and on the other, to deny the doctrine of special redemption.[26]

While not outright opposing evangelism and missions, this position certainly discourages them. This is true hyper-Calvinism.

(2) Some think that hyper-Calvinism is supralapsarianism (see Glossary).

(3) Others think hyper-Calvinism is a denial of the "well-meant offer of the gospel." The "well-meant offer" is the teaching that God *desires* the salvation of all men, even reprobates, although He has purposed to save only the elect. This teaching, which has come to prominence in Reformed circles, is based on the misunderstanding that God desires some things that He has not been pleased actually to bring to pass. This does not mean that God is frustrated by these unfulfilled desires, for He accomplishes all His will. Is this confusing? Reformed professors John Murray and Ned Stonehouse explain:

> We have found that God himself expresses an ardent desire for the fulfillment of certain things which he has not decreed in his inscrutable counsel to come to pass. This means that there is a will to the realization of what he has not decretively willed, a pleasure towards that which he has not been pleased to decree. This is indeed mysterious. . . .[Mysterious? No! Rather, it is baffling!][27]

Dr. John Gerstner comments:

> This is not "mystery" but bald contradiction, as these two fine Reformed theologians well realized. . . . Since we know that God does not desire what God does not desire, for this is evident on every page of Scripture, as well as in the logical nature of God and man, we know this exegesis is in error. . . .

21

John Murray and Ned Stonehouse . . . have difficulty offering a limited Atonement unlimitedly. But
what is the problem? The evangelist says, as ever,
"Whosoever will, let him come." "Believe on the Lord
Jesus Christ and thou shalt be saved." There never was
any other offer of the gospel and there never need be
any other. Surely, the limited Atonement in no way
limits *that* offer, and that is the only offer there ever
was or will be.[28]

Any who oppose this idea of a "well-meant offer" (which is
an accommodation to Arminian doctrine) are called *hyper-*
Calvinists, even though such a view has never been entertained as
genuine Calvinism.

(4) Many evangelicals teach that hyper-Calvinism is believing
all or most of the "five points." One writer, though not consistent in
his definition, seemed to define hyper-Calvinism as a belief in
more than one point: "Those whom we call hyper-Calvinists
usually outline their doctrinal position as represented by the letters
TULIP."[29] Most evangelicals side with one point of Calvinism
because they reject the notion that one may lose his salvation.
However, they hold that believing the "Calvinistic position of the
'Five Points'"[30] is excessive or extreme—*hyper*-Calvinism. That
also is not hyper-Calvinism. That misunderstanding leads to confusion, especially when a "five-pointer" speaks negatively of
hyper-Calvinism.

How do five-point sovereign-grace teachers (Calvinists) explain
hyper-Calvinism? Kenneth Talbot and Gary Crampton say:

Hyper-Calvinism, as the name indicates, is a perversion of Calvinism. It goes over or beyond (hyper)
what Calvinism teaches. It stresses the sovereignty of
God to the exclusion of man's responsibility. In its
attempt to exalt the honor and glory of God, hyper-
Calvinism so emphasizes His irresistible grace, that it
essentially eliminates the need to evangelize. The
secret will of God is so accentuated, that the revealed
will is de-emphasized. The result is a truncated view of
the free offer of the gospel.[31]

Hyper-Calvinism is not wrong doctrine so much as wrong application of doctrine.

WAS SPURGEON A HYPER-CALVINIST?

To demonstrate the sort of confusion that exists over the label *hyper-Calvinism*, consider the treatment of Charles Haddon Spurgeon, the Baptist pastor of the great Metropolitan Tabernacle in London during the latter half of the nineteenth century. Although he died a hundred years ago, Spurgeon, through his writings, remains very popular with multitudes of Christians today. He was a sovereign-grace gospel preacher. In his sermon "Christ Crucified," Spurgeon wrote:

> I have my own private opinion that there is no such a thing as preaching Christ and Him crucified, unless you preach what nowadays is called Calvinism. I have my own ideas, and those I state boldly. It is a nickname to call it Calvinism; Calvinism is the gospel, and nothing else.[32]

The late evangelist and writer, Dr. John R. Rice (1934-1980), published a tabloid periodical called *The Sword of the Lord*.[33] In the paper he printed sermons from both past and contemporary preachers. The sermons of Charles Spurgeon appeared regularly. Rice's treatment of Spurgeon is, therefore, confusing.[34] Spurgeon was what Dr. Rice would, by his own definition, term a hyper-Calvinist because of Spurgeon's belief in predestination as defined in the "five points." Spurgeon produced a little volume called *T-U-L-I-P*, in which he wrote, "We believe in the five great points commonly known as *Calvinistic* . . . five bright emanations springing from the glorious covenant of our triune God, and illustrating the great doctrine of Jesus crucified."[35]

Dr. Rice redefines Spurgeon's theology based on his own erroneous definition of hyper Calvinism:

> Charles Spurgeon, great and blessed London preacher, was a Calvinist though he spoke against "hyper-Calvinism," and called it that; and his hyper-Calvinist friends criticized him for preaching that "whosoever will" may come. . . . So Spurgeon did not really believe all the points of hyper-Calvinism, did not believe that some sinners are not called [n]or could repent.[36]

Dr. Rice's conclusion that Spurgeon did not believe all the points of TULIP is based on (1) the fact that Spurgeon "spoke against 'hyper-Calvinism,' and called it that" because Rice defined *hyper-Calvinism* as belief in "all the [five] points." (2) Spurgeon preached "that 'whosoever will' may come," something Rice concludes cannot be preached by one who believes in the five points because that would mean "some sinners are not called" to repent. Why call them?

We answer: (1) Spurgeon did believe all five points. Since hyper-Calvinism is properly defined as failure to evangelize, Spurgeon spoke against those Calvinists who neglected the duty of evangelism by over-stressing God's sovereignty. Spurgeon's balance in stressing both God's sovereignty and human responsibility is easy to observe. (2) Preaching "whosoever will" is both biblical and Calvinistic.[37] That Calvinists do practice biblical evangelism is also clearly evidenced by Spurgeon.

Dr. Rice sought to minimize Spurgeon's Calvinism:

> Some Christians, like Charles H. Spurgeon, have *nominally* held to Calvin's position without spending much time on it and without having their lives ruined by it. Spurgeon lived in a time when the two great clashing systems of religious thought were Arminianism and Calvinism. Spurgeon believed in the great doctrines of grace, of man's fallen condition, that man could be saved only by grace without works, and that God keeps those He saves. So Spurgeon *nominally* accepted Calvinism. And so there is an *occasional reference* to election and predestination in Spurgeon's preaching. But it was *not with him a major matter.* He had a burning heart, the fullness of the Spirit, and so he pressed always to get sinners saved [emphasis mine].[38]

Was Spurgeon only "nominally" a Calvinist? *Nominally* means "in name only; not really." Dr. Rice was wrong, and his attempts to use the Calvinist/Arminian controversy to explain away Spurgeon's Calvinism is also wrong. That is like saying a fundamentalist warrior like W. B. Riley was not really a fundamentalist. He was only "nominally" a fundamentalist because he did not want to be known as a modernist in the controversy with theological liberalism!

The truth is that the youthful Spurgeon preached his Calvinism in the New Park Street Chapel at a time when orthodoxy was dead and Arminian influence was strong in the evangelical churches of England. In a letter to a friend written in 1855, Spurgeon wrote: "My position, as pastor of one of the most influential churches, enables me to make myself heard and my daily labour is to revive the old doctrines of Gill, Owen, Calvin, Augustine and Christ."[39]

Some have suggested that he softened his views in his latter years during the "Downgrade" controversy, when he stood with non-Calvinists in opposing modernism in the Baptist Union. But in his newsletter, "The Sword and Trowel," December 1887, he wrote, "We do not conceal our Calvinism in the least."[40]

This clearly shows that controversy over God's sovereignty in salvation is not new. We have our critics; Spurgeon had his critics. In his sermon entitled "Election," Spurgeon defended his position by arguing that

> [W]hilst I may be railed upon as a heretic and as a hyper-Calvinist, after all, I am backed up by antiquity.
>
> If a handful of us stand alone in an unflinching mainte-nance of the sovereignty of our God, if we are beset by enemies, ay, and even by our own brethren, who ought to be our friends and helpers, it matters not, if we can but count upon the past; the noble army of martyrs, the glo-rious host of confessors, are our friends; the witnesses of truth stand by us. With these for us, we will not say that we stand alone: but we may exclaim, "Lo, God hath reserved unto himself seven thousand that have not bowed the knee unto Baal!" But the best of all is, *God is with us.*
>
> The great truth is always the Bible, and the Bible alone. My hearers, you do not believe in any other book than the Bible, do you? If I could prove this from all the books in Christendom; if I could fetch back the Alexandrian library, and prove it thence, you would not believe it any more; but you surely will believe what is in God's word.[41]

Not only was Dr. Rice wrong in his definition of hyper-Calvinism, but also was he guilty of wishful thinking. Dr. Rice edited Spurgeon's sermons, expunging his Calvinism. Is that not dishonest? A man who knew Dr. Rice once told me that Dr. Rice felt justified in editing Spurgeon because "he knows better now and would approve." Rice simply could not conceive of a Calvinist who was a successful soul winner. Nevertheless, an honest reference to a man's theology requires a thoroughly researched and factual presentation.

Is there a deliberate attempt to impugn the sovereign-grace gospel as hyper-Calvinism? Probably. While some mistakenly define "hyper-Calvinism" as considered above, others do seek deliberately to offend. Many free-willers use the term in a slanderous or derogatory sense.

25

Hyper-Calvinism sounds so menacing: "So-and-So is a *hyper*-Calvinist!" This false label, whether its application is mistaken, misdirected, or slanderous, offends those who rightly understand the difference. Let us all accurately define terms; otherwise, confusion abounds. Many evangelicals would prefer to dispense with labels altogether. It is easier to get along with everyone else if one does not specifically identify oneself.

"I AM A BIBLICIST!"

Evangelicals and fundamentalists insist that they are neither hyper-Calvinists nor Arminians but that they hold a third position. However, this third position is never shown to be a true third position and is given a nebulous identification. *Biblicist* is one such appellation. It is a noble term, for it associates the user with the Bible. The difficulty with this term is that all "Christians" claim to get their doctrines from the Bible.

There can be only two sides to this question. A third position, instead of being different, would actually be a *synthesis* of the two sides. *Biblicism* does not succinctly identify itself as something different from both "excessive Calvinism" and Arminianism, nor does it identify a synthesis of the two positions. Rather, the term appears to be an attempt either to hide one's true position or to avoid the controversy altogether.

In order to determine whether there is a "Biblicist" position on the way of salvation, consider the following comparison. It is essential, first, to establish the identity of the positions of sovereign-grace and free-will salvation. Then, by comparing these positions, one should be able to see how a Biblicist view would differ from these two standard positions.[42]

1. **Can a sinner make a choice for salvation without first being regenerated?**
   Sovereign grace says, "No."
   The sinner is dead in sins. Therefore, he is both unwilling and unable to choose for salvation without a spiritual resurrection—regeneration.
   Free will says, "Yes!"
   Though corrupted by sin, the sinner is able to repent and believe by his own power when confronted and convicted by the Spirit of God.
   Biblicism says, "?"
   (What comes first: faith? regeneration? or —?)
2. **Is the sinner totally disabled by sin?**
   Sovereign grace says, "Yes."
   Man is responsible for any demand that God may put on him. His will, however, is in bondage to his nature. He can neither change

26

his nature nor make choices contrary to his nature. He is dead in his trespasses and sins.

Free will says, "No."

Man's depravity has not left him in a totally helpless state. His will is not affected by sin. He is free to choose salvation: he has the ability to repent and believe the gospel. His eternal destiny depends on how he uses his free will.

Biblicism says, "?"

(Either the sinner is totally disabled spiritually, or he is not. Is there a third possibility?)

3. **Has God chosen a people He intends to save?**

   Sovereign grace says, "Yes."

   God, for righteous reasons not revealed but according to His own pleasure and purpose, chose an innumerable people unto salvation before the foundation of the world.

   Free will says, "No."

   God chooses those who were willing to choose Him. "Election" is based on God's knowing that they will believe of their own free accord.

   Biblicism says, "?"

   (Either God chooses sinners unto salvation or sinners choose for themselves. What else is there?)

4. **Did Christ die for all of lost humanity?**

   Sovereign grace says, "No."

   The intention of Christ's work was the actual redeeming of the elect. In the sacrifice of His Son, God limited His purpose (to the elect) but not His power. His death secured the salvation of all for whom He died.

   Free will says, "Yes."

   Christ's death was "sufficient" for all but "efficient" only for the ones who would believe. It had an unlimited purpose but a limited power (limited by man's free will). It merely made men savable; it did not actually secure the salvation of anyone.

   Biblicism says, "?"

   (Again, Christ's death is either for every sinner or for the elect only.)

5. **Can sinners resist God's saving grace?**

   Sovereign grace says, "No."

   The external call to salvation given to all who hear the gospel can be rejected and often is. However, the internal call made by the

Spirit to the elect cannot be ultimately resisted. Neither is the sinner coerced. The Spirit graciously causes the elect sinner to repent willingly and believe the gospel.

Free will says, "Yes."
God wants to save everybody, but inasmuch as the sinner is free, he can resist God's will. The Holy Spirit can save only those who allow Him to save them—those who are first willing to believe. Therefore, God's grace in salvation can be resisted.

Biblicism says, "?"
(You do begin to see the point now, do you not?)

6. **Can a believer lose his salvation?**
   Sovereign grace says, "No."
   While the saint is preserved by God, true faith will persevere, even though the believer may, yea, will stumble and fall. However, when he falls, he cannot remain long in that condition. He will arise and go on in faith. He is eternally saved.

   Free will says, "Yes."
   Believers who are truly saved can lose their salvation by failing to keep up their faith. A Christian must persevere to the end or be lost. (Some Arminians, however, do hold that believers are eternally secure.)

   Biblicism says, "?"

Modified Calvinism—Hypothetic Universalism
   Another attempt to dodge being labeled a "hyper-Calvinist" is to blur one's position so that he can find acceptance with both sides. One such effort is a conditional atonement called *hypothetic universalism*. The Scotch theologian John Cameron at the university in Saumer advocated it in the early 1600s. George Smeaton describes this view:

> It was a revolt from the position maintained at the Synod of Dort, under the guise of an explanation; for the propounders of the theory would not allow that they were out of harmony with its decrees. Not content to affirm, with the canons of Dort, that the intrinsic value of Christ's atonement was infinite, and capable, had God so pleased, of being extended to all mankind, they maintained that, along with a sufficiency of value, there was a certain destination of Christ's death, on the part of God and of the Mediator, to the whole human race.[43]

The theory has survived under the name of Cameron's disciple, Moise Amyraut, and is known as Amyraldianism. It teaches that there are two conflicting decrees: a general decree by which God wills the salvation of all men; and a specific decree by which God wills the salvation of the elect, those whom He chose in Christ for salvation. Thus, on the one hand, Amyraldianism alleges a rejection of Arminianism by insisting on a sovereign election of God, while, on the other hand, it charms Arminianism by holding forth an Arminian gospel appeal.

In reality, it is a subtle sabotage of the truth in an effort to make God and His purposes more palatable to those at enmity with God. It treats all sinners as if God loves them and longs for their salvation on the condition that they will repent of their sins and believe on a Christ who died for them and eagerly longs to be their Savior if they will have Him. However, as Arthur Pink has aptly stated, "To tell the Christ-rejecter that God loves him is to cauterize his conscience as well as to afford him a sense of security in his sins. The fact is, the love of God is a truth for the saints only, and to present it to the enemies of God is to take the children's bread and cast it to the dogs."[44]

This blurred Calvinism is *hypo-Calvinism*, to use a term coined by author David J. Engelsma.[45] It is widely held by many who claim to be Calvinists but are embarrassed by Calvinism. Also, many who claim to be "four-point" Calvinists might better call themselves Amyraldians and would do well to compare their definition of election with that of the Arminians. They may find that they are in agreement with the Arminians that God elects to salvation all those whom He foresees will trust in Christ.

3

A MAN-MADE SYSTEM?

If the critics of the sovereign-grace gospel are correct in their assumption that "Calvinism" is a "man-made doctrine," who invented Calvinism? Was it John Calvin? This seems to be the general understanding. It is amusing to me to read the little books and pamphlets of anti-Calvinists who cite the five points, saying something like, "By irresistible grace, Calvin meant. . . ." The problem is, they never quote directly from Calvin on "irresistible grace." I would challenge these "scholars" to show where John Calvin listed "his" so-called "five points" as such. It is obvious the critics have not read Calvin's writings. To attack a man without reading his books is inexcusable.

It is also erroneously assumed that "Calvinism" summarizes itself in the "five-points."[46] It is actually Arminianism that summarizes itself in five points. The so-called five points of Calvinism were actually responses to the five points of Arminianism. Sixteenth- and seventeenth-century Protestant churches held to Calvinistic theology. This era regarded Arminian doctrine a novelty and an error.

DEFENDING THE FAITH

The Antagonists

Whenever truth is challenged, God raises up able men to defend it. Often these defenders' names become attached to the positions they defend. There is an important lesson here that Christians need to understand. The great doctrines that form our theology were extracted from Scripture, defined, summarized, and polished in controversy by the defenders of the faith. The doctrines of grace were *not* invented by theologians but derived from Scripture, defined, and summarized into the system that now bears Calvin's name.

All the great confessions of faith were written because false teachings and heresies challenged the beliefs that were commonly held. The churches convened councils after the pattern of Acts 15. In these councils, theologians debated the issues, searched the Scriptures, assembled the thus-clarified doctrines into succinct form, and issued creeds.

John Calvin (1509-1564) was one such defender of the faith. A Swiss reformer, Calvin was a great Christian who had a fervent love for God and men. His personal seal was a flaming heart with an out-stretched helping hand. Even most non-Calvinists regarded Him as a great Christian and theologian. Historians have called Calvin "the most Christian man of his generation." He was described as "equally great in intellect and character, lovely in social life, full of tender sympathy and faithfulness to his friends, yielding and forgiving toward personal offenses."[47]

Jacob Hermann, a Dutch theologian and pastor, lived in the late sixteenth century (1559-1609). He is better known by his Latin name, Jacobus (James) Arminius. Sixteen years after Calvin's death, Arminius studied theology under Theodore Beza, Calvin's successor at the University of Geneva. In 1602, Arminius was invited to replace the deceased Francis Junius at the University of Leyden. When questions of his orthodoxy surfaced, Franciscus Gomarus (a bulwark of ortho-doxy at Leyden) interviewed him and publicly declared Arminius to be sound in his theology. In 1603 Arminius joined the faculty at Leyden.

However, questions about Arminius's theology dogged him throughout his ministry. In 1608, a year before his death, he published his "Declaration of Sentiments," which he presented to the state assembly at The Hague.[48] This document is his most definitive state-ment of beliefs and reveals his tendencies toward Pelagianism and conditional salvation.

Arminius was a follower of the teachings of Martin Luther's adversary, Erasmus (1466-1536), a priest of Rome whose humanistic ideas are still quoted today, and Augustine's adversary, Pelagius, a fifth-century British monk, who taught that men are born innocent and that they sin by following the example of Adam. Since Arminius did not go to the extremes of Pelagius in his theology, his views were called "semi-Pelagianism." However, his teachings followed the very *man-centered* focus of Erasmus.

After the death of Arminius in 1609, his followers began to chal-lenge openly the accepted doctrinal standards of Dutch Protestantism. They argued that the theology of the Reformed church focused too much on God's sovereignty in salvation. They argued that the Belgic Confession and Heidelberg Catechism portrayed God as a cruel tyrant with no thought for the will of His creatures. Arminians favored a more humanistic theology of "free will."

In 1618 the Arminian remonstrants sued the church of Holland with five reprimands or "remonstrances" (protests). They became known as the *Five Points of Arminianism* (see Chapter 1). In response to these reprimands, the state of Holland convened the Synod of Dort. For seven months learned theologians debated the issue. Their conclusion was that Arminianism was contrary to Scripture. Their written "verdict," subsequently called the Canons of Dort, has survived to become known as the "five points" of Calvinism as identified in the acrostic *TULIP*.

So, through historical review, we see the "five points" were legitimately set forth to clarify the position of orthodox Christianity in the face of adjudged Arminian error. Neither Calvin nor anyone else invented Calvinism. It is legitimate collective theological doctrine emerging from this seventeenth-century controversy by legitimate means.

The Continual Assault

Arminianism became more polished and increasingly popular because of its humanistic appeal of "free will." In spite of the synod's renunciation of Arminianism, the Arminian/Calvinist controversy not only did not die; it grew. Out of this controversy, however, God has raised up other theologians than John Calvin. The English Puritan divine John Owen (1616-1683) is considered by many scholars to be the greatest theologian of all time. It is my own conviction that one cannot reject Calvinism without studying and refuting Owen. Unfortunately, most Christians today seem to have little time for personal Bible study, to say nothing of studying John Owen.[49] But on the other hand, no one ought out of hand to reject a system of theology, which was held by churches for hundreds of years and ably defended by godly men, because some twentieth-century preachers label it "a man-made philosophy not found in Scripture."[50] To do so is to admit not only ignorance but also arrogance.

BAPTISTS AND SOVEREIGN GRACE

Long Live Sectarianism!

The sovereign-grace gospel is not only attacked as a "man-made philosophy" but also as "a sectarian doctrine."[51] One critic charges:

> A sectarian viewpoint is fatal to an unbiased approach to the Scriptures. Any doctrine to be accepted by Bible believers ought to be one which is plainly found in the Bible itself by honest seekers with open hearts, whether from any denomination or no denomination. . . . A strict denominational pride would color everything found in the Bible and make one's teaching unreliable.[52]

As we pointed out in the preface, the sovereign-grace gospel is regarded as indistinguishable from Reformed Theology ("Calvinism"). Thus, Reformed denominations, such as the Presbyterians, are at least nominally Calvinistic. Just so, the above criticism fails to distinguish the soteriology of sovereign grace from the denominational distinctives of a particular sect. The problem is further compounded by the presumptions inherent in the charge. The accusation here is that the beliefs held by any "denominational" group are necessarily at odds with the Bible. This charge also assumes that to hold a specific doctrinal (denominational) standard makes one not an "honest seeker with an open heart."

Is a specific doctrinal standard, then, unreliable because the critic says so? Who is the judge of whether someone is full of sectarian pride and therefore biased? What if it is the critic's teachings that are unreliable? If sectarianism "colors" what one finds in the Bible, would not anti-sectarianism also color one's interpretation? Could not one also be guilty of a *non*denominational pride? Of course, the Scriptures are to be the sole judge of whether anyone's teachings are true.

In defending Bible truth from the extremes of those who renounce either God's sovereignty or human responsibility in the gospel, Spurgeon answers the critic's charge of sectarianism:

> The great controversy which for many ages has divided the Christian Church has hinged upon the difficult question of "the will." I need not say of that conflict that it has done much mischief . . . but I will rather say, that it has been fraught with incalculable usefulness . . . I believe there is a needs-be for this . . . The natural lethargy of the Church requires a kind of healthy irritation to arouse her powers and stimulate her exertions. The pebbles in the living stream of truth are worn smooth and rounded by friction. . . . I glory in that which at present day is so much spoken against—sectarianism, for "sectarianism" is the cant phrase which our enemies use for all firm religious belief. . . . Success to sectarianism, let it live and flourish. When that is done with, farewell to the power of godliness. . . . When we cease each of us, to maintain our own views of truth, and to maintain those views firmly and strenuously, then truth shall fly out of the land, and error alone shall reign. . . .[53]

Where Did the Reformers Get Their Doctrine?

"Do Baptists believe in 'The Five Points of Calvinism'?"[54] After asking the question, Dr. John R. Rice proceeds to argue that, but for a "handful of Primitive Baptists," all the other "millions of Baptists . . . repudiate hyper-Calvinism [by which he means the sovereign-grace gospel]."[55] His observation may accurately describe the current scene, but he fails to consider the history of Baptists and their roots in sovereign-grace tradition. Sadly, modern Baptists have retreated from this heritage. In fact, most uninformed Baptists today would vigorously deny that Baptists ever held to the sovereign-grace gospel in the strict sense. What is an even more startling truth is that the reformers got their doctrine of salvation from the same source as the Baptists, as we shall see!

Very few Baptists understand their spiritual heritage. There are at least a couple of explanations for this. (1) Many Baptists are embarrassed to admit such a Calvinistic heritage. They would like to obscure their roots, if not deny them altogether. (2) History interests very few people. This is tragic, for history is essential to our understanding of our present position. How can we maintain a right course if we have lost our compass? I suggest that we have done just that.

The pre-Reformation Baptists held the doctrines of grace before Luther and Calvin expounded them. These early Baptists and their forebears did not call themselves Calvinists for at least two reasons: (1) These truths were not then known as Calvinism: they were held long before Calvin lived. (2) The pre-Reformation Baptists were heavily persecuted not only by the Roman church but also by the Calvinistic reformers themselves.[56]

To demonstrate the sovereign-grace doctrine of pre-Reformation Baptists, Baptist historian, T. W. Leach writes:

> On September 12, 1532, a brief Waldensian confession of faith was made with the general consent of the ministers and the heads of families of the churches of the Valleys of Piedmont, assembled in Anorogne, France. This document reaffirms the earlier confession [1120 A. D.], but expressed itself more freely concerning its historic views of the absolute sovereignty of God. In reading this confession, the reader must keep in mind that it was written shortly after Luther began to make himself known in the western world, and before Calvin had risen to power. [Luther published his *On the Bondage of the Will* in 1524. Calvin did not publish the first edition of his *Institutes of the Christian Religion* until 1536.][57]

The above-mentioned Waldensian Confession (1532) reads:

> That God, saves from that corruption and condemnation [mentioned in Article 10] those whom he has

34

chosen from the foundation of the world, not for any disposition, faith or holiness that he foresaw in them, but of his Son; passing by all the rest, according to the irreprehensible [that for which no fault can be found to censure] reason of his free will and justice (Article 11).[58]

Several Catholic bishops, apologists, and a pope (Genebrard, Lindanus, Gaulter, Ecchius, and Pope Pius II), all contemporaries of the reformers, corroborate that the doctrinal views of Luther and Calvin were those of the early Baptists.[59] A French historian of that period, Sieur de la Popeliniere, also confirms that the doctrines called Calvinism could be traced to the 1100s as principles of the Waldenses.[60]

Post-Reformation Baptists were also Calvinistic. The mainline Baptists in England (from 1616) were known as Particular Baptists because they held to particular redemption (limited atonement) in opposition to the Arminian general redemption views of the General Baptists. The premier Baptist theologian of America, A. H. Strong, in discussing the history of doctrine under the section entitled "British Theology," lists three men as representing English Baptist theology: John Bunyan (1628-1688), John Gill (1697-1771), and Andrew Fuller (1754-1815). Each of these is a Calvinist.[61] The Arminian Baptists (the General Baptists of England and the General Free Will Baptists of America) have never been regarded as either the mainline Baptist movement nor representative of Baptists in "general" (pun intended). It is indeed sad that in the last hundred years those who are the successors of Baptist orthodoxy, the present-day Calvinists, are looked upon as being aberrant and heretical in their theology.

Samuel E. Waldron in his book *Baptist Roots in America* traces the growth of the "Regular" (Particular or Calvinistic) Baptists (not to be confused with the group today called General Association of Regular Baptists) in the American colonies from four churches in 1660 to four hundred fifty-seven by 1780.[62] These churches were strong and evangelistic. They also made a major contribution to the greatness of the American Experiment in fighting for the establishment of "soul liberty" and freedom of religion.

Four churches in the Philadelphia, Pennsylvania, area became concerned with the Arminian drift of Baptists in America. To stem this tide, they formed the Philadelphia Baptist Association in 1707. In 1742 the association adopted, with minor modifications, the London Confession of the Particular Baptists of England, renaming the document the Philadelphia Confession of Faith. Edward T. Hiscox, whose *New Directory for Baptist Churches* is the standard guide for Baptist church conduct, said of this confession that it "is a most admirable statement of Christian doctrine."[63] Three brief excerpts from that confession demonstrate its sovereign-grace flavor:

> Chapter III, Of God's Decrees, 3. By the decree of God, for the manifestation of his glory, (I Tim. 5:21; Matt. 25:41) some men and angels are predestinated or foreordained to eternal life, through Jesus Christ, to the (Eph. 1:5, 6) praise of his glorious grace; others being left to act in their sin to their (Rom. 9:22, 23; Jude 4) just condemnation, to the praise of his glorious justice.

> Chapter IX, Of Free Will, 3. Man, by his fall into a state of sin, hath wholly lost (Rom. 5:6; 8:7) all ability of will to any spiritual good accompanying salvation; so as a natural man, being altogether averse from that good, and (Eph. 2:1, 5) dead in sin, is not able, by his own strength, to (Titus 3:3-5; John 6:44) convert himself or to prepare himself thereunto.

> Chapter X, Of Effectual Calling, 2 This effectual call is of God's free and special grace alone (II Tim. 1:9; Eph. 2:8), not from anything at all foreseen in man, nor for any power or agency in the creature, co-working with his special grace (I Cor. 2:14; Eph. 2:5; John 5:25), the creature being wholly passive therein, being quickened and renewed by the Holy Spirit, he is thereby enabled to answer this call, and to embrace the grace offered and conveyed in it, and that by no less (Eph. 1:19, 20) power than that which raised up Christ from the dead.[64]

The Philadelphia Confession was replaced by the New Hampshire Confession in 1833 for the Baptists in the North and East. The New Hampshire Confession is much shorter and, as Hiscox says, less "abstruse" (hard to understand) than the Philadelphia Confession. It is interesting that Hiscox ignores the Arminian Baptist confessions and cites only these two confessions as the standards of the Baptists in America. The New Hampshire Confession was written not only to simplify the confession but also to stand against the pressure of the Arminian "Free Will" Baptists to join with Regular Baptists. The following excerpts demonstrate its Calvinistic orientation:

36

IV. God's Purpose of Grace. We believe the Scriptures teach that *election* is the eternal purpose of God, according to which He graciously regenerates, sanctifies and saves sinners; that being perfectly consistent with the free agency of man, it comprehends all the means in connection with the end; that it is a most glorious display of God's sovereign goodness, being infinitely free, wise, holy and unchangeable; that it utterly excludes boasting, and promotes humility, love, prayer, praise, trust in God, and active imitation of His free mercy. . . .

VIII. Of Faith. We believe the Scriptures teach that *faith*, as an evangelical grace wrought by the Spirit, is the medium through which Christ is received by the soul as its sacrifice and Savior.[65]

A group called the "Separate" Baptists[66] originated in the first Great Awakening in America in the 1740s. They were vigorously evangelistic, following the zeal of Jonathan Edwards. However, they tended to regard creeds and confessions of faith as unnecessary because of their insistence on the Bible only as a rule and guide. The Separates merged with the Regular Baptists in the 1780s when they agreed to adopt the Philadelphia Confession. Nevertheless, their "anti-creedal" tendency plagued Baptists and eventually allowed Arminian theology to take over the churches.

The Decline of Calvinistic Baptist Churches

Waldron lists seven factors which he believes contributed to the decline of Calvinistic Baptist churches in America.[67] Of the seven, I consider two to be the main causes.

The Doctrine of Individual Liberty

Many founding fathers of our nation were deists and believed in the need of individual freedom for development of the human potential. Deists limited divine providence to God's working through nature's laws. Therefore, since they thought that God could not be relied upon to intervene directly in human affairs, they sought to protect human rights by human law—the Constitution. Of course, the concept of individual freedom is a good thing as long as "rights" are controlled and managed by a strong emphasis on responsibility and an understanding of man's fundamental moral and spiritual depravity. The Bill of Rights safeguards freedom from all kinds of tyranny, especially religious tyranny. James Madison, Thomas Jefferson, and others wisely understood this and enlisted the cooperation of Virginia Baptists (Isaac Backus, John

Leland, and others) in drafting this document. But without the balance of the authority of and man's responsibility towards the Word of God, "rights" quickly degenerate into the anarchy of individualism.

Our founding fathers envisioned a republican government of law, not a "rights"-focusing democracy. Government of law focuses upon principles; democracy, upon the whim of the people. True and pure democracy is as fickle and changeable as the human nature it serves. Waldron states:

> In all that was good about the United States, there was an unholy emphasis on inalienable rights, human freedom and hatred of authority which emerged as a reaction against Calvinism. The full revelation of this anti-God spirit and its ugly fruits would be later manifested in the "Abortion-Rights'" and "Gay-Rights'" movements of the later 20th Century.[68]

Anti-Creedalism and Anti-Sectarianism

Creeds have always clarified the positions which men hold regarding the Word of God. But the spirit of anti-creedalism (the resistance to reliance upon creeds or confessions to define what one believes) and the spirit of anti-sectarianism (the reluctance to stand firm on doctrine) that led to the interdenominational movement in America have also allowed Arminianism to become the doctrinal system in vogue. Cooperation of all Christians in the revival movements necessitated the minimizing of doctrine, and this price proved to be very costly to truth. Inclusivism is always a compromise in which truth suffers and error gains. Waldron cites Marcus Dods:

> A man may accept as the rule of his faith the same inspired books as yourself, while he rejects every important article of the faith you find in these books. If, therefore, we are to know who believe as we do, and who dissent from our faith, we must state our creed in language explicitly rejecting such interpretations of Scripture as we deem them to be false. Papists, Unitarians, Arminians, all profess to find their doctrines in Scripture; but they do not find them in the Westminster Confession.[69]

Waldron shows indisputably how this attitude of anti-creedalism enabled the modernists to gain control over the conservatives in the 1922 Northern Baptist Convention.[70] This ought to be a lesson for Baptists in our day! The "Arminian idol," free will, inevitably leads to compromises with liberalism because both Arminianism and liberalism have the same philosophy—humanism. Because Baptists were reluctant to stand firm and insist that those who would fellowship with them must adhere to their doctrinal statement, Arminianism opened the door to compromise and before long liberalism took over.

Another reason for this minimizing of doctrine was that fundamentalists, who insisted on Biblical inerrancy, saw it wise to reduce their confessions of faith to a bare minimum (called the "fundamentals") in order to cooperate in their stand against modernism. The test of fellowship was limited to an adherence to these few fundamentals. Any discussion of doctrinal differences was rebuked as "majoring on the minors." Sectarian ideas were regarded as wickedly divisive. The controversy was no longer Calvinism versus Arminianism but fundamentalism versus modernism.

A third reason for minimizing doctrine is that many Calvinistic Baptists have found it necessary to conceal their doctrine in order to avoid rejection and censure from brethren who are rabidly anti-Calvinistic. Naturally timid about being the instigators of contention and controversy, many preachers would prefer to avoid negative outbursts and the turmoil that accompanies them. Neither does one care to be labeled as extreme and questionable in his orthodoxy. Therefore, fearing controversy, persecution, and perhaps disassociation, many who hold the doctrines of grace are understandably reluctant to declare themselves.[71]

Others, fearing that Calvinistic doctrine is too strong and will hurt weak Christians and discourage sinners who may desire to be saved, have taken the position that election is a "family secret" that should not be preached or taught openly. Their contention is that these doctrines should not be taught to any but mature believers who are ready to receive them. But this silence—is it caution, or is it evasion? In his reply to "moderates" of his day, John Calvin aptly stressed,

> But for those who are so cautious or fearful that they desire to bury predestination in order not to disturb weak souls—with what color will they cloak their arrogance when they accuse God indirectly of stupid thoughtlessness, as if he had not foreseen the peril that they feel they have wisely met? Whoever, then, heaps odium upon the doctrine of predestination openly reproaches God, as if he had unadvisedly let slip something hurtful to the church.[72]

Again, Calvin wrote, "Evasion is never excusable."[73]

39

Another reason for the reluctance of many men to express openly their belief in the doctrines of grace is the fear of causing division in their churches. Calvinistic truths are divisive. "Calvinism tears up churches" is an oft-repeated cliché which strikes terror in the sensitive natures of God's servants.[74] Why is it that these doctrines cause such vehement explosions in some people? Why do some people become irrational, abandoning their commitments and leaving their churches at the mere suspicion of "Calvinism"? If it were only that "new" ideas should be viewed with caution, one might understand caution. But abandonment? Is caution justification for division? Paul wrote to the Galatians, *"It is good to be zealously affected always in a good thing"* (Galatians 4:18). But should caution produce anger and hostility? I submit that the truth always elicits hateful responses in carnal minds. Consider how religious men treated Christ and the apostles. Paul appealed to the Galatian believers because of their negative response to his ministry: *"Am I therefore become your enemy, because I tell you the truth?"* (Galatians 4:16).

Sadly, the result of this minimizing of doctrine is the covert access by which Arminian humanism has become the foundation of current evangelical doctrine. Consider the popularity of Christian psychology with its *humanizing* of Christianity by focusing on the individual and his needs. Much contemporary teaching views God as a divine attendant, duty-bound to cater to human whims in order to ensure happiness and prosperity. A good self-image seems to be the goal of this version of the gospel.

With doctrine dismissed as impractical, we have been excused from our duty to deny ourselves, take up our cross, and follow Him. God's standards are shrugged off as inconvenient, and obedience has become optional.

How far from true Biblical Christianity have we come? No wonder the sovereign-grace gospel is despised, for it focuses on God and *His* rights as well as our obligations to Him.

4

CONTROVERSY

The Reformation emerged from the desire of God's people to reclaim the true gospel from the errors of Romanism. This reclamation established a theology born in the fires of controversy and nurtured in the caldrons of persecution. It was a theology hammered out on the anvil of an ardent zeal to defend *"the faith which was once* [for all] *delivered unto the saints"* (Jude 3). In turn, it shaped and molded a people whose burning passion was to know God in all His glory and to serve Him with all their hearts.

God has, according to His sovereign purpose in every age, called a people for Himself. It is a people whose one longing is for God and His glory: *"And I will give them an heart to know me, that I am the* LORD: *and they shall be my people, and I will be their God: for they shall return to me with their whole heart"* (Jeremiah 24:7). *"I will say . . . bring my sons from far, and my daughters from the ends of the earth; Even every one that is called by my name: for I have created him for my glory, I have formed him; verily, I have made him"* (Isaiah 43:6, 7). It is a people whose cry is, *"Whom have I in heaven but thee? and there is none upon earth that I desire besides thee. My flesh and my heart faileth: but God is the strength of my heart, and my portion for ever"* (Psalm 73:25, 26).

The work of God in calling this people to Himself produced the gospel (good news). Entrusted to man, the gospel became corrupted by humanism and salvation by works. This corruption called for a "reformation" to restore the gospel to the sweet sovereignty of God. However, stopping the natural tendency of fallen humans to reshape the gospel into a man-centered perversion of the true gospel requires constant vigil. As John Piper so accurately assesses, humanists want a gospel that has as its driving force a God who needs *humans* "instead of tracing it back to sovereign grace that rescues sinners who need *God.* "[75]

Piper describes the true gospel of God:

> But the gospel is the good news that God is the all-satisfying end of all our longings, and that even though he does not need us, and is in fact estranged from us because of our God-belittling sins, he has, in the great love with which he loved us, made a way for sinners to

41

drink at the river of his delights through Jesus Christ. And we will not be enthralled by this good news unless we feel that he was not obligated to do this. He was not coerced or constrained by our value. He is the center of the gospel. The exaltation of *his* glory is the driving force of the gospel. The gospel is a gospel of *grace!*[76]

This was the "old" gospel revived in the Reformation and later called Calvinism.[77] For hundreds of years it flourished as the orthodox position of the churches. However, in the last hundred years or so the sovereign grace gospel has become nearly extinct in evangelical circles. Although there are signs of its revival today, most contemporary fundamental and evangelical Christians continue to treat a sovereign-grace, God-centered gospel as false teaching. Why is this?

THE ISSUE

A Clash of Philosophy

As noted earlier, many characterize the sovereign-grace gospel called Calvinism as "a man-made philosophy not in the Scriptures."[78] That evaluation is correct in only one point—Calvinism is, in a sense, a philosophy. The question as to whether it is "man-made" and "not in the Scriptures," however, must be decided on more than the critic's say-so. Opposition to Calvinism's gospel finds its source in a clash with one's own philosophy. In the opening paragraph of his book *Predestined for Hell? No!,* Dr. John Rice states, "Nobody is predestined to be saved, *except as he chooses, of his own free will,* to repent of sin and trust Christ for salvation."[79] This statement succinctly sets forth the teaching of the "new" man-centered gospel in which the *sinner* has the final say in the matter of his own salvation.

This new gospel must reject the teaching that, for reasons of *God's* own purpose and pleasure, He has chosen a number of Adam's condemned race to be the recipients of His mercy and grace in Christ Jesus to the praise of His glorious grace. How, then, do we determine which of these two versions of the gospel is truly biblical, since both claim biblical authority?

I submit that it is almost impossible for humans to be objective in approaching the Bible because everything, including the Bible, is interpreted by human prejudice. The trend today is for Christians to rely on personal subjective experiences in order to formulate views of God and truth. The Bible has become for many a mere collection of inspirational sayings. The saving work of Jesus Christ has become a

42

euphoric *experience*. Moral ethics are described in terms of "feeling good" or "feeling bad" rather than as objective standards—*"Thus saith the Lord."* The will of God is determined by "peace" in one's heart regardless of the teaching of the Word of God. These trends work together to form a Christian's philosophy of life. His philosophy becomes his "security blanket" to which he tenaciously clings for comfort. Just try to take away the security blanket.

The fact is all Christians have a philosophy,[80] and their philosophy colors their interpretation of Scripture. The issue, however, is whether the Scripture conflicts with one's philosophy, and if so, what a person will do about his philosophy. Since the Bible is the revealed truth of God, we must strive to square all our views with it.

Another problem in this struggle is presuming that the words in Scripture mean what we want them to mean. Every conflicting doctrinal view uses passages of Scripture for proof, but the very nature of God's revelation cannot allow the Bible to contradict itself. Therefore, in considering passages which seem to support conflicting doctrinal positions, one must realize that either one or the other position is a misinterpretation of the Scripture. Both positions cannot be right.

A Personal Experience

I used to be frustrated with many passages in the Word of God, especially the teachings of Jesus, because of their conflict with my presumptions of what they should say. An example is Christ's encounter with the rich young ruler (Mark 10:17-31). When the young man asked, *"What shall I do that I may inherit eternal life?"* I assumed he wanted to be saved. I saw this as an evangelistic opportunity. Therefore, I could not understand why Jesus told him to keep the commandments. Jesus' answer did not fit my view of soul winning. It never occurred to me that Jesus was not working for a "decision."

Obviously, Jesus knew what He was doing, but knowledge of this fact only heightened my frustration. Finally, I came to realize that my expectations of the situation prevented me from understanding what actually was taking place. I was blinded by my opinion of what *should be* rather than what *was*.

The Scripture itself is clear. When the disciples exclaimed their amazement, *"Who then can be saved?"* (Mark 10:26), the Lord responded, *"With men it is impossible, but not with God: for with God, all things are possible"* (Mark 10:27). God does the saving, and He uses means. The rich young ruler, in order to be saved, needed to repent of his covetousness before he could trust Christ. In order to see his need to repent, he needed to realize his "God-belittling sins."[81]

In order to live with these problems, I decided that some things in the Bible were too deep for my puny mind. I would simply ignore those troublesome texts in hopes that someday, when I grew more in the faith, I would understand them. It was not *time*, however, but *grace* that I needed. The "old" gospel of sovereign grace opened the Bible to me like the dawn bursting on the darkness of night. Mine was the experience of Charles Haddon Spurgeon.

> I can remember well the day and hour when first I received those truths in my own soul—when they were burned into me, as John Bunyan says—burned as with a hot iron into my soul; and I can recollect how I felt I had grown on a sudden from a babe into a man—that I had made progress in Scriptural knowledge, from having got hold once and for all of the clue of the truth of God.[82]

THE FUNDAMENTAL DIFFERENCE

God's Purposes and Human "Free Will"

The fundamental difference between the "old" gospel of sovereign grace and the "new" gospel of "free will" (or human ability) centers on God and His purposes. The "new" gospel perceives God's sole purpose in salvation as the recovery of as many sinners as possible. In this recovery operation, however, God must be careful to maintain His place. He can provide only the opportunity, but then He must wait on sinners to decide either to choose or to refuse the gospel. In this view, "power of choice" is the sinner's sacred and non-negotiable right. Is this Scriptural? No, for *"salvation is of the LORD"* (Jonah 2:9).

As wonderful as salvation is, it is not in itself the divine goal. The goal is God's desire to be glorified in all that He does. In creation God is to be praised for the glory of His power (Psalm 19:1). In providence God is to be praised for the glory of His faithfulness (Lamentations 3:23). In retribution and judgment He is to be praised for the glory of His justice (Romans 9:22). In salvation we *"praise the glory of his grace"* (Ephesians 1:6).

In Ephesians 3:10 the Apostle Paul explains God's purpose in salvation: *"To the intent that now unto the principalities and powers in heavenly places might be known by the church the manifold wisdom of God."* *"For mine own sake, even for mine own sake,"* God says, *"will I do it: for how should my name be polluted? and I will not give my glory unto another"* (Isaiah 48:11). In other words, "What I do is not for your sake, but for mine because I will not share my glory." No, all God does He does for the sake of His own glory.

A Question of Control

The new gospel of "free will" attributes to fallen humans a freedom of choice that cannot be warranted either by Scripture or human experience. If the will is said to be "free," from what is it free? The issue is rather *control*—who or what is in control? Are humans truly in control of their own destinies? This basic question has been a central theme of philosophies and religions since the beginning of time. Nor is the struggle between "fate" and "free will" the exclusive contention of Calvinism and Arminianism.

The non-Christian world also struggles with its theories of destiny. Many hold that life is at the mercy of random forces (purblind chance or luck) on an unplanned pilgrimage to an unknown end. Intelligent beings may plan, but they remain at the mercy of these accidental forces. Ruling contingencies limit people's choices. Take, for example, the freedom desires of a person living in an oppressive society. His will to be free is in the control of the contingencies that resulted in his being born in that society. A truly "free will" simply does not exist. This conclusion is the practical observation of all humans.

Determinism is another non-Christian view of destiny. "Fate" controls all things. People's "choices" are already predetermined and are just part of the outworking of all things to their inevitable end. But even in this view, "fatal optimism" leads people to think that somehow they may alter the course of destiny. If they could only "see" into the future, then they could make the choices that would affect their future more favorably. The psychics, astrologers, and fortunetellers get rich on this folly of humans, whose hopes actually contradict their own philosophy. Humans like to think that they are in control of their own destinies.

Is God in Control?

Biblical Christianity has added a new dimension to the question of control—the existence of a personal sovereign God who is the Creator and Upholder of the universe. Is God deterministic? If so, to what extent have humans freedom under sovereign rule? Also, is God Himself free of contingencies and human choices?

The Bible asserts that God is sovereign, being fully and wisely in control of all things, including human choices. All things exist because God willed them to exist and not because they are necessary to fulfill God in some way. God needs nothing to be complete. Paul emphasized that truth on Mars Hill: *"Neither is* [God] *worshipped with men's hands as though he needed anything"* (Acts 17:25). Why, then, were we created? God says, *"I have created him for my glory"* (Isaiah 43:7). The creation exists to glorify God. Such an idea is very humbling to those who think that God's happiness depends on them.

The Bible calls the reason for God's acts *"his good pleasure"* (Ephesians 1:9). Paul regarded, for example, God's purpose in the church as a *"mystery"* demonstrating His manifold wisdom (Ephesians 3:9; 1:8, 9). Paul, God's chosen instrument, was to reveal this mystery (Ephesians 3:1-5), but he understood that this concept of God's purposes was so foreign to human thinking that it required far more than a mere explanation of these truths. That is why Paul, when he began to set forth these truths in his Ephesian letter, prayed for the believers,

> *That the God of our Lord Jesus Christ, the Father of glory, may give unto you the spirit of wisdom and revelation in the knowledge of him: The eyes of your understanding being enlightened; that ye may know what is the hope of his calling, and what the riches of the glory of his inheritance in the saints, And what is the exceeding greatness of his power to usward who believe, according to the working of his mighty power* (Ephesians 1:17-19).

Only God's answering this prayer for us will enable us to begin to receive the truth.

In His *"manifold wisdom"* God disposes all things according to a predetermined plan that includes human choices. All things bring glory to God as they demonstrate His glorious attributes. Why does God predestine some sinners to be conformed to the image of Christ (Ephesians 1:5)? In order that they might be *"to the praise of the glory of his grace"* (Ephesians 1:6). *"When he shall come to be glorified in his saints, and to be admired of all them that believe . . . in that day"* (II Thessalonians 1:10).

High Knowledge
The biblical view of God's sovereign rule is largely incomprehensible. For this reason, some folks invoke Deuteronomy 29:29 (*"the secret things belong unto the LORD our God"*). Who will disagree that many things about God and His plans are secret? God is infinite, and therefore both God's person and His ways are incomprehensible to the finite mind. Only those things which He has chosen to reveal to us can we know. The secret things should not be the subject of speculation. However, God has revealed much about election and predestination; so they are not of the

46

"secret things." Only the unrevealed aspects of election remain secret and therefore not our concern (Romans 11:33). What God has revealed to us we not only have a right to know but are commanded to know so that *we may do all the words of this law"* (Deuteronomy 29:29). In other words, we are to know what God has revealed.

When faced with God's ways, David cried: *"Such knowledge is too wonderful* [Heb. *palee,* 'hard,' 'hidden'—beyond human comprehension]" (Psalm 139:6). Paul agrees: *"O the depth of the riches both of the wisdom and knowledge of God! how unsearchable are his judgments, and his ways past finding out!"* (Romans 11:33). This is "high" knowledge, and we should reverently treat it as such. Therefore, rather than seeking to limit God to conform to our selfish, humanistic interests, we ought to fall on our knees in submission and adoration.

GOD'S SOVEREIGN RULE QUESTIONED

Limited Limitlessness?

Sovereignty is not an issue raised by Calvinism. It is not an issue raised even by Christianity or the Bible. It is a basic, non-negotiable assumption. God cannot be God if He is not sovereign—the supreme authority, independent and unlimited. Attempts to limit God's sovereignty have no Scriptural basis and violate even the simplest definition of the word.

Everyone who faces the awesome sovereignty of Almighty God, however, struggles with his place under it. Apart from the Bible view that God is indeed sovereign, Christians have two other views of God's sovereign rule. First, some teach that God, the ultimate Being in the universe, is good but not really sovereign. He, like His creatures, is, to some degree, at the mercy of contingencies. This view grants humans the greatest amount of personal "freedom" of choice. It also absolves God of any risk of blame for the evils which abound in the world. What is left, however, is an anemic God with little power and no glory.

The second view holds that God is sovereign but has sovereignly chosen to limit His sovereignty in order to accommodate human choices. This is the view of the vast majority of Christians today. It differs from the first view in acknowledging that God is—or was—sovereign. What it gives on one hand it takes away with the other. It may ensure humans their "free will," but the result is a god, even if by his own choice, who is no longer sovereign. What comfort would such a god be in this world?[83]

Some will strongly argue for human rights to the point of blasphemy as is evidenced by this statement: "The Bible says many wonderful things

47

about God, but it never says that God is an absolute unlimited sovereign."[84] What about Isaiah 46:9-11; Psalm 33:10, 11; 115:3; Lamentations 3:37, 38; and numerous other Scriptures? Author Jerry Bridges has stated, "The sovereignty of God is asserted, either expressly or implicitly, on almost every page of the Bible."[85] The Bible could not be clearer on this issue. Limited sovereignty is a contradiction in terms.

Stating that God is not an absolute sovereign clearly demonstrates that the author of such a statement does not understand sovereignty. His error is compounded:

> The way hyper-Calvinists[86] use terminology about the "absolute sovereignty of God" as if God Himself were not bound by any moral obligations, as if He were not bound by His own nature, as if He were not bound by His acts and promises, is a false emphasis, contrary to that clearly taught throughout the Bible.[87]

Does this evangelical author think God is to be subject ("bound") to principles apart from Himself? Does he think "unlimited" sovereignty makes God a capricious being flitting from whim to whim as fancy takes Him? Will denying God His sovereignty assure us of His proper behavior? Whose "moral obligations" govern God? To whom will He answer?

"God Is Love," Or Is It "Love Is God"?

Let us see where the thinking that limits God's sovereignty leads. "God is love, and love limits absolute sovereignty."[88] Now, how does love limit sovereignty? Does love prevent God from doing what He would sovereignly "will" to do if He were not love? If so, love is a ruling factor to which God must yield His desires. This makes God accountable to an impersonal principle, effectively making the principle, love, to be god. If this is so, then we should read the statement, "Love is sovereign, limiting God to doing only what love wills."

No, God's love is part of His character. He does not struggle between His desires to love and to will. Love is God's intention to do good. Rather than love's limiting sovereignty, God's being sovereign assures that whatever He desires to do in love will be done. Without love there would have been no salvation of lost sinners. On the other hand, an absence of love would neither have increased nor decreased God's sovereignty.

God's will to show special love to some sinners, electing them to salvation, arises from God's purpose to demonstrate His *"manifold*

48

wisdom" in the *"praise of the glory of his grace"* (Ephesians 1:6). His purpose determines His will. God's motivation (what He loves) is within Himself and cannot be influenced by anything apart from Himself. If His purposes could be influenced from without, God, then, would no longer be immutable and thus would cease to be God.

It is important to remember that one cannot have a full and proper understanding of God's work of redemption apart from a like understanding of God's person. Also, in answering the question of God's sovereignty, we must understand that God is not like we are. He is self-existent and self-sufficient. We are created and dependent. He knows all and can do whatever He wills. As the ultimate universal Being, He has both the right and the ability to do so.

Humanizing God

Idolatry

Humans are not content with Scripturally proper and exalted views of God. Sinful beings tend to view God as an extended version of themselves. When God says that He made man in His image, humans understand that idea in a reverse perspective—God in man's image. Humans suffer limitations; so they think that God, too, must suffer limitations. Such thinking projects humanistic ideas on God. This is idolatry—worshipping God in a form other than what He has revealed Himself to be.

Egoism

Another tendency comes from fallen humans' self-centeredness, a tendency called "egoism," a theory that "one's own good either is or ought to be the sole motive operative in human choice."[89] Thus, self-centered humans reason that their own good should be the sole motive of God's purposes. This concept is projected on God's love and leads Him to "do wonderful things for people" if only they will let Him. Since salvation promotes human good, God is working to do the most good to the greatest number of Adam's fallen race. This means getting as many saved as possible. What many Christians do not seem to understand is that this thinking may lead to other erroneous conclusions, even a denial of hell.[90] This is not so far-fetched. Consider this argument: Does the punishment of sinners in hell advance their good? No. Should not a loving God rather be interested in a corrective therapy that promotes the welfare of sinners? Therefore, perhaps we should just throw out the doctrine of eternal punishment!

On the other hand, is God glorified in His wrath as well as in His mercy? *"What if God, willing* [His holy will disposes Him] *to shew* [to

49

display] *his wrath, and to make His power known,* [nevertheless] *endured with much longsuffering the vessels of wrath, fitted* [ripe] *for destruction"* (Romans 9:22). Paul is saying here that God is disposed to display His wrath and to reveal His power in punishing "vessels of wrath" that are ripe and ready for punishment. However, He is enduring vessels of wrath for now to fulfill other purposes (Romans 9:23). The point is (without going into great detail) God's purpose in either the salvation or punishment of sinners is not for their benefit but for His. God will be glorified by displaying His wrath (II Thessalonians 1:7-10).

Contingencies

Another tendency is to see God as subject to principles and laws outside of Himself because humans are subject to laws and principles. We know that God is omniscient and knows future events, but we think that God somehow does not absolutely control them. As we react to the contingencies of life—constantly adjusting our plans, failing at times, being "lucky" at other times—we see God doing the same, though perhaps better than we.

But God does not experience hopes, dreams, disappointments, and frustrations. *"God is not a man"* was the true statement of the false prophet Balaam. *"Hath he said, and shall he not do it? or hath he spoken, and shall he not make it good?"* (Numbers 23:19).

The sovereign-grace doctrine seeks to uphold the sovereignty of our great God and Savior. Free-will doctrine seeks to establish a human claim in God's dealings with people. I do not proclaim "Calvinism" to be error free. In the quest for doctrinal purity, the reformers did make mistakes, even persecuting those who dissented from their teaching. Zeal for the truth does not always come with perfect understanding, and sometimes the flesh gets the best of even the most mature saint. The path of the heart is often littered with errors of the head, as Christian history so abundantly demonstrates. However, mistakes are no cause to abandon the path of truth.

We all need to examine our presuppositions and see what they do to our view of God. If they are not honoring to God, we must discard them. Few people would argue that God is not sovereign. It is how He exercises that sovereignty that worries self-willed sons and daughters of Adam.

5

THE "HINGE"

The contentions over "free will" are not new: they are at least as old as the Reformation. In the fall of 1524, Desiderius Erasmus, a priest of Rotterdam, published his *Diatribe sue collatio de libero arbitrio (Discussion, or Collation, Concerning Free-Will)*. In it he defined free will as a power "by which a man may apply himself to those things that lead to eternal salvation, or turn away from the same."[91] This concept of free will is still in current vogue among the majority of evangelical and fundamental Christians. Although evangelicals would differ with Erasmus as to the nature of the "things that lead to eternal salvation," they would agree that the choice of salvation is in the power of a sinner to accept or reject.

Martin Luther responded to Erasmus in his classic *The Bondage of the Will*. In the conclusion of his book, Luther said to Erasmus:

> I give you hearty praise and commendation on this further account—that you alone, in contrast with all others, have attacked the real thing, that is the essential issue [free will]. You have not wearied me with those extraneous issues about the Papacy, purgatory, indulgences, and such like—trifles, rather than issues—in respect of which almost all to date have sought my blood . . . you, and you alone, have seen the hinge on which all turns, and aimed for the vital spot.[92]

This issue of human choice is indeed the "hinge on which all turns." The late Dr. Gordon H. Clark related the following experience:

> [In August of 1961] I attended an evangelistic service in which the evangelist introduced his prayer by a five-minute talk on free will. God offers us salvation, he said, but God cannot make us accept it. The will of man is inviolable; it is free from God. Now that God has made us the offer, all he can do is to sit back and wait and see who will accept it.[93]

Dr. Clark observed,

> In their [the evangelist's and his audience's] minds, a denial of free will would be tantamount to a denial of Christianity. . . . They were unaware that Protestantism began by denying free will. They were unaware that they had receded from the doctrine of the Reformation and had taken long steps backward to the theology of Romanism. Such is the ignorance of our day.[94]

Therefore, we need to examine whether the Bible teaches this supposed power of humans either to accept or reject God's offer of grace. The understanding of "free will" is, as Luther declared, "the hinge on which all turns."[95] Luther further declared, "You cannot know what 'free-will' is without knowing what ability man's will has, and what God does, and whether He foreknows of necessity."[96]

FREE WILL?

The Boss

The issue before us requires an understanding of the basic relationship between the Creator and His creatures who possess intelligence and power of choice. The Creator is the "boss," and His will is "free." Creatures are subordinate to God, but they do have volition. There is no argument that humans are volitional creatures. The argument is whether, being fallen sinners, they are able to use their power of choice to apply themselves to their salvation. Also, we must consider the question of how much volitional creatures are free to exercise their choices under God's sovereign rule. Must God adjust His will to human choices? These were the subjects of the debate between Luther and Erasmus. Luther subscribed to the position that the omnipotent and omniscient Creator operates according to a plan; therefore, all contingencies occur in harmony with the outworking of that plan.

> It is, then, fundamentally necessary and wholesome for Christians to know that God foreknows nothing contingently, but that He foresees, purposes, and does all things according to His own immutable, eternal and infallible will. This bombshell knocks "free-will" flat, and utterly shatters it; so that those who want to assert it must either deny my bombshell, or pretend not to notice it, or find some way of dodging it. . . .

So our original proposition still stands and remains unshaken: all things take place by necessity. There is no obscurity or ambiguity about it. In Isaiah, it says, "My counsel shall stand, and my will shall be done" (46:10); and any schoolboy knows the meaning of "counsel," "will," "shall be done," "shall stand"![97]

God does all things decently and in order. By His power He rules over contingencies. By His omniscience He knows no surprise. By His wisdom He has no "Plan B." In order to accomplish His will, it is necessary that God control the desires and acts of free agents. God does "all things according to His own immutable, eternal and infallible will" (Luther's "bombshell").

God is sovereign and could not be God if He were not sovereign. God's will and ways, however, are incomprehensible to us. They put God beyond our control! This scares us and, indeed, it should. That fear should produce worship. It should cause us to kneel in awe and wonder of His greatness!

Instead of submitting humbly to God's plan, many people balk at His sovereignty and assert the right of free will. "God must respect our rights," they say, declaring dogmatically what God can and cannot do. Nebuchadnezzar learned the hard way how God humbles the proud. He concluded, *"All the inhabitants of the earth are reputed as nothing: and he doeth according to his will in the army of heaven, and among the inhabitants of the earth: and none can stay his hand, or say unto him, What doest thou?"* (Daniel 4:35). Nebuchadnezzar's observation is supported in Isaiah 14:24 and 27: *"The LORD of hosts hath sworn, saying, Surely as I have thought, so shall it come to pass; and as I have purposed, so shall it stand: For the LORD of hosts hath purposed, and who shall disannul it? and his hand is stretched out, and who shall turn it back?"* No one who believes the Bible questions these statements about God's sovereignty, but when it comes to applying them, we have a different attitude. The old flesh begins to assert its "free will," and we start to babble about the fairness of God.

The Bible teaches that God sovereignly acts in three areas: (1) creation, (2) providence, and (3) salvation.

Creation

Generally, humans will allow that God is sovereign in creation. Who would question the right of the Creator to make whatever He wants? The Bible clearly teaches us this. *"For thou hast created all things, and for* [Gk. *dia,* 'by means of' or 'because of'] *thy pleasure*

[Gk. *thelema*, 'will'] *they are and were created"* (Revelation 4:11). This verse could be translated: "For thou hast created all things, and they exist and were created because of thy will."

Providence

For the most part, we will also let God be sovereign in His providence—His governing of creation. It comforts us to know that God is fully in charge of this world (Psalm 103:19). The providential government of God extends to every detail of life—from the sparrow's fall (Matthew 10:29) to the outcome in the casting of lots (Proverbs 16:33), including the weather (Psalm 135:5-7)—everything. He even controls the governments of the world (Daniel 4:17, 25, 32; 5:21). The Bible declares that in all things God works for the good of those *"who love him, to those who are the called according to His purpose"* (Romans 8:28).

The proof of His providential control is abundant in the Word of God. An example is recorded in Exodus 34:24. God required the men of Israel to appear before Him three times a year at the Tabernacle (and later the Temple). In order to obey this command, the men of Israel had to leave their homes and families unprotected and vulnerable to attack from their enemies. Encouraging the men to obey God in spite of this danger, God promised that their homes and cities would be safe from such attacks, and He worked in the hearts of Israel's enemies so that they would have no desire to attack them at those times. Now, how could God do this and not control the "free" wills of Israel's enemies? Did God force them to stay home? Did He violate their freedom of will in this? No. They willingly stayed home.

What about Philippians 2:13? How does God *"work in us to will and to do of his good pleasure"* if God cannot control what we will? Some might argue that God works only in those who will let Him, but this verse teaches that God works in us in order for us *"to will . . . to do his good pleasure."*

What about people who complain, "If God is good, why does He let this or that happen?" The very question itself demonstrates that people do recognize, although perhaps grudgingly, that God is indeed sovereignly controlling circumstances.

Salvation

The third area of His sovereign acting is in the saving of sinners (James 1:18). Here is where the natural enmity of humans to the sovereignty of God reveals itself. Here the line is drawn. *"We will not have this man to reign over us!"* (Luke 19:14). In the heat of passion many become disturbed and confused, not understanding the nature of the human will and its relationship to the divine sovereign will. While willing to concede God's sovereignty in creation and providence, they balk at or outright reject God's sovereignty in salvation.

Can Subordinates Have "Free" Will?

The Bible teaches both God's sovereignty and human free agency. The fact that both are taught creates a dilemma for people who see them as contradictory. In his book *Reclaiming Authentic Fundamentalism*, author Dr. Douglas McLachlan says many good things, but he is in error on this issue. In discussing the need to guard against what he sees as dangers to authentic evangelism, Dr. McLachlan lists "excessive Calvinism." He explains, "Without doubt, the matter of God's sovereignty and man's responsibility has boggled theologians from the beginning of time. Anyone who thinks he has all the answers on this matter simply has not yet heard all the questions!"[98]

Without claiming to have all the answers, we assert that it is possible for one to understand the biblical relationship between God's sovereignty and human responsibility. There is a problem only when we fail to see that God's free will is fulfilled without ever violating human will. No human is ever coerced into doing God's will, but everyone does God's will, even in one's efforts to rebel against God (Acts 2:23).

Dr. McLachlan concedes that divine election is taught in Scripture. But then he argues that "God has also granted His image-bearers an authentic exercise of their wills."[99] Seeing what he perceives to be a conflict between these two ideas, he adds, "This can only mean that there is in the matter of personal salvation an *inscrutable synergism*, a mysterious working together of the divine and human wills."[100] It is this notion of *synergism*—this "working together of the divine and human wills"—that raises the possibility of an unbiblical contradiction.

Salvation is a *monergism*—the sole operation of God's grace. Those who object to a monergistic salvation falsely conclude that it requires God to deny "an authentic exercise" of the sinner's will in the process. This error is a failure to understand that God works *behind* the sinner's will, changing the desires that control the will. With new desires, the elect sinner can willingly decide for Christ so that God has granted a legitimate exercise of human will while at the same time fulfilling His own immutable will. No contradiction must be surmounted.

McLachlan's calling his *synergism* a "mystery" enables him to avoid a perceived problem that does not actually exist. His *synergism*, however, poses another question: can creature will frustrate the divine will? If so, divine sovereign election is not possible because election demands the overriding supremacy of God's will. Simple logic dictates that God's sovereignty cannot be maintained if salvation is a *synergism*.

Not Absolutely Free

Of course, we do loosely speak of people having free wills. What we mean is that humans have intelligence and volition. Therefore, I personally prefer to view creature volition as the right and power of moral responsibility under the sovereign rule of God. But it is only as the grace of God enables sinners that they can exercise their proper spiritual responsibility to God. As John Piper so eloquently states, "Grace is the pleasure of God to magnify the worth of God by giving sinners the right and power to delight in God without obscuring the glory of God."[101]

There are three reasons why the subordinate creature's volition cannot be free. First, no human can be sovereign. There is only one Sovereign; God already claims that position. Satan and sinful men can only challenge God's claim.

Second, people are not *free* in their choices because the will is subject to influence. Men and women have the powerful influence of predispositions (habits, preferences, and fears). Myriad external appeals are constantly bombarding them, either pressuring them to make decisions or restraining them from action already decided upon. For example, a person has the choice to exceed or stay within the speed limit on the highway. He may be tempted to speed, but if a police car is following him, he has a strong motivation not to speed. The presence of the police car is a restraining influence that gives rise to desires that are greater than the original temptation. Thus, he chooses the stronger desire.

Third, no human is truly free because he can act only according to his nature. Our desires determine our choices, and these desires originate from a corrupted nature. Jesus asks,

> *O generation of vipers, how can ye, being evil, speak good things? for out of the abundance of the heart the mouth speaketh. A good man out of the good treasure of the heart bringeth forth good things: and an evil man out of the evil treasure bringeth forth evil things. But I say unto you, That every idle word that men shall speak, they shall give account thereof in the day of judgment. For by thy words thou shalt be justified, and by thy words thou shalt be condemned* (Matthew 12:34-37).

56

The "abundance of the heart" is the wellspring of desire. The condition of the heart, whether good or evil, determines the moral value of the desire—"good treasure" or "evil treasure." Jesus asks, "How can ye, being evil, speak good things?" This is a rhetorical question. Evil men cannot speak good things or seek good things. "Men loved darkness rather than light, because their deeds were evil" (John 3:19). How, then, can a sinner freely choose against his nature for God and righteousness without a prior work of grace?

Humans are not free in their choices because of the limits set by their spiritual disabilities. The unregenerate man cannot know spiritual things (I Corinthians 2:14). The unregenerate man cannot submit to God's standards (Romans 8:7). The unregenerate man cannot find acceptance with God (Romans 8:8). The unregenerate man cannot come to Christ (John 6:44). All the protests in the world will not change the clear statements of these Scriptures. Under the spiritual incapacitation of their evil natures, sinners *cannot* choose to be saved. This is why the Father must *draw* sinners to Christ (John 6:44) if they are to be saved.

Free to Do Evil

There is a sense in which fallen sinners are free: they are free to follow the course of their own lusts. I know a woman whose husband deserted her for another woman. She wanted to know why he could do that. She could not understand why God did not stop him. In this case, she was apparently willing for God to sovereignly exercise control over her errant husband. Her question is answered by the fact that, in His sovereign pleasure, God has left men to follow their own hearts' desires (Acts 14:16; Psalm 81:12; I Peter 4:3). Spurgeon said:

> God foreknew the mischief that he [the Syrian king Hazael] would do afterwards, when he came to the throne; and yet that foreknowledge did not in the least degree interfere with his free agency. Nor is this an isolated and exceptional case. The facts most surely believed among us, like the doctrines most clearly revealed to us, point all of them to the same inference. The predestination of God does not destroy the free agency of man, or lighten the responsibility of the sinner. It is true, in the matter of salvation, when God comes to save, His free grace prevails over our free agency, and leads the will in glorious captivity to the obedience of faith. But in sin man is free—free in the

57

widest sense of the term, never being compelled to do any evil deed, but being left to follow the turbulent passions of his own corrupt heart, and carry out the prevailing tendencies of his own depraved nature.[102]

Therefore, people do not have a "free" will, but they do have will (moral agency)—the ability to make decisions as to what they will do. Hyper-Calvinism makes the mistake of ignoring human will. Free-willers make the mistake of attributing to fallen creatures the ability to make good choices in spite of their sinful predisposition. If a sinner is able to make a good decision (for example, for salvation), then, as free-willers insists, divine sovereign election is not necessary. The problem is not whether humans have the power of choice but whether they can use that choice of themselves to be saved.

RECONCILE WHAT?

Imagining Contradictions
Some Scripture references seem to teach that men do have some power over God. For example, God promises to answer when we pray. But the Bible also teaches that God cannot be influenced by anything outside of Himself. If God is absolutely sovereign, why pray if there is no hope of changing God's mind or of influencing Him to act on our behalf? The Scriptures command and encourage us in our responsibility and privilege to pray by promising us that God will hear and answer our prayers. Actually, God's sovereignty assures us that God will answer our prayers. God is wise and has ordained that His people pray. Praying accomplishes God's will.

Another example of this seeming contradiction is the doctrine of election and God's commands to preach the gospel to every creature. Why evangelize if God has already sovereignly chosen some to salvation? The answer? Because God tells us to do it.[103]

These questions are resolved when we understand that there are two aspects to God's will: (1) His *secret* will, which is not fully revealed to us, has to do with God's eternal decrees—what *He* has purposed and intends to do: His *"good pleasure"* (Ephesians 1:9). (2) His *revealed* will involves what He has purposed and intends for *us* to do—His written commandments to His creatures.

Some aspects of election belong to God's secret will. God has revealed to us only *that* He has chosen some to salvation, but He has not revealed *why* he chose them nor *whom* He chose. Praying and evangelizing belong to the revealed will of God—commandments found in Scripture that are our duty. God can command us to obey Him in areas where He has already determined what He will do. We simply obey and trust His infinite wisdom. He does not owe us an explanation, and we have no right to demand one.

Have I All the Facts?

We make a problem of divine sovereignty and human responsibility because we expect things to be a certain way. When things do not work out the way we expect, we become frustrated and confused. Charles Spurgeon was once asked how he could reconcile divine sovereignty and human will. He replied with his usual witty candor, "I didn't know that they had had a falling out." Both are equally evident in Scripture, and there is no need to reconcile them. Any attempt to reconcile them is to assume that they are contradictory. Nothing contradictory can be reconciled. Therefore, to attempt to reconcile them forces one to explain one or the other away. That must not be done. There is no contradiction in Scripture.

These seemingly contradictory facts are called *antinomies.* They are only *seemingly* contradictory because we do not know enough about them to see their real harmony. Many of these antinomies are falsely identified because of our failure to define concepts properly. For example, if we define *free will* as the *power* of the creature to frustrate God's purposes, then we do have a contradiction. Under this definition, God's imposed will on the sinner would violate the sinner's supposed rights. However, if *free will* is defined as the power to make moral choices *under* God's sovereign rule, then we have harmony. God's sovereignty permits Him to override the choices of His creatures or to let them stand.

The harmony of these things is obvious in Jesus' words about Judas's betrayal: *"And truly the Son of man goeth, as it was determined: but woe unto that man by whom he is betrayed!"* (Luke 22:22). God sovereignly determined that Jesus would go to the cross, but *Judas was fully responsible for his choice in betraying Jesus to the Jews.* Does this mean that God made Judas betray Christ? Absolutely not! Judas acted without coercion, but at the same time God's will was fulfilled in his choice. Such workings are wondrous to behold. Only God could do this!

WHAT ISN'T "FAIR"?

Who Submits to Whom?

Why do people think they need to reconcile God's sovereignty and human will? The answer is that we want to put our right to choose on a par with God's will. Of course, few people would actually be brazen enough to admit outwardly that they think they are equal with God. However, when anyone regards God's sovereign acts as an imposition on human freedom, he is saying that human freedom and God's will are equally important. What we need to understand is that because God is sovereign, His will takes priority over human will. People are to be subject to the will of God.

The first sin in the universe was Satan's desire to be equal with God. To be equal means that the subordinate wants to be independent of the superior. This pirated and presumed independence we call "autonomy"—self-law—in which the creature acts as if he were free of responsibility and obligation to God and therefore free of judgment and punishment.

Original sin is another term which has suffered considerable abuse from ignorance. Many people have confused the act of eating the forbidden fruit with original sin. God's prohibition made eating the fruit a *transgression.* However, the original sin was the *condition* of self-efficiency into which Adam, through his disobedience, plunged the human race. Original sin is the *"iniquity"* that has cursed all of Adam's descendants. *"All we like sheep have gone astray;* [how?] *we have turned every one to his own way* [iniquity]; *and the LORD hath laid on him the iniquity of us all"* (Isaiah 53:6). Because of original sin, sinners presume rights which they think the Creator must acknowledge.

What Is God Doing?

An illustration of the difference between God's sovereign right and the creature's rights is the family unit. My children have desires of their own, but their desires are to be subordinate to my will as long as they are living at home. They are free to make choices within the boundaries of my will, which takes precedence. An act of trespass spells trouble for the trespasser in the form of consequences.

Take this idea a step further. Suppose I ask my daughter to do the dishes for five straight nights. What is the universal response of children? "It's not fair! Why don't my brothers have to do the dishes?" What is meant by *fair*? It is that I am not treating the children *equally*, which is correct. Nevertheless, I have a parental right to impose my will on each child differently.

God, too, has the right to impose His will upon His individual creatures. Life is not fair; all people are not treated equally. We can observe that not all people have the same responsibilities, privileges, and opportunities in life. This observation leads us to conclude either that God is not sovereign or that God's sovereign acts affect people differently as He wills.

Paul understood in Romans 9:20-23 that God's sovereign acts affect people differently. God did not treat Pharaoh the way He treated Moses, but He was just in His dealings with both. He did not call Hammurabi to be the father of His chosen nation, nor did He make the Hittites His chosen people. Even though Ishmael was Abraham's son, God rejected him from the covenant promise. God purposed that He would raise up His chosen seed through the miracle birth of Isaac: *"In Isaac shall thy seed be called"* (Genesis 21:12).

Now, it might be argued that God's choice of Isaac over Ishmael was because Hagar, the mother of Ishmael, was a slave. However, that certainly was not the case in God's choice of Jacob over Esau: they had the same mother.

God did not show *fairness* in choosing Jacob, the younger twin brother, over Esau, the elder. God's choice of Jacob was in spite of Esau's having the legal right to the inheritance. One cannot pass off this choosing (which some do) as God's merely foreseeing the eventual conduct of the boys and their descendants. The fact that Esau sold his birthright to Jacob must not be construed to be the reason God purposed that Jacob should have it. Nor did Jacob's crooked scheming to steal the blessing from Esau compromise God's original intention. God's purpose had nothing to do with their conduct. No, God's plans were not contingent on the conduct of either Jacob or Esau, even though He foresaw their conduct.

Before the children were born, God told Rebekah, *"The elder shall serve the younger"* (Genesis 25:23). Paul in Romans 9:11 and 12 adds, *"(For the children being not yet born, neither having done any good or evil, that the purpose of God according to election might stand, not of works, but of him that calleth;) It was said to her, The elder shall serve the younger."* Esau even changed his mind (Hebrews 12:16, 17). God, however, did not change his mind, for God's purpose must stand.

This whole story of Jacob and Esau illustrates a clear lesson: God's purposes, not our choices or conduct, determine His will regardless of the fact that God's omniscience foresees our choices. As the sovereign Lord of the universe, He does what He desires. *"I have purposed it, I will also do it"* (Isaiah 46:11). After all, God could have easily remedied the conflict between Jacob and Esau by letting Jacob be born first!

Romans 9, where Paul elaborates on God's sovereign dealings with Jacob and Esau, is probably one of the least-preached chapters in the Bible because it poses so many difficult problems to "rights"-insisting humans. Many commentators skirt the issue of the chapter as John R. Rice does when, after citing Benjamin Warfield, he says:

> Now where is Warfield's mistake? And Calvin's mistake?
>
> It is in one phrase. In the midst of the quotation above, Warfield says, "We are explicitly told that IN THE MATTER OF SALVATION it is not of him that wills, or of him that runs, but of God that shows mercy."
>
> But we are explicitly told nothing of the kind! That entire passage of Scripture we have read above [Romans 9:10-18] does not even mention salvation.[104]

Now, where is Rice's mistake? He interprets the passage as referring to God's choice of leadership for the nation of Israel: "When God chose Jacob instead of Esau to have the birthright and the headship of the nation, it had nothing to do with salvation."[105] In saying that, he misses the point of Paul's discussion (Romans 9-11), which is neither about salvation specifically nor about national leadership. Paul is arguing about the sovereign right of the Creator to carry out His plans, which include His purposes related to His creatures: *"That the purpose of God according to election* [sovereign choice] *might stand"* (Romans 9:11). Romans 9 answers those who saw the Jewish rejection of Christ as evidence that God's purposes could be frustrated by human choices. This is seen in the words, *"Not as though the word of God hath taken none effect* [ekpipto, 'to fall to the ground without effect']*"* (Romans 9:6). Paul's critics reasoned that Jewish unbelief had caused the Word of God to "fall to the ground"—to fail in its purpose. Paul responded by demonstrating clearly *from Scripture* that God is sovereign and that Israel's unbelief is in God's purpose. He stated, *"They are not all Israel, which are of Israel"* (Romans 9:6). God has a *"remnant according to the election of grace"* (Romans 11:5).[106]

The fact that his argument would be met by violent objections Paul anticipates and answers. These objections clearly prove that the subject of this discussion was *not* who would have national leadership of Israel—Jacob or Esau. Why would anyone question God's right to choose a man to be the head of a nation? However, one would expect complaint if God's choice involved one's eternal salvation!

"Is God Unrighteous?"

The first objection Paul anticipated was, *"What shall we say then? Is there unrighteousness with God?"* (Romans 9:14). It would appear to the observer that God was unfair in His dealings with Isaac's sons. After all, Esau did have the right of the firstborn. Would not God be unjust to take away Esau's rightful position and give it to Jacob for no apparent reason? Paul does not even try to explain this. Rather, he shows from Scripture (Exodus 33:19) that God has sovereignly bestowed His compassion and mercy as He wills (Romans 9:15, 16). Paul assumes that because God *is* righteous, His acts, which supersede supposed human rights, would also be righteous. It is only those infected by Adam's unlawful usurpation that find God's righteous acts at fault.

"Then, How Can God Hold Me Responsible?"

In the second objection, Paul anticipates the violent emotional protest of those who see in jeopardy their right to control their own destinies. If God's will is supreme and unhindered, then *"Why doth he yet find fault?"* If I am still a sinner, it is because I have been a recipient of God's hardening, not of His mercy (Romans 9:15-18). *"For who hath resisted his will?"* Therefore, how can God hold me responsible for my condition?

Paul replies, *"Nay, but, O man, who art thou that repliest against God? Shall the thing formed say to him that formed it, Why hast thou made me thus?"* (Romans 9:19, 20). He who makes something has power over what he makes:

> *Hath not the potter power over the clay, of the same lump to make one vessel unto honour, and another unto dishonour? What if God, willing to shew his wrath, and to make his power known, endured with much longsuffering the vessels of wrath fitted to destruction: And that he might make known the riches of his glory on the vessels of mercy, which he had afore prepared unto glory, Even us, whom he hath called, not of the Jews only, but also of the Gentiles?* (Romans 9:21-23).

Clay has no say in the potter's choice of what vessel it becomes. The creator of a vessel asserts his purpose over the clay without seeking the desire of the clay. Everyone accepts that as right and proper. Cannot God have the same power?

Now, in considering this right of the potter, however, please do not read into the passage what it does not say. Paul is not referring to *creating* clay—creating some good and some bad—but to working with clay that already is what it is. God is making vessels out of fallen, sinful, rebellious "clay." This is not a fatalistic dogma (like Islam) that has God *creating* the clay, some for heaven and some for hell.[107] Paul is not teaching fatalism, and Calvinism is not fatalism, though many seem to think it is. Why cannot God show mercy to one lump of clay and justice to another if both deserve justice? That is the issue!

Notice, Paul does not rebuke the objectors for their conclusion about God's sovereign choice (*"who hath resisted his will?"*) but for their wrong attitude about it (*"who art thou that repliest against God?"*). *"Is it not lawful for me to do what I will with mine own?"* (Matthew 20:15). People should be very careful about the implications of their protests. What right has any creature, especially a fallen creature, to question the actions of the righteous Sovereign of the universe? This ought to silence forever the fairness complaint, but it will not.[108]

Those who argue that God cannot show fairness by electing some to salvation are arrogantly seeking to discover God's infinite reason in the matter. God has not chosen to reveal this mystery to us. Therefore, we are not to judge God by some human moral principle of fairness that we use to judge ourselves.

Some cite Romans 2:11 to prove that God cannot make some *"vessels of honor"* and others *"vessels of dishonor"*; *"For there is no respect of persons with God."* God's Word does not contradict itself. To use Romans 2:11 against Romans 9:21-23 is to do injustice to the Word of God. The context of Romans 2:11 refers to God's justice, not His sovereign purpose to which justice is subordinate. Consider the context: *"Who* [God] *will render to every man according to his deeds . . . For there is no respect of persons with God"* (Romans 2:6, 11).

The crux of the fairness issue is the moral dilemma in which the human race finds itself—already in disobedience and liable for punishment. *"Therefore as by the offence of one* [Adam] *judgment came upon all men to condemnation"* (Romans 5:18). Judgment is a matter of justice; mercy is not. Mercy is an act of sovereignty, not justice. Even our human judicial system recognizes that heads of state have the authority to pardon and grant clemency. These acts of mercy supersede justice. However, even though God shows mercy to some people, He will still punish their transgressions. Justice requires that all transgressions be punished. While some people suffer their own punishment, others have had their punishment suffered by a Substitute. This is the gospel of grace. The free-will "hinge" turns on the pin of God's determination.

6

AGAINST GOD'S WILL

A love of the truth (II Thessalonians 2:10) requires that one always guard against his natural tendency to a predisposed opinion as to what one thinks the Bible should say. For example, many read John 10:26, *"Ye believe not because ye are not of my sheep,"* as "Ye are not of my sheep because ye believe not."

A lady once angrily accused me of twisting this Scripture. I had been preaching a series on the Gospel of John and was in the tenth chapter. Concerning John 10:26, I said in passing, "Please notice that Jesus gives the Jews the reason for their unbelief—because they were not His sheep." The lady accused me of using the verse to teach the doctrine of election, which she vigorously rejected. Opening my Bible with her, I read the verse. It reads just as I had preached it. That lady was perfectly capable of reading her Bible. The verse was perfectly clear. Her predisposition to reject the doctrine of election caused her to read the verse incorrectly.

An inflexible spirit also contributed to her anger in the matter. Such a spirit is dangerous. What, then, can we do to avoid prejudice in interpretation of the Scripture? How can we recognize when we are being pridefully stubborn rather than Scripturally convinced of the truth? One thing to help us to determine whether our spirit is wrong is to see whether we are violating the Christian graces—meekness, kindness, gentleness, forgiveness, mercy, peace, joy. Are we being angry and hateful? Are we unloving, critical, and judgmental? Only by acknowledging this propensity to a prejudiced view can we guard ourselves against it.

I, too, once hated the doctrines of God's sovereign grace in salvation. We are all initially Arminian because we are self-centered and believe we should have a say-so the matter of salvation. When I was confronted with the doctrines of grace, I struggled with them and resisted them.[109] However, I did want to know the truth. The more I studied, the more I became convinced of God's sovereignty in the gospel. I finally surrendered to the obvious. One day I said to my wife, "I believe I am a Calvinist." She replied, "Oh, no!"[110] It was the Scriptures themselves that drove me to the position I now joyfully champion.[111]

THE PROBLEM OF PREDISPOSITION
AND INTERPRETATION

The predisposition of modern evangelicalism with its insistence on humans' right of choice tends to confuse "who does what" in salvation. This confusion results in erroneous conclusions based on improperly defined terms. For example, as we observed in the last chapter, God's sovereign choice and human responsibility are seen as contradictory. Thus, in order to avoid contradiction, those inclined to humanism will explain away God's sovereignty in order to preserve human free will.

Another example of unnecessary confusion is faith and election. The "recognized scholar and an authority on the matter of Calvinism,"[112] anti-Calvinist Samuel Fisk, declares, "Any statement setting forth a condition on which a sinner may receive the forgiveness of sins through God's provision in Christ would belie unconditional election. . . . When conditioned on something, it is not unconditional."[113] Let us examine this statement.

Does the Command to Repent and Believe Belie Unconditional Election?

Let us look at the assumptions behind Fisk's comment: (1) If faith is a *condition* for salvation, then election cannot be *unconditional*. If this is true, the doctrine of unconditional election must be false. (2) Since faith is a condition for salvation, then the sinner, it is assumed, is *able* of himself to meet the condition. If that is true, then the doctrine of total depravity is false and the doctrine of election would be unnecessary. (3) In order for sinners to be able to exercise faith, they must have *freedom of choice*—to be free to refuse as well as accept Christ. If that is true, the doctrine of irresistible grace is false and the doctrine of election would be immoral. (4) Freedom of choice in salvation assumes that all have the *opportunity* to choose or refuse salvation. If that is true, then the doctrine of limited atonement is false and the doctrine of election would be unfair.

Now, let us examine the facts. First, Fisk has confused concepts. While election is unto salvation (II Thessalonians 2:13), it is not salvation. Salvation is *conditional* (it requires faith), but election is still *unconditional*.[114] However, the fact that faith is a condition of salvation does not contradict the fact that God unconditionally chose some sinners to salvation, not choosing them according to any faith foreseen in them. A condition for salvation and an unconditional election are not mutually exclusive.

66

Second, the fact that salvation requires faith as a condition does not assume that every sinner can meet that condition. Commands in Scripture only demonstrate responsibility, not ability. The unregenerate sinner will not believe because of the inherent enmity of his fallen nature toward God. The doctrine of total depravity is secure. Election is necessary if any sinners are to be saved. *"No man can come unto me, except it were given unto him of my Father"* (John 6:65).

Third, the task of preaching the gospel naturally focuses on the calling of sinners to repentance and faith. The Bible indeed teaches us that *no* sinner will ever be saved who does not freely respond in faith to the gospel offer. The sinner is responsible to *"believe on the Lord Jesus Christ,"* and in believing, *"thou shalt be saved"* (Acts 16:31). But Scripture also teaches us that believing the gospel is the fruit of the effectual inward call (irresistible grace, Romans 1:5, 6). The proof of one's election is his faith (Titus 1:1, *"the faith of God's elect"*). *"And . . . as many as were ordained to eternal life believed"* (Acts 13:48). To confuse these concepts and err on the side of humanism results in a denial of sovereign election and the freedom of God's will.

Let the Scripture Speak for Itself!

If one's predisposition holds that conditional salvation belies unconditional election, he must deny that election is *to salvation*—that God chose the sinners who will be saved. Samuel Fisk denies election to salvation in order to preserve human freedom of choice. He argues that those who teach that nobody would be saved without a sovereign election overlook God's foreknowledge.[115]

> That foreknowledge, while not pre-determinative, nevertheless sees the end from the beginning. We may say that God made His provision for the salvation of fallen human beings so wonderful, so complete, so surpassingly attractive, that He foresaw (without directly causing) that many would respond to the gracious invitation, would recognize the avenue of escape from certain doom so freely available, and would flee for refuge into the arms of the infinitely loving Savior."[116]

The fault with Fisk's thinking should be obvious. He never explains how salvation can be made "so surpassingly attractive" that sinners will "flee for refuge" to a Savior they naturally loathe. What is this that is so powerful that God needs only to "see" that some will believe? If God does not "cause" them to come, what does He do? Something must be done. Arminius argued that "sufficient grace must necessarily be laid down; yet this sufficient grace, through the fault of him to whom it is granted, does not always obtain its effect."[117] Even the Arminians agree that God must do something. They think He must not, however, interfere with the sinner's free choice, and He must be willing to take refusal. The assumption is that if the gospel with its commands and exhortations is preached in someone's hearing, the hearer must be *able* to respond if he will. God must give him sufficient grace to enable him but not to save him.

On the other hand, when sovereign-grace doctrine teaches "inability" to repent and believe the gospel, the reference is not to the *natural* capacity for believing but to the *moral* frame that makes one unwilling. Jesus said, *"And ye will not come to me that ye might have life"* (John 5:40). This unwillingness is behind the declaration in John 6:65 that *"no man can come unto me, except it were given unto him of my Father* [in election]." The sinner *will not*, therefore *cannot*, come to Christ.

The question remains: can unregenerate people obey the gospel in their unregenerate state? Is their inability physical or moral? Does the sinner's inability to obey the gospel relieve him of his responsibility in it? The arguments go round and round on this issue. To sort them out, one must define what kind of ability is in view. When Christ commanded the man with the withered hand to stretch it forth (Matthew 12:10-13), we have something of an illustration on this point. In this instance, the command was accompanied with physical healing, but suppose Christ had not healed the physical problem. Could He have held the man responsible for not obeying? What if the man's inability to obey Christ was a moral refusal in spite of his physical difficulty? His refusal could not then be justified by any defect in his hand. He could be held responsible. Just so, salvation comes in the "healing" of the will (Psalm 110:3).

God still commands that all men repent and believe the gospel because every sinner has the ability to hear the gospel and understand God's requirement of him. Because sinners do not have the heart to receive the gospel, however, they will not. God is not unrighteous to require repentance and faith. He holds accountable in judgment all those who refuse to repent and believe (Acts 17:30, 31). At the same time, however, obeying the command is *morally* not possible without divine enablement. Even free-willers themselves admit that no one comes to Christ without the conviction and enlightenment of the Holy Spirit.

Sovereign grace takes this process one step further, believing that conviction and enlightenment alone are insufficient without the sinner's disposition first being changed in regeneration. Any theology that puts limits upon God, even if it cites supposed Scriptural support, must be viewed as dangerous. God's will does not play second fiddle to human will.

CAN ANYONE MAKE GOD DO WHAT HE IS NOT WILLING TO DO?

The other side of this question of ability is what supposed "free will" does to the sovereignty of God. Can human will frustrate the Divine will? Can anyone or anything make God do what He is unwilling to do? Of course, most people will immediately say no because they view God as sovereign and all-powerful. When it comes to the issue of salvation, however, many will insist that God wants all sinners to be saved but that sinners are free to choose or refuse salvation. This means that in the matter of salvation God can be made to do what He is unwilling to do—let unrepentant sinners perish. "Yes," they consent, *"the Lord is . . . not willing that any should perish, but that all should come to repentance"* (II Peter 3:9). Does this verse not prove that it is God's will that everyone be saved?

The Typical Interpretation of II Peter 3:9

God's longsuffering, the theme of II Peter 3:9, concerns sinners who are in imminent danger of judgment at Christ's coming because of their sin. These sinners need to repent in order to escape judgment. The typical "free-will" interpretation of this passage is as follows: "Christ's delayed coming shows His patient waiting for sinners to repent. He wants to save all sinners if only they will repent. He wishes every sinner to repent even if He knows eternally that many will not."[118]

If it is God's will for all to be saved, why do both God's Word and experience teach us that not everyone is going to be saved? We know that multitudes have lived and died without Christ. Neither have all been given even the opportunity to be saved. If God purposed to save as many as could be persuaded (assuming that they could be persuaded), should not all be given this opportunity, which we know they have not been given? Now, we may either find fault with God, or we may accept the fact that we have been wrong about our interpretation of the verse.

Preliminary Considerations

In order to interpret this verse properly, we must first deter-
· mine whether the Scriptures reveal God as desiring what He cannot

have. As we have previously noted, people tend to view God as like themselves, a view encouraged by the many Scripture references which use anthropomorphic terms to describe God. These references must be understood in a metaphorical sense and *not* in a literal sense—that God actually has, for example, eyes (I Peter 3:12). We must not take God literally where we should not do so or else we will be giving God limitations that "literally" take away His deity. *"God is not a man"* (Numbers 23:19). With this understanding in mind, read II Peter 3:9. Also, be careful not to read into the verse what it does not say. Unfortunately, many who should know better err in this very point.[119]

We do observe this fact: not all have come to repentance. We must, then, conclude that either God is not willing for all to repent or He is not able to accomplish universal repentance. Which is it: God is not willing to save all? or since God is not wishing any to perish, He is not able to save all? Can Christ-rejecting sinners frustrate God's will? If so, then what does God mean when He says, *"So shall my word be that goeth forth out of my mouth: It shall not return unto me void* [empty], *but it shall accomplish that which* I *please, and it shall prosper whereto I sent it"* (Isaiah 55:11)? The typical interpretation of II Peter 3:9 contradicts Isaiah 55:11 and makes it read like the empty boast of a braggadocio who cannot do what he wants to do because his hands are tied by the exigencies of human free will. He would love to save perishing sinners if only He could get their cooperation.

God's Purpose

In the context Peter has explained that in the last days there would be scoffers who would deny Christ's coming. They would view God's patience as weakness or failure to keep His Word. They would mock at God's threats of judgment and brazenly continue in open sin and rebellion. Peter exhorts the believers not to be discouraged at the brazenness of the mockers. God "puts up" with these mockers because He has a purpose to fulfill concerning *"us."*

What is God not willing should happen? The word *boulomia* (*"willing"*) means "to will," as of purpose.[120] It refers to God's *determinative will*. The key to understanding what God is not willing to do are the words *"to us-ward,"* or better, "concerning us (believers)." Consider the phrase *"not willing that any should perish."* Not *any* what? Here is where many read into the passage. *"Any"* is generally read to mean all sinners. This verse does not say that. It says only *"any."* One must find in the passage itself the antecedent for *"any."*

The closest antecedent is *"us"*: "God is longsuffering concerning us." *"The Lord is not willing that any* [of us] *should perish."*

Now, to whom does *"us"* refer? Although, linguistically, *"us"* could refer generally to anyone, contextually *"us"* must refer to the recipients of Peter's letter—the elect *"that have obtained like precious faith through the righteousness of God and our Saviour Jesus Christ"* (II Peter 1:1, 2). It refers to those *"beloved"* with *"pure minds"* (II Peter 3:1) who are being exhorted to remember the words of the prophets and the commandment of the apostles (II Peter 3:2). Peter was warning *"us"* not to be intimidated by the scoffers.

"Us" refers to the believers contrasted with the *"scoffers."* Peter encourages believers: *"Account that the longsuffering of our Lord is* [your] *salvation"* (II Peter 3:15). *"Therefore, seeing ye know these things before, beware lest ye also, being led away with the error of the wicked* [regarding God's longsuffering as weakness or lack of purpose] *fall from your own steadfastness"* (II Peter 3:17).

Therefore, the *"any"* and the *"all"* of verse nine simply refer back to *"us."* The Lord's promise that He would return is secure. His delay is only apparent. His purposes must first be fulfilled. Therefore, Peter gives the believers this encouragement: *"The Lord is not slack* [slow] *concerning his promise* [of returning], *as some men count slackness; but is longsuffering* [in bearing with brazen sin and rebellion] *to* [Gk. *eis,* 'with respect to'—referring to purposes related to believers] *us-ward, not willing that any* [of us, His elect] *should perish, but that all* [of us, His elect] *should come to repentance."* God will gather in all whom He has given to Christ to save before He comes again. Christ promised that all whom the Father had given Him He would raise up in the last day (John 6:36-44).

Peter is explaining that God is doing exactly what He wills, and He will come when it is time for Him to do so. His Word is true and reliable. We are not to be discouraged by the ranting of skeptics and the waning of years. But He will not come before bringing all of His elect to repentance (II Timothy 2:10) and in His own good time.

To sum up, free-willers twist the doctrine of election, making God to look anemic by willing what He cannot have because He is forced to submit to the unwillingness of His creatures to cooperate with His desires. Anything else, they surmise, would be to make God out to be unrighteous and unfair.

An old friend, Doug Bookman, wrote the following in an excellent article that appeared in *Masterpiece* magazine to correct the notion that there might be unfairness in God:

71

We must not misconstrue God's electing activity as partiality, as though He were being fair to some and not to others. That would be to assume all men have a claim upon salvation but that God designed to grant it only to some—a grotesque and man-centered distortion of biblical truth. It views God as choosing to save only a few of a greater number of innocent unfortunates, who, through no fault of their own, found themselves shipwrecked and drowning when all were equally deserving of rescue, and when God might have saved them all. The clear and emphatic teaching of Scripture is rather that God has sovereignly and graciously chosen to rescue part of a great company, none of whom have any just claim upon God's goodness and all of whom have wickedly, deliberately, and repeatedly resisted God's every attempt to prevent their spiritual self-destruction.[121]

7

CHOSEN? TO WHAT?

There is no question that election is a Bible doctrine: *"And as many as were ordained to eternal life believed"* (Acts 13:48). However, the controversy concerning the doctrine has been long and bitter. One writer speaks for many who see election as "precious beyond words and a great nourishment for Christlikeness of faith."[122] But a multitude of Christians seem to agree with another writer who calls it "akin to blasphemy," being a "totally unscriptural," "monstrous thing" that "presents God as a Being of injustice and maligns His holy character."[123] There is no neutral ground on this issue.

While unconditional election is indicted as a "man-made doctrine not in the Scripture,"[124] the nature of the doctrine itself could hardly support the charge. The mere mention of election, even the quoting of a biblical reference without comment, will send some people into a sputtering rage. With this kind of reaction, a human origin of election is hardly feasible, its being so repulsive to human reasoning. Why is this? The answer is very simple. In the words of Martin Luther, "This bombshell knocks 'free-will' flat, and utterly shatters it."[125] You see, any doctrine which denies the exercise of what may be constituted a sacred "rite" (free will) will be met with vigorous opposition.

A "TAMED" ELECTION

Free-Will Election Defined

Opposition to the doctrine of unconditional election does not always take on a vehement nature. Most efforts raised against the doctrine do not seek to disprove it but rather seek to "tame" it. Those who find the Calvinistic definition of election obnoxious must necessarily redefine the term to make it acceptable to their sensibilities. The late Baptist theologian Dr. Henry C. Theissen did this very thing. Although he would probably have vigorously denied it, his view of election is the Arminian view.[126] In his book on systematic theology, Theissen wrote: "By election we mean that sovereign act of God in grace whereby He chose in Christ Jesus for salvation all those *whom He foreknew would accept him* [emphasis added]."[127] That, whether Theissen realized it or not, is the historic Arminian definition of election. A seventeenth-

73

century disciple of Jacobus Arminius, Corvinus, wrote: "God hath determined to grant the means of salvation unto all without difference; and according *as He foresees men will use those means,* so he determineth [elects] them [emphasis added]."[128] Theissen and Corvinus, along with most modern evangelicals, agree that election is based on God's foreseeing the sinner's "free" exercise of faith in Christ.

Free-Will Election Developed

In explaining this view of election, Theissen says:

> Since mankind is hopelessly dead in trespasses and sins and can do nothing to obtain salvation, *God graciously restores to all men sufficient ability to make a choice* in the matter of submission to Him. This is the salvation—bringing the grace of God that has appeared to all men. *In His foreknowledge He perceives what each one will do with this restored ability, and elects men to salvation in harmony with His foreknowledge of their choice of Him* [emphasis added].[129]

What is this "restored ability"? Here Theissen departs from the semi-Pelagianism of Arminius and takes the same path as John Wesley. Wesley agreed with Calvinists on "total depravity." He believed that "because of original sin, the natural man is 'dead to God' and unable to move himself toward God or to respond to him."[130] Therefore, Wesley believed that salvation had to be *all* of grace.

Calvinists teach that if the sinner cannot by any means find his way to God for salvation, then the logical "next step" is that God must predestine him to salvation. Wesley, however, rejected the doctrine of predestination. Therefore, in order to break the "chain of logical necessity" (eliminating predestination),[131] Wesley adopted a two-pronged view of grace that forms two "steps" in the saving process. First, he argued for "prevenient grace,"[132] which restores to every sinner the *ability* to choose freely to be saved. Wesley saw this grace as the *"light, which lighteth every man"* (John 1:9). If this grace is encouraged and not resisted, the now-enabled sinner can then be introduced to "convincing grace," which comes by the gospel and actually leads the sinner to salvation. Convincing grace can also be resisted. God cannot "force" even an enlightened sinner to be saved. According to Wesley, God may be willing to save all, but He can save only those who willingly of themselves choose to be saved.

Wesley's doctrine of grace is based on these two points: (1) that all mankind is by nature sinful and separated from God, being unable to return to God without intervening grace; (2) that God gave His Son to die for every man and that Christ enlightens every man in order to enable him either to accept or to reject His offer of mercy.[133] The first point agrees with the reformers, but the second effectively denies Reformation theology and leans back towards Romanism. Author Colin Williams demonstrates this direction in Wesley:

> His [Wesley's] view is synergistic [a "working together"] in the sense that God creates in man the freedom to receive or resist His grace. Man is given responsibility by God's grace. This recognition, that man is given freedom to receive or resist the gospel, would seem to have a double significance: (1) It provides the way for reconciling the Classic Protestant tradition of justification by faith through grace alone, with well-nigh universal abandonment of the logical framework of double predestination. (2) It enables an adequate answer to be given to the strong suspicion, particularly among those of the catholic and liberal traditions, that the Classical Protestant view leads to a certain quietism [a passive reliance upon God, which ultimately leads to antinomianism] and to a lack of concern for present personal social transformation [humanism].[134]

What is Theissen's "restored ability" but Wesley's "prevenient grace"? This "grace" enables the "totally depraved" to exercise "free will" in salvation without the necessity of the doctrine of predestination. With Wesley, Theissen believes that "depravity has produced a total spiritual inability in the sinner in the sense that he cannot of his own volition change his character and life so as to make them conformable to the law of God, nor change his fundamental preference of self and sin to supreme love for God."[135] The sinner "has a certain amount of freedom left. . . . Freedom of choice with . . . limits . . . is not incompatible with complete bondage of the will in spiritual things."[136] How is this possible? Theissen and Wesley have invented a doctrine of "restored ability" to improve the condition of every sinner by removing "total" from his depravity. Christ's death saved every sinner just enough for the sinner to save himself, if he wants to. It is a universal "almost" salvation.

This view of Theissen and Wesley, which is nothing but a varnished Arminianism, is clearly in evidence today. I heard a fundamental Baptist preacher say that Christ's death made it possible for God to give everyone enough faith to believe the gospel. Sinners need only to decide to use that faith in order to be saved. This same preacher would be horrified if he were called a Wesleyan-Arminian, but his message is what John Wesley taught. It is what H. C. Theissen taught. It is what Arminius taught. However, contrary to all these, the Bible teaches that complete bondage of the will makes freedom of choice impossible in spiritual things (I Corinthians 2:14).

Satisfying Our Sense of Justice?

Theissen argues that his view of election answers the "persistent demand of the heart for a theory of election that does commend itself to our sense of justice and that harmonizes the teachings of Scripture concerning the sovereignty of God and the responsibility of man."[137] Did you catch that? This view answers the "persistent demand of the heart" to have an election that "satisfies *our* sense of justice"! There it is! That is the motive for emasculating the biblical doctrine of unconditional election. The whole philosophy behind Theissen's theology with its "restored ability" and "conditional election" is the notion that God's justice requires Him to give every sinner a second chance—an opportunity to reconsider his rebellion. That is humanism—pure humanism! No careful exposition of Scripture is used to demonstrate this conclusion. It is rather concerned with giving the spiritually dead a way to exercise free will short of regeneration while absolving God of the charge of playing favorites.

What proof did Dr. Theissen offer for his man-satisfying doctrine of election? He argues, "In the minds of some people, election is a choice that God makes for which *we can see no reason* and which we can hardly harmonize with His justice."[138] If nothing else so far, surely *this* statement reveals Theissen's anti-God humanism. In light of this error, I ask, whose view of election is "man-made" and "not in the Scriptures"?

Free-Will Election Answered

1. Election Based on Foreknowledge

Theissen's doctrine of election is correctly based on God's foreknowledge (I Peter 1:2). However, his definition of foreknowledge is that God merely *foresees* human choices but does not determine them. If God foresees the sinner's faith in Christ (He sees the individual "getting saved"), then what purpose does election serve? It appears to be a redundancy. Why does the sinner need to be elected to what God foresees the sinner has already done? This view makes God look foolish in doing the unnecessary!

There are at least three problems with the view that election is based on God's foreseeing the individual's faith: (1) It makes God a mere third-party observer. Since God is not the determiner of the event, who is? The event must be certain if God foresees it. (2) What power outside of God can so influence and affect the mind of a sinner that he changes his desires against his own nature (I Corinthians 2:14)? (3) If God's choice of the sinner is merely a consequence of the sinner's choosing Christ, then God's choice is no choice at all, seeing He is under the necessity of choosing the chooser. Thus, salvation would not be of free grace but would be rather a reward of debt, which Paul flatly denies (Romans 4:4).

2. Election and God's Invitations

Theissen believed in a universal atonement. He reasoned, therefore, all sinners should be given the opportunity to accept or reject what Christ accomplished for them in His death. He argued that an unconditional election would make a mockery of God's universal invitation. To answer, God's commands to sinners to repent of sin involve the sinner's moral responsibility to God and cannot be construed as insincere even though God knows that they will never be obeyed. We have discussed this and will do so again. Besides, the elect must hear the gospel in order to be saved. Unconditional election is not incompatible with universal preaching of the gospel.

3. Election and God's Justice

His view, Theissen argues, absolves God of the injustice that unconditional election seems to thrust on God. He says, "It is difficult to see how that God can choose some . . . and do nothing about all the others, if, as we read, righteousness is the foundation of his throne."[139] Actually, it is not justice that is at issue here but "fairness." If all deserve to be punished, then God is just to punish all. If God showed mercy to one and saved him, He is still just to punish the rest. It is not justice but supposed *unfairness* that is at question here.

The Puritan Thomas Manton puts this concern into perspective:

> Our understandings are not the measure of God's justice, but his own will. . . . God's freedom is a riddle to reason, because though we will not be bound to laws, yet we are willing God should be bound. God's actions must not be measured by any external rule; things are good because God willeth them, for his will is justice itself.[140]

The real issue, again, is not God's justice but His sovereign freedom. God's justice cannot be called into question over His saving anyone—some, all, or none. Justice could be called into question only if God had failed to satisfy His own demand for sin's payment in the saving of sinners.[141] It is God's sovereign freedom to show mercy and compassion to some but not all sinners that provokes the protest of fairness.

Arguing that unconditional election poses a problem to God's fairness reveals more than a difference of theological opinion: it reveals the carnal propensity in fallen humans toward enmity with God. As Charles Spurgeon pointed out,

> There seems to be an inveterate prejudice in the human mind against this doctrine [election], and although most other doctrines will be received by professing Christians, some with caution, others with pleasure, yet this one seems to be the most frequently disregarded and discarded. In many of our pulpits, it would be reckoned a high sin and treason to preach a sermon upon *election*.[142]

That prejudice is rooted in the belief that humans deserve a voice in God's dealings with them. We have not lost our determination to impose our supposed equality with God.

As we noted in Chapter 5, Paul, in Romans 9:19, dealt with this very attitude of prideful enmity toward God's freedom of will. Paul does not seek to explain the fairness of God's sovereign acts of mercy but rather rebukes the objectors for their rebellious outburst: *"Nay but, O man, who art thou that repliest against God"* (Romans 9:20). The very sad fact is that many reject the doctrine of unconditional election because they *loathe* a God who is free to implement such an election. Sinners are still guilty of *"changing the glory of the uncorruptible God into an image"* of their own liking (Romans 1:23).

4. Election and Missionary Motive

Theissen concludes, "This [Theissen's view of election] tends *logically* to great missionary endeavor [emphasis added].["143] But I ask, how would this view *"logically"* contribute to obedience in missions more than the view of sovereign election? The doctrine of election assures the missionary that there will be a harvest of souls. *"I have much people in this city,"* God assured Paul (Acts 18:9, 10).

Missionary endeavor is based on God's command to preach the gospel to every creature (Mark 16:15). Obedience to God's command is based on God's authority to issue the command, not on the command's *reasonableness*. We are to obey God, and we trust *Him* for the results. Only rebellious human hearts "demand" that authority justify commands before they are obeyed.

UNCONDITIONAL ELECTION

Unconditional Election Defined

What is the biblical view of election? The Bible teaches *unconditional* election—that God chose a host of people in eternity past to be the recipients of His saving grace (Ephesians 1:3-10). This election was made on the basis of His own freedom—what the Bible calls *"the good pleasure of His will"* (Ephesians 1:4, 5). God did not choose or reject anyone because of anything good or bad that He foresaw in them. His choice was made before any were born, before any sinned, even before there was a creation (Ephesians 1:4). This election was neither an arbitrary selection nor an obligation to reward foreseen faith.

Election is simply choosing. *Unconditional* means that the choice was made without any reference to condition. God made a choice in eternity past to choose some of the human race, predestining them to be conformed to the image of His Son (Ephesians 1:4, 5). Only the will and purpose of God, not even foreseen faith in the sinner, is the motive of election. Those not chosen to salvation are left to suffer the just consequences of their sin.

Unconditional Election Biblically Defended

Consider I Peter 1:2: *"Elect according to the foreknowledge of God the Father, through sanctification of the Spirit, unto obedience and sprinkling of the blood of Jesus Christ."* *"Elect"* is a description of the Christians to whom Peter is writing. In I Peter 2:9 Peter calls them *"a chosen* [same meaning as *elect*] *generation."* Believers are called *"elect"* or *"chosen."* No one questions this fact because it is obviously biblical language. The question centers on why believers are called *"elect"* and how they are chosen.

The word that is translated *"elect"* in I Peter 1:2 is the noun form of *eklegomai*, which means "to choose." Some have argued that this word cannot be used to prove a divine, sovereign election. They insist that it means only a choice of someone to something but not to salvation. This is partly true because election itself is not salvation; however, unconditional election does *result* in salvation. In fact, I Peter 1:2 cannot be interpreted to mean anything else. Even a casual reading of I Peter 1 shows that the whole context speaks of salvation: *"Receiving the end of your faith, even the salvation of your souls"* (v. 9); God has *"begotten us again* [the new birth, cf. v. 23] *unto a lively* [living] *hope"*

(v. 3); we are *"kept by the power of God unto salvation"* (v. 5); we are redeemed by the *"precious blood of Christ"* (vv. 19, 20).

In II Thessalonians 2:13 we have a different word with a different emphasis: *"But we are bound to give thanks always to God for you, brethren, beloved of the Lord, because God hath from the beginning chosen* [Gk. *haireo*] *you to salvation."* Calvinists, Samuel Fisk argues, ought not use this verse to support their doctrine because the word *"chosen"* is not the usual word (*eklego*) for choosing[144] but rather is a rare word (*haireo*) used only here of God's electing to something other than salvation—to sound Christian living.

Actually, *haireo* is a stronger word than *eklego*. Here the force of the Greek word is on the result of the choice—to elect someone to something: *"to salvation."*[145] Paul definitely and strongly teaches that God chose the Thessalonian believers *"to salvation."* The dictionary meaning of *haireo* (*"chosen"*) is a choice "in the sense of taking for oneself" (in the middle voice, as it is here).[146] *When* He chose believers for Himself is also clear—*"from the beginning* [of the world]."[147] *How* He brought His chosen ones to Himself follows in the next verse: *"Through* [the means of] *the sanctification of the Spirit* [God's work] *and belief in the truth* [gospel work] *whereunto he called you* [effectual calling requiring regeneration] *by our gospel"* (II Thessalonians 2:14).

In arguing against this view of election, Fisk points out that Paul uses *haireo* for his indecision in Philippians 1:22: *"But if I live in the flesh, this is the fruit of my labour: yet what I shall choose* [*haireo*] *I wot not."* All this verse says is that Paul at that point in his ministry did not know what choice he preferred—whether to depart this life and be with Christ or to remain and continue his ministry for the benefit of the churches. But *haireo* still means a "choice." Philippians 1:22 does not support Fisk's rejection of election to salvation in II Thessalonians 2:13. His diverting attention to Paul's indecision in no way reduces the impact of God's definite choice of the Thessalonian believers to salvation. Diversion is not a legitimate method of Bible interpretation.

Unconditional Election and Foreknowledge

Foreknowledge Defined

A proper biblical understanding of foreknowledge is essential for a proper view of election. Peter tells us that the *"elect"* were chosen through the *"foreknowledge of God the Father"* (I Peter 1:2). There are three applications of the word *foreknowledge*: (1) to know the relative certainty of an event because of planning, experience, or speculation; (2) to "see" the certainty of events ahead of time, which would require omniscience or prescience; (3) to determine, decree, or "foreordain" events ahead of time according to a plan. The certainty of the event would be in proportion to the power of the planner: God is omnipotent.

The verb form for *foreknowledge* appears five times in the New Testament, and the noun form appears twice. Of these seven times, it is used five times concerning God and Christ and twice concerning man. Our problem is to decide which of the above three ideas applies to *foreknowledge* in I Peter 1:2. It is unlikely that anyone who understands anything about God would suggest that God only guesses the outcome of events. Even the prevalent evangelical view of foreknowledge in election is that God at least foresaw who would believe. Obviously, God knew all about those who would believe; He is omniscient. But Scripture shows that God not only saw that they would believe; He *ordained* that they would believe (Romans 8:29).

One of the rules of interpretation of Scripture is to let the author of a book explain how he uses a word. Peter interprets *"foreknowledge"* (I Peter 1:2) for us in I Peter 1:19-21, where he explains how God predetermined Jesus' death: *"Who verily, was foreordained before the foundation of the world, but was manifest in these last times for you."* The word here translated *"foreordained"* is the same word that is translated *"foreknowledge"* in I Peter 1:2. Did God foresee that Jesus would die on the cross and then choose Him to die? Of course not! Before the world began, God determined that Jesus would die on the cross. God planned for Christ's death to happen.

In Acts 2:23 Peter, preaching on the day of Pentecost, said, *"Him, being delivered by the determinate counsel and foreknowledge of God, ye have taken, and by wicked hands have crucified and slain."* Notice the phrase *"by the determinate counsel and foreknowledge of God."* The Granville-Sharp rule in Greek grammar states that when two words are joined together by *"and"* and the first word has a definite article but the second does not, the second word means the same as the first. In other words, Peter uses *"determinate counsel"*[148] to mean the same as *"foreknowledge."* Thus, in I Peter 1:2 Peter's use of *foreknowledge* is to be understood as God's plan, determined in the counsel of the Godhead before the world began (I Peter 1:20), to choose a people for Himself and to bring them to Himself by the sanctifying work of the Holy Spirit and the sacrificial death of Christ. Election is the sovereign act of God in which He in eternity past chose certain of Adam's condemned race to be the recipients of His mercy, which resulted in their salvation from wrath and sin.

Foreknowledge Biblically Illustrated

The biblical view of foreknowledge that we have just set forth can be illustrated in Romans 11. In dealing with the rejection of Israel, Paul answers some questions about the permanence of that rejection. *"Hath God cast away his people* [Israel]*? God forbid! . . . God hath not cast away His people which He foreknew"* (Romans 11:1, 2). Notice again the phrase *"which He foreknew."* It cannot mean that God elected Israel by foresight of Israel's response to God, for what kind of response did God foresee? *"Ye stiffnecked and uncircumcised in heart and ears, ye do always resist the Holy Ghost: as your fathers did, so do ye"* (Acts 7:51). No, in spite of Israel's being a rebellious people, He *determined* to make them His people. Now, upon what basis did God choose Israel to be His people?

> *For thou art an holy people unto the LORD thy God: the LORD thy God hath chosen thee to be a special people unto himself, above all people that are upon the face of the earth. The LORD did not set his love upon you, nor choose you, because ye were more in number than any people; for ye were the fewest of all people: But because the LORD loved you, and because he would keep the oath which he had sworn unto your fathers, hath the LORD brought you out with a mighty hand, and redeemed you out of the house of bondmen, from the hand of Pharaoh king of Egypt* (Deuteronomy 7:6-8).

This passage is important because it shows that God's setting His love upon someone is the same as His choosing them. Deuteronomy 7:6-8 is the first biblical reference to the love of God. It is important because it establishes what God means when He says that He loves us.

In Romans God says, *"Jacob have I loved, but Esau have I hated"* (Romans 9:13). What does this mean? "A woman once said to Mr. Spurgeon, 'I cannot understand why God should say that He hated Esau.' 'That,' Spurgeon replied, 'is not my difficulty, Madam. My trouble is to understand how God could love Jacob!'"[149]

If the thought of God's loving one brother and hating the other troubles one, it may be that he lacks a biblical understanding of man's sinful condition. It is more likely that he does not have a proper understanding of God Himself. We must learn to divorce our notions of love and hate as being responses of passion from the biblical idea of God's love and hate. In God, hate is an action of purpose and choice. In other words, God's *hating* Esau was not a passionate reaction to Esau's disagreeable character, actions, or attitudes. God's *hating* Esau was not a reaction to Esau at all. The choice of Jacob necessitated the rejection of Esau.

God's choosing Israel to be His chosen people is an earthly illustration of the truth of election (I Corinthians 10:11). Although privileged (Romans 3:1, 2; 9:4, 5), the Israelites were not a spiritual people (Romans 10:1-3, 18-21). This fact is used by some against the doctrine of unconditional election to salvation. But this objection does not change the fact of Israel's being a special object of God's love, which is election.

Israel's existence began when God chose Abraham out from the peoples of the world in order to make a special people for Himself. No other nation was given the privileges Israel enjoyed (Psalm 147:20). But even within the nation, there was a spiritually elect people, for in the setting aside of the nation in this gospel age, Paul argued, *"There is a remnant according to the election of grace"* (Romans 11:5).

What is God's motive in the New Testament gospel age in choosing a people for His name? Love.

> *"Behold, what manner of love the Father hath bestowed upon us* [His elect], *that we should be called the sons of God: therefore the world knoweth us not, because it knew him not"* (I John 3:1).

> *"Herein is love, not that we loved God, but that he loved us* [His elect], *and sent his Son to be the propitiation for our sins"* (I John 4:10).

Foreknowledge and Faith

Believers are not chosen to salvation as a reaction of God to some foreseen "decision" by them. Such a thing would not be election at all but the rewarding of virtue in the sinner. That kind of salvation is not of grace. Rather, in eternity past God purposed to set His love upon some, choosing them for His own. Christ came to redeem the elect by His substitutionary work in their behalf. Faith in His finished work is the means whereby the elect are brought into the experience of their salvation.

Faith's being the gift of God is rejected by those who argue that while sinners are saved *"by grace,"* this salvation is *"through"* faith—that faith being the sinner's response to God's grace. *"For by grace are ye saved* [past perfect: *have been saved*] *through faith; and that not of yourselves: it is the gift of God: Not of works, lest any man should boast"* (Ephesians 2:8, 9). This faith, they argue, originates with the sinner and is *foreseen* as the means of election. To rebut this notion, consider the following arguments.

Faith Is God's Gift to the Elect

There are two proofs from this passage (Ephesians 2:4-10) that show faith is God's gift. First, Paul plainly teaches that *"faith"* is *"not of yourselves,"* being *"the gift of God"* (2:8). Believing is the evidence of God's choice, not the source of it. Second, Paul's purpose to magnify God in the wonderful grace of salvation falls flat if faith is produced on our part. Let us elaborate.

I can hear those who will try to expose my ignorance of Greek at this point. (I make no claim to be a Greek scholar.) I should know that the demonstrative pronoun *"that"* (better, "this"—*"this not of yourselves"*) is *neuter* and cannot refer either to *"grace"* or *"faith,"* which are both feminine.[150] However, those who use this argument to prove that faith is not a gift either do not know Greek or ignore the facts. It is not at all unusual in Greek grammar for the feminine, especially an abstract feminine like *"faith,"* to take a neuter pronoun.[151] The gender, however, is not the only grammatical consideration.

Faith is the most logical noun reference of the pronoun *touto* (*"that"*) for the following reasons. First, *touto* usually refers to the noun immediately preceding it, in this case *"faith."*[152] This antecedent is also logical because *faith* is the only noun mentioned in the verse which we might be tempted to claim as coming from ourselves. We could hardly claim that either grace or salvation itself was *"of"* (*ek,* "out of") ourselves.

Third, the phrase begins with *kai* (*"and"*), which, when coupled with *touto,* gives it an added emphasis ("and this *too*"), which underscores faith's being the antecedent of *touto.* It is a reminder to the reader that, should he be inclined to think otherwise, his faith is also the gift of God.

A fourth consideration is that the emphasis of the verse is not salvation but the grace that brought salvation. The verse is an explanation of Paul's interjection in verse five—*"for by grace you have been saved."* Paul's purpose in this passage is to exalt God for His wonderful grace in salvation. Faith is the gift of that grace.

Fifth, the reason Paul gives for God's grace in saving us and giving us faith is that no one can boast about it. If one's believing is of himself, then he can boast at least of his willingness to believe God. Paul is saying that people cannot boast even about their faith because God gave it to them.

The Main Emphasis: Grace

But if the preceding argument is not convincing, remember that salvation is *all* of grace. Paul emphasizes in verses four through ten the exaltation of God's amazing grace. This glorious grace stands in vivid contrast to the condition of spiritual death and ruin of the human race under Satan's power. Grace *"quickened us"* when we were dead in trespasses and sins, *"raised us up,"* and *"seated us in Christ"* in the heavenlies in order that *"in the ages to come"* God could display *"the exceeding riches of his grace in his kindness to us in Christ."* In other words, this whole passage explains how God's quickening salvation by grace contrasts with our former dead, hopeless estate.

Now, if faith is our part in salvation and if that faith originates in us, then Paul's lavish praise of God's grace topples here. Paul's argument would have to read something like this: "Oh, the wonderful mercy of God in His great love to us—that He has raised us up from spiritual death and has given us box seats in heaven to wonder at His marvelous kindness to us throughout the coming ages. What marvelous grace this is, but it could not save you without you. You contributed the vital part! You see, *you*, not God, supplied the deciding factor, the necessary ingredient. Your faith made it possible for His grace to succeed. As great as His grace is, it is worthless without your faith!" Such an idea is unthinkable! God alone must be glorified because even faith was a gift of His grace.

Other verses, such as Ephesians 1:19, Philippians 1:29, and Colossians 2:12 show that faith is the gift of God. Merely gathering proof texts, however, is not satisfactory. We must look at the whole argument. The question is not whether the Bible supports the idea of faith's being a gift but why faith must be a gift. The first thing to settle is whether it is *possible* for sinners to exercise faith on their own, not whether they ought to (which is not in question). The commentator R. C. H. Lenski amplifies this thought:

> Faith is not something that we on our part produce and furnish toward our salvation but is produced in our hearts by God to accomplish his purpose in us.
>
> Col. 2:12 states this directly: "through the faith of the operation of God." One often meets careless statements such as: "Grace is God's part, faith is ours." Now the simple fact is that even in human relationships faith and confidence are produced in us by others, by what they are and what they do; we never produce it ourselves. There is no self-produced faith; faith is wrought in us.[153]

Three Elements of Faith

What is faith? The reformers taught that saving faith has three elements: (1) knowledge (*noticia*) of the facts of the gospel (I Corinthians 15:1-3), (2) assent (*assencia*) to the truth of the gospel, and (3) trust (*fiducia*) in or commitment to the Savior.

Sinners refuse the facts of the gospel because they are blind. Sinners do not assent to the truth of the gospel because the gospel must be spiritually received (I Corinthians 2:14). Faith is trust, and sinners do not trust Christ because they are at enmity with Him due to their rebellious nature (Romans 8:7). As the saying goes, "The sinner is looking for God the way a thief is looking for a policeman." When God, in grace, removes the enmity and changes the sinner's nature, Jesus Christ is then seen as lovely and wholly worthy of trust.

When we say that faith is the gift of God, we do not mean that faith is something God puts in the sinner's heart. The sinner trusts Christ when his heart is changed in regeneration and Jesus Christ is no longer rejected as unnecessary or undesirable. Thus, faith is said to be the work of God or the gift of God.

CONCLUSION

God chose the Israelites on purpose because He loved them. God chose believers in this gospel age on purpose because He loved them. If God saves men because He foresees that they will believe, then grace becomes a reward of faith and not the means of faith. Merited grace is not grace. In his commentary on Romans, William R. Newell writes:

> Now let us just frankly bow to God's plain statement that His purpose according to election is likewise not of human works. That is to say, that favor of God to the children of the promise (to those whom He has given to Christ) is not procured by their response to God's grace, but contrariwise, their response to God's grace is because they have been given to Christ.[154]

The gift of salvation is of God's grace and *"by means of faith."* It is God's enabling us to trust Him after He grants to us understanding and willingness to trust (Psalm 110:3). Therefore, since faith is part of the gift, it cannot be viewed as the *cause* of God's electing the sinner. Charles Haddon Spurgeon illustrates this:

> "But," says [sic] others, "God elected them on the foresight of their faith." Now, God gives faith, therefore

he could not have elected them on account of faith, which he foresaw. There shall be twenty beggars in the street, and I determine to give one of them a shilling; but will any one say that I determined to give that one shilling; that I elected him to have the shilling because I foresaw that he would have it? That would be talking nonsense. In like manner, to say that God elected men because he foresaw they would have faith, which is salvation in the germ, would be too absurd for us to listen to for a moment. Faith is the gift of God. Every virtue comes from him. Therefore it can not have caused him to elect men, because it is his gift.[155]

Paul assures us that our salvation rests upon a more secure footing than our believing. To rest the assurance of my salvation upon the election of an unchanging God brings absolute security. *"Nevertheless the foundation of God standeth sure, having this seal, The Lord knoweth them that are his"* (II Timothy 2:19). *"Knoweth"* means sovereign election.

Therefore, Scripture demonstrates that (1) God is sovereign and has the right to impose His will upon His creatures for whatever reason and to whatever purposes He may have, including salvation. (2) Election is the exercise of God's right to impose His will by free grace in bringing many, but not all, undeserving sinners to salvation. The sinner's believing is not the cause of his election but the evidence of it. *"And as many as were ordained to eternal life believed"* (Acts 13:48).

8

LEFT TO THEMSELVES,
WHAT CAN SINNERS DO?

The doctrine of election is founded on the fact that in the fall mankind has been spiritually disabled. The doctrine of total hereditary depravity makes election to salvation both logical and necessary. However, there is such distaste for election that many seek to "break the chain of logical necessity." Rather than resort to election, they invent a teaching that "restores" to every sinner sufficient ability to choose for himself whether he will be saved or not. This, in effect, removes "total" from his depravity. It is simply the error of Pelagianism.

Others assault election by making the doctrine extremely odious in order to offend sensibilities. This tactic accuses God of terrible tyranny and conjures images of chains and slavery—people being forced against their wills. Evangelist Robert Sumner, retired editor of the periodical *The Biblical Evangelist*, is one who uses this line.

> Summed up, the unconditional election theory says in effect: "God brings a baby into this world. He has done neither good nor evil. Yet that baby is going to grow up and go to Hell and be damned forever. There is absolutely nothing he can do to keep from going to Hell. *God will not permit it.* God arbitrarily decided in eternity past that the baby would grow up, never be saved, and go to Hell and be tormented forever. This decision was not made upon anything the baby would or would not do; God simply did not select him to be saved." It is, as the late Dr. Gaebelein charged, "totally unscriptural" and "akin to blasphemy."[156]

Dr. Sumner sounds righteously indignant about this outrageous teaching, but what he actually objects to is the negative side of unconditional election, reprobation. However, he has misrepresented the facts of reprobation as well. To correct this abuse, let us consider what the Bible reveals to us about predestination, positive and negative.

ELECTION AND PREDESTINATION

Akin to Blasphemy?

Those who are indignant over the doctrine of predestination obviously do not understand the doctrine. In the quote above, what Dr. Sumner calls unconditional election is in reality a grossly distorted view of predestination. Several points show his distortion. (1) Dr. Sumner ignores the fact that sin is the culprit here, not God. Sin is an odious offense that a holy and righteous God must punish. The sinner's wanton defiance of God's will has rightly earned him a place under God's righteous wrath. (2) It is God who is has been offended, not the sinner. Sinners are not innocent victims who deserve some kind of second chance—a *right* to be saved. God is not *obligated* to sinners. (3) Dr. Sumner says, "There is absolutely nothing he can do to keep from going to Hell." This is wrong. No sinner is forced to suffer the flames of eternal hell against his will. *"Have I any pleasure at all that the wicked should die? saith the Lord God: and not that he should return from his ways and live?"* (Ezekiel 18:23). It is the sinner who refuses to repent of his sinful ways. (4) Ignoring the sinner's depravity, Dr. Sumner assumes that any "poor sinner" may *want* to be saved (which is, by the way, an espousal of Arminian doctrine and an ignoring of the typical response of sinners to the gospel). Such a view as Sumner has ascribed to election certainly would be "akin to blasphemy." Thankfully, this perverted view is not true of unconditional election.[157]

Unconditional election does not teach that God created evil in this baby, then damned it forever. Bible election teaches that God abandons the reprobate to his evil nature, letting it take its vile course to inevitable ruin in hell. God may also provoke the wicked and aggravate the natural rebellion of his heart. But whatever God does, the result is righteous.

Vital Questions

What is *predestination,* and how does it differ from *election*? Theologically, predestination is the determination of God that events will occur as He planned them. Dr. R. C. Sproul writes:

> What predestination means, in its most elementary form, is that our final destination, heaven or hell, is decided by God not only before we get there, but before we were even born. It teaches that our ultimate destiny is in the hands of God. Another way of saying it is this: From all eternity, before we even existed, God decided to save some members of the human race and to let the

89

rest of the human race perish. God made a choice—He chose some individuals to be saved into everlasting blessedness in heaven and others He chose to pass over, to allow them to follow the consequences of their sins into eternal torment in hell.[158]

Election has to do with God's choosing of the *individuals* who are predestined. *Predestination* is the goal to which the *elect* are chosen. Ephesians 1:4 tells us that some were *"chosen in him, before the foundation of the world."* Then in verse five we read that these *"chosen"* were *"predestinated"* that they would be *"holy and without blame before him."*

But what happens to the nonelect—to those who are not predestined to glory? This seems to be the great concern of those who reject predestination. Unless one totally rejects election to salvation or unless one believes that all mankind will be saved, there must be a negative side to predestination—a "double predestination." But did God "elect" people to be damned to hell? Does God actively work evil in the hearts of the reprobate and prevent them from coming to faith in Christ? Absolutely not! This idea is what Dr. Sproul calls a "positive-positive" schema of double predestination—believers predestined to salvation and unbelievers predestined to damnation.[159] This view goes beyond what the reformers taught and certainly beyond what the Bible teaches.

So, then, are the nonelect "predestined" to hell? Only in the sense that God determined beforehand that those who sin would suffer His wrath and justice. Although God did not *elect* people to be sinners, He did predestine sinners to perdition (Romans 9:22; Jude 4). This view is what might be called the "positive-negative" view of double predestination. It is unnecessary for God to elect the lost to condemnation; He simply leaves them to themselves. Those whom God did not elect to salvation are not harmed by their nonelection. Any harm that comes to them is of their own choice of sin and rebellion. God does not deal with them as nonelect but as sinners.

REPROBATION
On the basis of their choice of sin, God gives sinners over to their own desires: *"And even as they did not like to retain God in their knowledge, God gave them over to a reprobate mind, to do those things which are not convenient"* (Romans 1:28). The Bible term for this "giving up" of sinners is *reprobation*: *"Examine yourselves, whether ye be in the faith; prove your own selves. Know ye not your own selves, how that Jesus Christ is in you, except ye be reprobates?"*

(II Corinthians 13:5). The word translated *"reprobate"* is *adokimos* in the Greek (used eight times in God's Word). It means to be "judicially rejected"—to be given up by God; to be excluded from grace and salvation; to be left to continue on one's course of willful sin and ruin. *"Reprobate"* is the Bible term for the nonelect.

Now, God does use reprobates to accomplish His own ends. However, His working with these nonelect sinners should never be regarded as His trying to bring them to repentance and salvation. On the contrary, as God actively intervenes in mercy to bring the elect to salvation, He may also actively intervene to harden reprobates in their own evil. *"Therefore hath he [God] mercy on whom he will have mercy, and whom he will, he hardeneth"* (Romans 9:18).

In demonstration of this truth, the Bible says that God hardened Pharaoh's heart (Romans 9:17). How did God do this? Since Pharaoh naturally resisted God's will, Pharaoh in essence hardened his own heart. God's intervention involved His commanding Pharaoh to let the children of Israel go out of Egypt. This command was contrary to Pharaoh's natural inclination and aggravated his stubbornness. Pharaoh greeted the divine request with, *"Who is the LORD, that I should obey his voice to let Israel go? I know not the LORD, neither will I let Israel go"* (Exodus 5:2).

D. M. Lloyd-Jones writes, "God does not create evil or put it there, but He aggravates what is there for His own great purpose."[160] The more God pressured Pharaoh, the more Pharaoh resisted. Paul tells us that the law does the very same thing—it provokes the sinner in accord with his nature. The law aggravates the evil already present and, in effect, causes the heart to sin (Romans 7:7-12). *"Sin, taking occasion by the commandment, deceived me, and by it [the commandment] slew me"* (Romans 7:11). Does that make the law evil? Paul asks, *"Was then that which is good made death unto me? God forbid"* (Romans 7:13). The rebellion in Paul's own heart reacted to the commandment by sinning, but the law itself remains pure. *"For we know that the law is spiritual: but I am carnal, sold under sin"* (Romans 7:14).

God's purpose in this aggravation is fulfilled. In Romans 9:22 and 23 we read, *"What if God, willing to shew his wrath, and to make his power known, endured with much longsuffering the vessels of wrath fitted to destruction: And that he might make known the riches of his glory on vessels of mercy, which he had afore prepared unto glory."* The purpose of *"the vessels of wrath fitted to destruction"* is for the displaying of His wrath and power. This display forms the background

91

for showing His wealth of glory on *"vessels of mercy . . . afore* [beforehand] *prepared unto glory."*

The text does not say *who* fitted (*katartizo*, "to prepare") these "vessels" for destruction. It certainly does not say that God did the fitting. Paul merely responded in advance to the anticipated objection to God's showing mercy to some and hardening others (Romans 9:18, 19). Paul illustrates this freedom of God by showing God's sovereign purpose for putting Pharaoh on the throne of Egypt (Romans 9:17). In His rule over the affairs of mankind, God chose a reprobate Pharaoh to the throne of Egypt in order to display His own awesome power to the world. The passage shows Pharaoh as a reprobate—a "vessel prepared for destruction." This is the negative side of predestination.

THE FALLEN NATURE, SICK OR DEAD?

The doctrine of election and predestination teaches that God chose some to be saved from their sins by the finished work of Christ. The doctrine of reprobation teaches that God chose not to save the remainder of humanity. None of this occurs against anyone's will. In order to save the elect, God regenerates them, thereby enabling them to be willing to be saved. Regeneration must precede faith; faith cannot possibly precede regeneration.

The Serious Condition of Mankind as a Result of the Fall

To understand why regeneration must precede faith, we must understand the nature of the sinful human condition. We must take into account the seriousness of man's depravity as a result of his fall. We previously mentioned that self-will (independence from God) is the root of man's failure with God. Iniquity makes it impossible for a person to submit his will to God without divine enablement.

One of the great problems in theology involves the origin of sin. If God cannot be the author of sin, then from where did sin come? We know that Satan introduced it to Adam, but how did Satan sin? There was no devil to tempt Satan. Also, evil and good did not eternally coexist as necessary entities in the universe, as dualism teaches. From where, then, did Satan's sin come?

The answer is fairly obvious. God created angels and the first human beings (unlike Adam's descendants) with freedom to exercise moral responsibility (will)—to love God and serve Him. God's very position and being demand that all His creatures yield willing obedience to Him. *"Fear God and keep his commandments: for this is the whole duty of man"* (Ecclesiastes 12:13). However, moral freedom for these first creatures also involved the virtual certainty that they would act independently of God. God permitted this for His glory. This independence is *iniquity*.

In Ezekiel 28 a prophecy is addressed to the king of Tyre. Most Bible commentators agree that the message is addressed to the power behind the king, Satan himself.

> *Thou art the anointed cherub that covereth; and I have set thee so: thou wast upon the holy mountain of God; thou hast walked up and down in the midst of the stones of fire. Thou wast perfect in thy ways from the day that thou wast created, till iniquity was found in thee* (Ezekiel 28:14, 15).

Iniquity is the disposition of the heart in acting independently of God's authority. Satan said, *"I will be like the most High"* (Isaiah 14:14). He did not want to be in submission to God; neither did he want to dethrone God. He just wanted to enthrone himself and be equal with God—to have the same authority as God. He did not want God telling him what to do. He wanted independence; so he led a rebellion in heaven and became God's archenemy.

Satan also introduced the spirit of independence into the human race through Adam. In the Garden of Eden Satan sold Adam on the equality doctrine. Adam also chose independence from God's authority, and the result is that the whole human race is in *"the snare of the devil"* and is *"taken captive by him at his will"* (II Timothy 2:26). Now Satan is *"the god of this world"* (II Corinthians 4:4). Original sin was not an *act* of transgression but a *disposition* of independence from God—iniquity.

By One Man

Paul writes, *"Wherefore, as by one man sin entered into the world, and death by sin; and so death passed upon all men, for that all have sinned"* (Romans 5:12). All die, Paul reasoned; therefore, all sinned in Adam. Adam was the head of the race and disobeyed for the race.

The doctrine of original sin is not popular. Arminius wrote, "It is perversely spoken, that original sin makes anyone guilty of death,"[16] but Paul said, *"In Adam all die"* (I Corinthians 15:22). Many modern evangelicals, while agreeing that the fall made the race sinners, say that mankind is not completely corrupted by Adam's sin—not guilty of Adam's sin, nor totally disabled by it.

We can see this reluctance to own Adam's sin as we read Dr. John R. Rice, who, referring to I Corinthians 15:22, wrote:

This Scripture plainly teaches that *all men potentially became sinners by Adam's sin*, so all that are ever born are *potentially* made alive in Christ.

That means that no one ever went to Hell because of Adam's sin. Whatever was lost in Adam was regained in Christ!

Read that passage again and see that just as universally "as in Adam all die," just as universally "so in Christ shall all be made alive." In both cases the death and salvation are potential, for the race of sinners was not yet born when Adam sinned, *but his sin potentially made all sinners* [emphasis added].[162]

Whoa, Dr. Rice! Did you say that no one "ever went to hell because of Adam's sin"? That is what Arminius taught. It seems that the doctrine of the imputed sin of Adam to his posterity is still difficult to swallow. People cannot see how God could condemn the whole race because Adam disobeyed God by eating some forbidden fruit. They do not understand. It was not Adam's eating of the forbidden fruit that condemned the race. Adam's disposition to act on his own corrupted his nature. This corrupt nature is what is imputed to all Adam's children. Dr. Rice apparently rejected this doctrine.

Is John R. Rice a Pelagian?

Dr. Rice's interpretation of I Corinthians 15:22 is seriously flawed. He argues that both *"all's"* in the verse mean the same—the whole human race. This means that the whole human race is saved, because *"all . . . shall be made alive."* To avoid this absurdity, Rice is forced to add to the Scriptures the word *potential*. However, by this addition Rice creates a greater error. He teaches that *sin* is only a "potential" threat to the human race. "[Adam's] sin *potentially* made all sinners."[163] Apparently, then, Adam's sin did not cause the whole race to die spiritually. Consequently, is it possible for a person not to sin? Have people ever been born who did not follow Adam's example? Such people would not need a Savior. Surely, Dr. Rice did not believe that!

Further, by using the word *potential*, Dr. Rice teaches that sin is a threat that becomes a reality only *if* we actually *choose* to sin—"his sin potentially made all sinners." In other words, we become sinners by sinning. This teaching must be rejected as unbiblical for two reasons. First, infants, who are innocent of actual personal sin, can *die* because death is the wages of sin (Romans 6:23). Second, the Word of God clearly teaches that babies are born sinners: *"Behold, I was shapen in iniquity; and in sin did my mother conceive me"* (Psalm 51:5). *"The wicked are estranged from the womb: they go astray as soon as they be born, speaking lies"* (Psalm 58:3). *"Yea . . . thou . . . wast called a transgressor from the womb"* (Isaiah 48:8).

No, Dr. Rice was dangerously wrong in his interpretation of I Corinthians 15:22. Both *all*'s do not mean the same thing, and there is nothing in this verse that suggests anything "potential" (death or life). In order to interpret this verse correctly, we must see the terms *"in Adam"* and *"in Christ"* as keys to our understanding. The verse "plainly" states that *"in Adam all die."* It "plainly" states that *"in Christ shall all be made alive."* The question is, to whom do the *"all's"* refer? Obviously, *"all"* in Adam refers to the whole human race, for the race originated in Adam. However, the *"all"* in Christ refers to a new race, God's elect children, given to Christ and redeemed out of Adam's race.

The principle taught in I Corinthians 15:22 is simply that the action of one person as a representative or substitute acts for all for whom he is a representative. *"For as in Adam all* [the human race] *die, so in Christ shall all* [believers who are *'in Christ'*] *be made alive"* (I Corinthians 15:22). Paul cites this principle in II Corinthians 5:14: *"We thus judge* [conclude], *that if one died for all* [as a substitute], *then all died* [in their substitute]. *"*

Three Strikes and You're Out!

Every person "in Adam" is born into the world with three strikes against him. The first strike is that he is already condemned as guilty of Adam's sin, having inherited Adam's nature. All sinned in Adam (Romans 5:12; Psalm 51:5). All are sinners by nature. Two very strong evidences show that people are sinners by nature: (1) their being subject to death—the penalty of their sin, and (2) their wicked actions—the fruit of their sin. Sinning does not make us sinners. We sin because we *are* sinners; we act out what we are by nature. Three times in the New Testament Paul refers to the nature of sinners as *"children of disobedience"* (Ephesians 2:2; 5:6; Colossians 3:6). As sinners we *"walked according to the course of this world, according to the prince of the power of the air, the spirit that now worketh in the children of disobedience"* (Ephesians 2:2).

The second strike is that all "in Adam" inherit a disposition to self-will (iniquity) that renders them incapable of obeying God's will or law (Romans 8:7, 8; Matthew 7:21-23).

The third strike is that all "in Adam" have a propensity to personal acts of sin so that he cannot *not* sin (*"If ye, then, being evil"*—Luke 11:13; John 8:44; I Kings 8:46; I John 1:8).

95

These three strikes make all "in Adam" liable for punishment. They are subject to God's wrath *"for because of these things cometh the wrath of God upon the children of disobedience"* (Ephesians 5:6). Death is the wages of sin (Romans 6:23). *"The soul that sinneth, it shall die"* (Ezekiel 18:4). *"But the scripture hath concluded all under sin"* (Galatians 3:22). There is no question on this. Death is not only the *penalty* (spiritual death and hell) of man's sin, but it is also the *nature* (physical dying) of sin's corruption. God warned Adam, *"But of the tree of the knowledge of good and evil, thou shalt not eat of it: for in the day that thou eatest thereof thou shalt surely die"* (Genesis 2:17). The Hebrew reads literally, *"Dying, thou shalt die."* God warned that if Adam sinned, he would experience the corruption that sin brings—both physical death and spiritual alienation from the life of God. By *one* man's [Adam's] sin all die, being subject to sin's *corruption* (physical death), sin's *depravity* (spiritual death), and sin's *penalty* (eternal death—hell).

The History of Israel

In order to understand this natural, persistent, sinful resistance of humankind, one need only examine the history of Israel. Israel was called to be a holy people unto the Lord: *"Ye shall be holy: for I the LORD your God am holy"* (Leviticus 19:2). God gave the Jews His law, an expression of His holiness and character, which they were required to keep. They promised they would: *"And he took the book of the covenant, and read in the audience of the people: and they said, All that the LORD hath said will we do, and be obedient"* (Exodus 24:7). Over fifty times in the Old Testament, God commanded, exhorted, and warned the children of Israel to obey His commandments. However, in the face of all their promises to Him to obey the law and in spite of all His appeals to them, they persistently disobeyed.

Patiently, God waited for them to repent: *"All day long have I stretched forth my hands unto a disobedient and gainsaying people"* (Romans 10:21). What was the conclusion?

> *But they and our fathers dealt proudly, and hardened their necks, and hearkened not to thy commandments, And refused to obey, neither were mindful of thy wonders that thou didst among them; but hardened their necks, and in their rebellion appointed a captain to return to their bondage* (Nehemiah 9:16, 17).

God had patiently dealt with the nation of Israel, giving them His law and His Word. He showed signs and wonders among them, per-

96

formed many mighty acts, sent His prophets to correct and inform them. Their history of response Stephen summarizes in Acts 7:51: *"Ye stiffnecked and uncircumcised in heart and ears, ye do always resist the Holy Ghost: as your fathers did, so do ye."* A review of Israel's history shows clearly that God does not arbitrarily elect poor helpless sinners to perdition. Rather, it sounds as if sinners always refuse God *with their wills*, even when God gives them abundant opportunity to do otherwise.

A New Heart Required

Why did Israel fail to live up to her responsibility to God's commandments even after she pledged to keep them (Deuteronomy 5:28)? God Himself predicted her failure: *"Oh that there were such an heart in them, that they would fear me, and keep all my commandments always, that it might be well with them, and with their children for ever!"* (Deuteronomy 5:29). Israel's downfall was not because she lacked the faculties to obey but because she had no heart to obey. *"The carnal mind is enmity against God: for it is not subject to the law of God, neither indeed can be"* (Romans 8:7). How, then, can a man obey the law when he has no heart to do so? He can obey only as God Himself provides enabling by grace.[164]

I heard a radio preacher talking about the need of his listeners to respond to the gospel with their hearts. The heart, he insisted, was the key to acceptance with Jesus. He was right; God does expect us to have a good heart toward Him. However, the preacher seemed to plead with his hearers on the basis of a presumed ability in them to have a good heart (Jeremiah 13:23). This is just the problem. Sinners have stony hearts that cannot please God (Romans 8:8). How can they be expected to have a good heart?

Many try to encourage a good heart by promises or threats. Oh, to be sure, everyone would like the "perks" that accompany salvation—joy, peace, and heaven—but dangling these benefits before them will not change their hearts. Neither will threats of judgment, wrath, and hell scare them into change. God used the promise of blessings and the warning of cursings with Israel (Deuteronomy 7, 8); yet, Israel, with the exception of a godly remnant, was not affected by these pleadings of God and His prophets.[165] Why? *"The Lord hath not given you a heart to perceive, and eyes to see, and ears to hear, unto this day . . . that ye might know that I am the LORD your God"* (Deuteronomy 29:4, 6). God did not give them a heart to obey Him; rather, He left them to their own devices to keep His commandments. They could not obey, and they found that there was no power in the law to change their stony hearts (Romans 8:3).

God, however, promised to make that change: *"And I will give them an heart to know me, that I am the LORD: and they shall be my people, and I will be their God: for they shall return to me with their whole heart"* (Jeremiah 24:7). *"And the LORD thy God will circumcise thine heart, and the heart of thy seed, to love the LORD thy God with all thine heart, and with all thy soul, that thou mayest live"* (Deuteronomy 30:6). This is the New Covenant promise. To the New Covenant believers in Philippi, Paul commanded obedience to the gospel (Philippians 2:12), which he declares they are able to do because *"it is God which worketh in you, both to will and to do of his good pleasure"* (Philippians 2:13). In salvation, God gives a new heart with both a willingness and an ability to obey (Ezekiel 36:25-29; Hebrews 10:16-24).[166]

Can Dead Sinners Be Saved with a Little Enlightenment and Encouragement?

Most Christians will acknowledge that people are incurably wicked and rebellious, but at the same time they refuse to believe they will never cooperate with God in their salvation. Evangelist Robert Sumner, for instance, agrees that humans are totally depraved, incurably wicked, rebellious, and spiritually dead. He cites verses that support this truth.[167]

What is the spiritual death that results in inability to respond to God? Sumner argues that "spiritual death is not annihilation, but simply separation from God."[168] Yes, spiritual death is separation from God, but Sumner here infers that sinners are able to respond to the gospel call—that they are, in some sense, alive. "It is true," Sumner writes, "that the dead *corpse* cannot hear, speak, or move—*but the corpse is not the man!* The man [we assume he means the soul], even though physically dead, is still able to hear, see, move, act and be cognizant of things."[169]

What kind of "death" is it that leaves a man "able to hear, see, move, act and be cognizant of things"? It is the kind of death that is required if one wants to get sinners saved without the necessity of an unconditional election. Sumner's hatred for election is obvious: "If you will forgive us for saying so, *unconditional election* is the kind they have in Communist Russia, Red China, and Fascist Spain—*it is a stuffed ballot box!*"[170] So, according to Sumner, what is the condition of a lost sinner? Sumner seems to think that the sinner is "able to hear, see, move, act and be cognizant of things." He doesn't sound as if he is dead; he doesn't sound as if he is even sick! Paul said, *"And you . . . were* dead *in trespasses and sins"* (Ephesians 2:1).

Paul uses the term *"dead"* to signify a condition of spiritual inability that can be overcome only by the "quickening" of grace. The sinner, in his spiritual death, has not lost his natural faculties nor his ability for receiving information because he is not physically dead. Physically dead people have no physical ability to "hear, see, move, act and be cognizant of things." Spiritually dead people do not have spiritual ability to "hear, see, move, act and be cognizant of things." Concerning spiritual things, God says of the sinner, *"Neither can he know them"* (I Corinthians 2:14).

Consider this illustration of a sinner's inability without grace: The air is filled with myriad sounds and pictures that the natural faculties of a human being cannot discern. However, if a person has the proper devices for reception of these signals—radio or television—he can make use of them. In the same way divine enablement clearly requires infinitely more than some kind of divine assistance. It requires the enabling of the proper spiritual "devices" for the reception of spiritual truth. That enabling is nothing short of regeneration—the giving of a new heart.

Sumner does admit that God *must do something* or the sinner cannot or will not choose to be saved:

> The Word of God teaches that, while man is totally depraved and totally unable to help himself, our Lord draws *every man sufficiently* and enlightens every man *as much as necessary* for that individual to make a decision of his own free will.[171]

Does this sound familiar? We have here another Baptist/Wesleyan/Arminian. Sumner believes in a universal "almost" salvation that gives sinners a fair shake and absolves God from the charge of playing favorites. Both Sumner and Rice, along with Dr. Theissen and the Arminian Corvinus, agree that enlightenment and enabling allow every sinner freely to choose or reject Christ. "His Love, Enlightenment, Enabling, and Invitation Reach Every Sinner" reads the fifth chapter title of Dr. Rice's book against predestination.[172]

If it is not enlightenment for all, as these men insist, what is the *"light which lighteth every man"* (John 1:9)? It is the Lord Jesus Christ Himself, who gives the knowledge of God and eternal life (John 17:3). John develops this enlightenment to show that where gospel light shines, it makes a distinction among individuals, bringing *judgment* to those who reject the light. This is how God puts a difference between individuals. This is how He shows who are His own and who are not.

99

And this is the condemnation, that light is come into the world, and men loved darkness rather than light, because their deeds were evil. For every one that doeth evil hateth the light, neither cometh to the light, lest his deeds should be reproved. But he that doeth truth cometh to the light, that his deeds may be manifest, that they are wrought in God (John 3:19-21).

Jesus Christ does bring His people to salvation, but the same light that brings salvation to some condemns the rest. John says that the light causes the evildoer to scurry for the darkness like a cockroach. Light condemns those who practice evil; however, those who are of God (John 1:13) come to the light. Light gives evidence that the deeds of the doers of the truth originate from God. The wicked hate the light; Christians love it. The light distinguishes persons as to their relationship to God.

Sumner's teaching poses some interesting questions. How much is "sufficiently" and "as much as necessary"? Is God's help just enough to put sinners into a position where they can help themselves? If so, who really saves the sinner? Is not God, then, actually only helping the sinner to save himself? Under this system, Jesus is not a Savior: He is just a helper.

God's enabling of dead sinners must be more than enlightenment and wooing. His help must be regeneration, a resurrection of the dead. Only when the sinner is made alive can he be enlightened and wooed.

DRAWING SINNERS

Sinners need more than just a little help and encouragement from God if they are going to come back to God. Man is *dead* in trespasses and sins. He is more than separated from God: he is *alienated* [Gk. *apallotrioo*, "an estrangement due to enmity"] from God:

Having the understanding darkened, being alienated from the life of God through the ignorance that is in them, because of the blindness of their heart: Who being past feeling have given themselves over unto lasciviousness, to work all uncleanness with greediness (Ephesians 4:18).

John Rice wrote, "God can bring the pressure of loving invitation or stern warnings, to cause a man to weigh the consequences and the moral issues and decide."[173] Paul wrote that sinners are *"past feeling"* and *"have given themselves over to work all uncleanness with greediness"* (Ephesians 4:18). Sinners in that condition are not influenced by a little "pressure of loving invitation."

In speaking of his own experience, Paul tells us in Romans 7:5, 10, and 11,

> For when we were in the flesh, the motions of sins, which were by the law, did work in our members to bring forth fruit unto death. . . . And the commandment, which was ordained to life, I found to be unto death. For sin, taking occasion by the commandment, deceived me, and by it slew me.

Consider these Scriptures:

> Can the Ethiopian change his skin, or the leopard his spots? then may ye also do good, that are accustomed to do evil (Jeremiah 13:23).

> The heart is deceitful above all things, and desperately wicked: who can know it? (Jeremiah 17:9).

> For to be carnally minded is death; but to be spiritually minded is life and peace. Because the carnal mind is enmity against God: for it is not subject to the law of God, neither indeed can be. So then they that are in the flesh cannot please God (Romans 8:6-8).

Believers also know by their own experience that, were it not for their new nature, they would not and could not live in obedience to God. Believers are in a constant battle that they seem frequently to be losing rather than winning. Galatians 5:17 states, *"For the flesh lusteth against the Spirit, and the Spirit against the flesh: and these are contrary the one to the other: so that ye cannot do the things that ye would."*

Christians love the Lord, have the Holy Spirit, and are regenerated; yet, they still battle the flesh, always agreeing with Paul in Romans 7:15-20:

> For that which I do I allow not: for what I would, that do I not; but what I hate, that do I. If then I do that which I would not, I consent unto the law that it is good. Now then it is no more I that do it, but sin that dwelleth in me. For I know that in me (that is, in my flesh) dwelleth no good thing: for to will is present with me; but how to perform that which is good I find not. For the good that I would I do not: but the evil which I would not, that I do. Now if I do that I would not, it is no more I that do it, but sin that dwelleth in me.

If Christians, who have a new nature and power to do right, have so much trouble, how can the sinner, who loves darkness, loves his sin, loves his independence from God, and is in helpless bondage to sin and Satan, turn to Christ with a little "wooing"?

Effectual Grace, Not Help

I will deal with one more passage before concluding this chapter. Non-Calvinists quote John 12:32 as proof that Jesus Christ is "drawing" all men to himself: *"And I, if I be lifted up from the earth, will draw all men unto me."* By this they mean that Jesus Christ is lovingly seeking by wooing, warning, and enlightening to bring all sinners to Himself. But we must ask two questions: (1) Who did Jesus mean by *"all"*? and (2) What does the term *"draw"* mean?

In the context of this passage, which runs back into John 11, we have (1) the final rejection by the Jews of Christ, their King (John 11:47, 48); (2) this rejection made official in the issuing of Christ's death warrant (John 11:57); (3) Greeks (Gentiles), in contrast, now requesting to see Jesus, indicating a change of ministry emphasis (John 12:20-23); (4) the Lord's response to the Gentiles' request (*"The hour is come that the Son of man should be glorified,"* John 12:23); and (5) all this in light of the prophecy of Caiaphas (John 11:49-52, quoted below). God's timing is on schedule. It is now time for Jesus to die. He uses the term *"Son of man"* to show that His emphasis will now shift from Israel as a nation to the church, which includes the Gentiles, as indicated by those who were now seeking Him.

The Jews as a nation rejected Him, but individual God-fearing Jews and Gentiles desired Him. To bring these to God, He must go to the cross as Caiaphas predicted: *"And not for that nation only* [Israel]*, but that also he should gather together in one the children of God* [the elect, both Jew and Gentile] *that were scattered abroad"* (John 11:52). Therefore, *"all"* in John 12:32 should be understood as *"the children of God that were scattered abroad,"* not every person in the world. *"All"* means *"my sheep"* [the elect of Israel] and *"other sheep* [elect of the Gentiles] *I have which are not of this fold* [Israel]*"* (John 10:14, 16). It was for these that Jesus said, *"I lay down my life"* (John 10:15).

"Draw" is the Greek word *helkuo* and means "to draw" or "to drag off"; metaphorically, it means "to draw by inward power; to lead; to impel." It is used in John 6:44: *"No man can come to me, except the Father which hath sent me draw him: and I will raise him up at the last day."* This verse teaches that no one can ever come to Jesus on his own. He must be literally "impelled" by divine force—dragged out of his sin and self to salvation and Christ by supernatural power. By the

way, it should be noted that the last phrase of the verse *("I will raise him up at the last day")* is neglected by those who want to argue that *draw* means only wooing. That phrase clearly teaches that all who are drawn to Christ by the Father will be raised by the Son. This phrase is synonymous with salvation (see vv. 40 and 54).

Every reference in the New Testament supports this same definition of *draw*. In John 18:10 it is used of Peter's drawing the sword: *"Then Simon Peter having a sword drew it, and smote the high priest's servant."* In John 21:6 and 11 the disciples dragged in the fishing net: *"They cast therefore, and now they were not able to draw it for the multitude of fishes. . . . Simon Peter went up, and drew the net to land."*

Note these references: *"And when her masters saw that the hope of their gains was gone, they caught Paul and Silas, and drew* [wooing?] *them into the marketplace unto the rulers"* (Acts 16:19). *"And all the city was moved, and the people ran together: and they took Paul, and drew him* [by pressure of loving invitation?] *out of the temple"* (Acts 21:30). *"Do not rich men oppress you, and draw* [drag—a legal summons is not voluntary] *you before the judgment seats?"* (James 2:6). In not one of these places could *draw,* even in the most remote sense, mean to woo lovingly by invitation, warning, or whatever.

It is impossible for sinners to be "influenced" into believing in Christ for salvation by mere wooing and pleading. Salvation requires the monergistic operation of God's grace in regeneration, changing the inherent nature of the sinner so that the reborn person may now exercise his will in a favorable response to the gospel. With that regeneration, conviction, and invitation (gospel work), the sinner willingly and joyfully responds to Christ: *"They . . . gladly received his word"* (Acts 2:41).

9

CAN A MAN PAY
WHAT HE OWES TO GOD?

In Revelation 14:6 God summons an angel to preach the everlasting gospel to those who dwell on the earth. His message is *"fear God, and give glory to him . . . and worship him"* (Revelation 14:7). In this message is summed the whole responsibility of man. Solomon wrote, *"Let us hear the conclusion of the whole matter: Fear God, and keep his commandments: for this is the whole duty of man"* (Ecclesiastes 12:13).

Did you ever wonder why certain passages seem to teach salvation by works? For example, Paul tells us in Romans: *"To them who by patient continuance in well doing seek for glory honour and immortality, eternal life. . . . Glory, honour, and peace, to every man that worketh good . . . For there is no respect of persons with God"* (Romans 2:7, 10, 11). On the other hand, *"Unto them that are contentious, and do not obey the truth, but obey unrighteousness, indignation and wrath"* (Romans 2:8). What is the *"well doing"* in which we are to continue patiently? It is *"the commandment of the everlasting God"* (Romans 16:26). Is this salvation by works?

The prophet Micah asks,

> *Wherewith shall I come before the LORD, and bow myself before the high God? shall I come before him with burnt offerings, and with calves of a year old? Will the LORD be pleased with thousands of rams, or with ten thousands of rivers of oil? shall I give my firstborn for my transgression, the fruit of my body for the sin of my soul? He hath shewed thee, O man, what is good; and what doth the LORD require of thee, but to do justly, and to love mercy, and to walk humbly with thy God* (Micah 6:8).

Is a man saved by *"well doing"*? No, the Bible clearly teaches otherwise (Ephesians 2:8, 9) and does not contradict itself. These references do not indicate how a man may be justified with God: they do not present the way of salvation. These references do tell what God requires of His creatures. They describe what people owe to God.

God has been robbed. Sin is the robber.[174] Justice requires punishment of the offender. God judges sinners, not because they are unsaved but because they have offended God and have failed to render to God what they owe to Him. They have not feared God, glorified, nor worshiped Him.

GOD REQUIRES REPENTANCE

Salvation Means to Repent and to Return

When humans fail in their duty to God, He expects them to repent—see the error of their ways (Luke 15:17); experience remorse in their deed (Luke 15:18); and, leaving their sin, return to the Father to correct the error (Luke 15:19, 20). Indeed, God *commands* sinners to repent. In describing the ignorance of the heathen in times past concerning their false ideas about God, Paul urged, *"But* [God] *now commandeth all men every where to repent"* (Acts 17:30).

Yes, salvation is the deliverance of an offending sinner from the penalty of his failure, but there is more. This deliverance also requires the sinner's leaving the course of his former failure in order to return to God the duty that he owes to God. *"Thus saith the Lord GOD; Repent, and turn yourselves from your idols"* (Ezekiel 14:6). Christ saves men from their sins in order to restore them to obedience to God. *"For they . . . shew . . . how ye turned from idols to serve the living and true God; and to wait for his Son from heaven"* (I Thessalonians 1:9).

When rejecting the empty-hearted worship of the Israelites (a great offense to God), God called the people to a repentance and return to obedience:

> *Wash you, make you clean; put away the evil of your doings from before mine eyes; cease to do evil; Learn to do well; seek judgment, relieve the oppressed, judge the fatherless, plead for the widow. Come now, and let us reason together, saith the LORD: though your sins be as scarlet, they shall be as white as snow; though they be red like crimson, they shall be as wool. If ye be willing and obedient, ye shall eat of the good of the land: But if ye refuse and rebel, ye shall be devoured with the sword: for the mouth of the LORD hath spoken it* (Isaiah 1:16-20).

Paul described his ministry as *"testifying both to the Jews, and also to the Greeks, repentance toward God, and faith toward our Lord Jesus Christ"* (Acts 20:21). There should be no question that repentance is required of God and is therefore an essential part of salvation. Note a few of the many Scriptures that teach this truth:

105

> *But go ye and learn what that meaneth, I will have mercy, and not sacrifice: for I am not come to call the righteous, but sinners to repentance* (Matthew 9:13).

> *The time is fulfilled, and the kingdom of God is at hand: repent ye, and believe the gospel* (Mark 1:15).

> *I tell you, Nay: but, except ye repent, ye shall all likewise perish* (Luke 13:5).

Luke's account of the Great Commission stresses repentance: *"And that repentance and remission of sins should be preached in his name among all nations, beginning at Jerusalem"* (Luke 24:47).

If Repentance Is Commanded, How Do Sinners Obey?

Repentance verses use the Greek imperative, showing a command, but how does any sinner *obey* a command to repent? Many evangelicals teach that obligation necessitates ability. Are sinners naturally unable to obey God? Romans 3:12 answers, *"There is none that doeth good, no, not one."* This is precisely why sinners need a Savior. However, spiritual inability to obey God does not free the sinner from the obligation to turn from his sinful lifestyle unto God in obedience.

The Israelites were commanded to keep the law God gave them from Mount Sinai (Deuteronomy 5:32, 33), but was it possible for them to do that? Obviously not, and, as we discussed in the previous chapter, the missing element was a willing heart (Deuteronomy 5:29), which God did not give to them (Deuteronomy 29:4). That missing element is promised in the New Covenant (Jeremiah 24:7). Nevertheless, the lack of a willing spirit did not free them of their responsibility to the law.

Many anti-Calvinists argue that Calvinism makes God, who knows that sinners cannot of their own volition obey the gospel, dishonest in offering salvation to the nonelect.[175] But to my knowledge, none of these anti-Calvinists ever suggested that God was dishonest in requiring Israel to keep the law, which He knew they had no heart to do.

Repentance Is the Gift of God.

Sinners are not in morally neutral territory while God waits for them to "make a decision" for Christ. The divine picture is that all are on a broad way leading to destruction:

> *Enter ye in at the strait gate: for wide is the gate, and broad is the way, that leadeth to destruction, and*

many there be which go in thereat: Because strait is the gate, and narrow is the way, which leadeth unto life, and few there be that find it (Matthew 7:13, 14).

Thus, a call to salvation is a call for men to leave the broad way upon which all are presently moving in the inevitable course to ruin. This call to salvation, then, is a call to repentance—to change course, to turn around, to be an overcomer (Revelation 3:12). It means leaving the *"broad way"* in order to *"enter"* in at the *"strait gate"* into the *"narrow"* road that leads to life.

Although the Bible is filled with verses that command repentance, many verses also show repentance as a work of God. For example,

Him hath God exalted with his right hand to be a Prince and a Saviour, for to give repentance to Israel, and forgiveness of sins (Acts 5:31).

When they heard these things, they held their peace, and glorified God, saying, Then hath God also to the Gentiles granted repentance unto life (Acts 11:18).

In meekness instructing those that oppose themselves; if God peradventure will give them repentance to the acknowledging of the truth (II Timothy 2:25).

However, even though God does not grant repentance to all sinners, repentance is still every sinner's responsibility. This is clearly implied in Paul's rebuke of the Jews in Romans 2: *"Or despisest thou the riches of his goodness and forbearance and long-suffering; not knowing that the goodness of God leadeth thee to repentance?"* (Romans 2:4). Even though it was the will of God to keep the Jews in ignorance and unbelief, nevertheless, their responsibility to repent of their ignorance and unbelief remained unchanged (Romans 11:8-11). Paul charged them that in the prideful presumption of their privilege, they mistook God's goodness as deserved blessing and not as mercy.

GOSPEL RESPONSIBILITY

Choices
Every sinner is responsible to repent and return to God. God, in mercy, grants repentance and life to some, but not all sinners. No one's will is ever violated in this process. Everyone who is saved wanted to

be saved. No one who came to Jesus was turned away. Jesus said, *"Him that cometh to me I will in no wise cast out"* (John 6:37). The gospel message is plain, *"Whosoever believeth in him should not perish, but have everlasting life"* (John 3:16).

William R. Newell shows how many confuse election and gospel truths.

> I asked an intelligent man in western Michigan if he had believed on the Lord Jesus Christ. He burst out into loud laughing, saying, "If I am elect, I will go to heaven; and if I am not elect, there is no use in my worrying about the question!" I rebuked him sternly, with these words: "God commandeth men that they should *all everywhere repent*: inasmuch as He hath appointed a day in which He will judge the world in righteousness by the Man whom He hath ordained." "God's commands are His enablings," and if you will hearken to Him, you will be saved. But you will not dare to say to God in that day, I could not come because I was not of the elect; for that will not be true! The reason you refuse to come, will be found in your *love of sin*, not your non-election! God says, "Whosoever will," and the door is open to *all*, absolutely *all. God means "Whosoever":* and that is the word for *you*, sinner; and not *election*, which is God's business, not yours![176]

No one goes to heaven simply because he is one of God's elect. The elect, because they are sinners, must first believe and obey the gospel. Therefore, the gospel must be preached and sinners invited.

The Gospel Is Preached to Sinners

The sinner's concern is with the *gospel*, not election. The gospel relates to individuals as *sinners*. The sinner needs to be converted because he is a sinner—he has departed from the living God, going the way of iniquity. He must be converted, and in order to be converted, he must have the gospel preached to him (Romans 10:14-17). Any sinner who will believe the gospel by coming in repentance and faith to Christ will be saved. The gospel is the sinner's hope. It is also the sinner's responsibility. No one will ever die and go to Hell because he is not one of the elect. His condemnation centers on his love of sin and his failure to repent and obey the gospel (John 5:38-40).

EFFECTUAL CALLING

The General Call

We must keep in mind that the gospel has two sides: man's (gospel responsibility) and God's (effectual calling). These sides must not be confused. As the gospel is preached, a call goes out to sinners. This "call" involves two levels. First, there is a general outward call to all sinners. This call is implied in the Great Commission of the Gospel of Mark, *"Go ye into all the world and preach the gospel to every creature"* (Mark 16:15). This general call is inseparably tied to the gospel that is to be authoritatively "preached" (Gk. *kerusso,* "heralded, or proclaimed") to every creature. *"How then shall they call on him in whom they have not believed? and how shall they believe in him of whom they have not heard? and how shall they hear without a preacher?"* (Romans 10:14).

The gospel message (Gk. *kerygma*) contains three elements. These elements are (1) historical facts (I Corinthians 15:3, 4); (2) a theologically correct interpretation of those facts (Romans 5:8); and (3) a summons to appropriate the facts personally by faith (Acts 3:19). Invitations, exhortations, and commands for sinners to choose Christ and life accompany this summons. *"And the Spirit and the bride say, Come. And let him that heareth say, Come. And let him that is athirst come. And whosoever will, let him take the water of life freely"* (Revelation 22:17).

The general call of God by the preaching of the gospel assumes every sinner who hears it is under responsibility to obey it, being obliged to repent of sin and turn to the Savior. Everyone who hears the gospel responds in some fashion, either by believing, rejecting, or neglecting to do anything (Acts 17:32-34). Most people respond with indecision. This is very dangerous. Indecision is rejection because indecision is continued unbelief with no overt act. Indecision is a decision to postpone decision and is thus disobedience to the gospel (II Thessalonians 1:8). The necessity of obedience to the gospel is clearly implied in the words *"must be saved"* (Acts 4:12). Whoever will respond to the general call of the gospel will be saved (John 5:24). The question is, who will come?

The Effectual Call

Besides the general call of the gospel, a second level, an inward "effectual" call, is directed to God's elect. It is this inward call of the Holy Spirit whereby God's elect are brought willingly to repentance and faith in the Lord Jesus Christ. The term *"call"* in Scripture usually refers to the "effectual call."

109

In Romans 1 Paul gives a brief description of the purpose of his ministry in the gospel: *"for obedience to the faith among all nations for his name"* (Romans 1:5). He introduces the Roman believers to their place in the gospel purpose: *"Among whom are ye also the called of Jesus Christ"* (Romans 1:6). These Roman Christians were among *"the called ones belonging to* [genitive—possessive] *Jesus Christ"* (Romans 1:7). They were Christ's own, called out of the world by the gospel. To the Corinthians Paul made it even clearer: *"God is faithful, by whom ye were called unto the fellowship of his Son Jesus Christ, our Lord"* (I Corinthians 1:9). No one will be saved who is not effectually called.

"Many are called [in the outward gospel call], *but few are chosen* [in the effectual inward call]*"* (Matthew 20:16; 22:14).[177] "Effectual calling" involves regeneration—the initial saving act of God in bringing sinners to choose willingly the salvation which God has provided for them. This process is evident in the "golden chain" of Romans 8:30: *"[W]hom he did predestinate, them he also called."* Through the preaching of the gospel, God's elect are brought to Christ. God does not just "save" these elect sinners without their experiencing repentance and faith. So, while the gospel is outwardly declared to all, only those who are effectually and inwardly called believe on Christ. Therefore, it is God who does the saving, which is evidenced by the sinner's willingness to come to Christ.

Saved and Called for the Glory of God

The Scriptures tell us *how* the elect are effectually called: *"Who hath saved us and called us with an holy calling, not according to our works, but according to his own purpose and grace, which was given us in Christ Jesus before the world began. But is now made manifest . . . through the gospel"* (II Timothy 1:9, 10). The Scriptures tell us *why* God effectually calls his elect: *"That no flesh should glory in his presence"* (I Corinthians 1:21-31—read the whole passage). Only God is to receive glory for salvation. He will not share this glory with sinners.

When it is insisted that God must not only do the saving but also initiate the process, people balk. Without exception, one hears, "But we have a choice!" or, "We have a free will!" Well, just when does this choice come? Does it come before or after regeneration? Also, does this choice include the freedom to refuse God's invitation to trust Christ? The Bible declares, *"Salvation is of the Lord"* (Jonah 2:9), not of human choice.

Paul rebuked the Corinthian believers for their attitude of pride: *"Who maketh thee to differ* [Gk. *diakrino,* 'to make a distinction'] *from another? and what hast thou that thou didst not receive? now if thou didst receive it, why dost thou glory, as if thou hadst not received it?"* (I Corinthians 4:7). If salvation is not solely a work of grace— if the believer must initiate his faith—then there is room for the believer to glory in his initiating that faith. Paul is rejecting just that idea. He is insisting that it is the grace of God and not faith that makes the distinction between believers and unbelievers.

Two people are sitting under the same gospel message. One repents and believes the gospel; the other does not. Why? Many will answer, "Because one believed, and the other did not."[178] True, but why did that one believe? Was he somehow better—more alert, more sensitive to God—than the one who did not believe? Is the unbeliever a greater sinner or more hardhearted because he does not believe? If one's believing makes the difference, then one's believing gives one room to glory. This, Paul argues, is not the case. He does not ask, What *"maketh thee to differ?"* (is it faith?) but *"Who maketh thee to differ?"* (is it God?). Believing does not make the difference. God makes the difference, and the sinner's believing the gospel merely reveals this difference.[179]

Humans are prone to limit their understanding only to gospel responsibility. On gospel responsibility, both Calvinists and Arminians essentially agree: sinners must repent of their sins and believe on Christ. There is no disagreement that a choice must be made by the sinner. It is when election truths are introduced with the necessity of effectual calling that Arminians violently disagree.

God Forces No One to Be Saved!

Arminians view effectual calling or irresistible grace as God's coercing sinners to be saved. Coercion involves forcing someone against his will. The persistent error of anti-Calvinism is its failure to understand that the issue is *not* with the ability of humans to make choices but rather with the *moral* ability of sinners to make the right choices. In order for sinners to make the right choices in spiritual matters, they must first experience God's power in regeneration (Psalm 110:3).

The necessity for regeneration to precede faith is wonderfully illustrated in the ninth chapter of John's Gospel. Jesus first gave sight to the blind man. When the Jews charged Jesus with being a sinner, the man replied, *"Whether he be a sinner or no, I know not: one thing I know, that whereas I was blind, now I see"* (John 9:25). Later in the Temple Jesus asked him, *"Dost thou believe on the Son of God?"* (John 9:35). He replied, *"Who is he, Lord, that I might believe on him?"* (John 9:36). When Jesus revealed Himself to him, the man said, *"Lord, I believe. And he worshipped him"* (John 9:38).

111

The spiritual significance of this order—that he first received his sight, then he believed on Jesus—is seen in the next three verses (John 9:39-41). Christ came into the world *"that they which see not might see; and that they which see might be made blind."* When the Pharisees asked Him, *"Are we blind also?"* Jesus replied, *"If ye were blind* [if you understood you were blind], *ye should have no sin* [you would be forgiven]*: but now ye say, We see* [not understanding your spiritual blindness]; *therefore your sin remaineth."*

Believing requires regeneration of the sinner first in order that the "eyes" of darkened understanding be opened. Believing is the sinner's responsibility in the gospel, but it cannot take place without regeneration, the work of God.

God's Word clearly reveals both God's and man's sides of the gospel. For example, *"All that the Father giveth me shall come to me; and him that cometh to me I will in no wise cast out"* (John 6:37). *"All that the Father giveth me shall come to me"* is God's side of salvation and speaks of election. All sinners whom the Father chooses He gives to Christ to save. *"Him that cometh to me I will in no wise cast out"* is the sinner's side of the gospel. The sinner who freely chooses to come to Jesus will not be turned away. However, this promise must be understood as qualified by John 6:44 and 65: *"No man can come to me, except the Father which hath sent me draw him: and I will raise him up at the last day."*

Matthew 11:27-29 emphasizes the same thing: *"All things are delivered unto me of my Father: and no man knoweth the Son, but the Father; neither knoweth any man the Father, save the Son, and he to whomsoever the Son will reveal him* [that is God's side in election]. *Come unto me, all ye that labour and are heavy laden, and I will give you rest* [that is the gracious invitation and promise to all sinners who will come]. *"*

A Summary of Gospel Responsibility

Election has to do with God's purpose relating to certain individuals who now are part of a sinful race. The fulfillment of election is complicated because both the elect and nonelect are sinners. Both justly deserve God's wrath. Both are equally incapable of changing their miserable state, even if they were willing and desiring to do so. Thus, it is God who must act to save those whom He will.

Calvinism teaches that gospel grace is God's showing mercy to some undeserving sinners according to His will: *"Of his own will begat he us with the word of truth, that we should be a kind of first-fruits of his creatures"* (James 1:18). By His will He saves some from their sin, rebellion, and condemnation by changing their nature and transforming them into obedient children with a glorious destiny. In order to do this, God frees these sinners' wills from the bondage of sin and Satan by the new birth. God then appeals to the sinner's will via the gospel. The new nature, free of spiritual enmity, seeing the desirability of the Savior, freely and willingly responds to Him.

But what about those whom God does not elect? Are they given no choice? Of course they are. Over and over again in Scripture, God not only calls men to repentance but commands them to repent. The fact is, sinners *will not* respond: *"And ye will not come to me, that ye might have life"* (John 5:40). As Newell said, on judgment day no sinner can argue that he is lost because he was not elect. He is lost because he willingly chose to sin against God. Sinners who have the gospel preached to them and refuse Christ do so because they love their sin, not because they are not elect. No, "the door [of salvation] is open to all [who will], absolutely all [who will]."[180]

The Bible view of the sinner is that he is a rebel—unwilling, and because unwilling, unable to repent on his own. The sinner will never respond to God's general invitation without divine enablement (regeneration). Nevertheless, repentance is still required of every sinner because the sinner's failure has not removed his responsibility to render to God all the duty which he owes to God.

10

JUST WHAT DID GOD INTEND?

We stand on a simple principle—*"that Christ Jesus came into the world to save sinners"* (I Timothy 1:15). We argue that all for whom Christ died partake of the benefits of His dying. By His death our Lord accomplished exactly what the Father intended that He should—the saving of His elect:

> *But we see Jesus, who was made a little lower than the angels for the suffering of death, crowned with glory and honour; that he by the grace of God should taste death for every man* [the word *man* is an interpolation; so, the text actually reads "every one"—"every one" of whom? Every one of the *"many sons"* who are brought to glory]. *For it became him, for whom are all things, and by whom are all things, in bringing many sons unto glory, to make the captain of their salvation perfect through sufferings* (Hebrews 2:9, 10).

> *Even as the Son of man came not to be ministered unto, but to minister, and to give his life a ransom for many* (Matthew 20:28).

> *And she shall bring forth a son, and thou shalt call his name JESUS: for he shall save his people from their sins* (Matthew 1:21).

The death of Christ is a clear demonstration of the redemptive love of God (Romans 5:8), but how does God love sinners? Does He love them by making a provision which sinners may *take* or *reject* at will? Or, rather, is the sinner's appropriation of the provision a *fruit* of this merciful love of God? Is not God's love more properly expressed in the actual saving of sinners?

The Word of God clearly teaches that what God sovereignly purposes He always accomplishes. When God purposes to save people, He saves them. The death of Christ was the *means* God used to accomplish this saving work: *"In whom we have redemption through his blood, the forgiveness of sins, according to the riches of his grace"*

(Ephesians 1:7). The cross is, therefore, the vanguard of the controversy between Calvinism, modified Calvinism (Amyraldianism), and Arminianism (see Glossary for these terms).

ONE OR THE OTHER

Calvin on the Atonement

John Calvin himself did not address the extent of atonement specifically in terms of the "five points."[181] Calvin understood the death of Christ in its mediatorial application—Christ, as a priest for His people, served as both the offerer and the offering. If God elected to save certain sinners and if He chose the death of Christ as the propitiation (satisfaction of God's wrath) to accomplish salvation, then, logically, Christ's death was for only those to whom He was given as a priest to save.

Comments on I John 2:2 attributed to John Calvin's more mature thought are often quoted by advocates of unlimited atonement to show that he softened his views in later life. Augustus H. Strong cites James Richards, who quotes Calvin,[182] and John Rice cites Calvin's supposed quote from Strong.[183] However, I myself have never been able to confirm the attributed statement directly to Calvin. On the contrary, in my edition of Calvin's commentary on I John 2:2, Calvin argued clearly and succinctly *against* the idea of unlimited atonement:

> Here a question may be raised, how have the sins of the whole world been expiated? I pass by the dotages of the fanatics, who under this pretence extend salvation to all the reprobate, and therefore to Satan himself. *Such a monstrous thing needs no refutation.* They who seek to avoid this absurdity, have said that Christ suffered sufficiently for the whole world, but efficiently only for the elect. Though then I allow that what has been said is true, yet I deny that it is suitable to this passage; for the design of John *was no other than to make this benefit common to the whole church . . .* those who should believe [John's immediate audience] as well as those who were scattered through various parts of the world [all other believers].[184]

Even if John Calvin had modified or softened his views, we should not follow Calvin but rather the Scriptures. Although we do read what men have written on the issue in order to learn and profit from their studies, we know that men make mistakes; the Bible does not.

The extent of the atonement was not a primary issue with Calvin, but it certainly was with John Owen.[185] This point was, in fact, hotly debated in his generation. Dr. Owen set forth his views in the *Death of Death in the Death of Christ,* a powerful polemic in defense of the biblical view of the atonement against the humanistic corruption of Arminianism and Socinianism. The book, written after Owen had diligently studied the subject for seven years, is the most thorough and biblical examination of the atonement ever written. It cannot be answered. If ever there was a time when this book was needed, it is in today's world with its mishmash of contradictory theology.[186]

Two Views

Excluding universalism, only two views of the atonement seek to answer the question of what God intended to accomplish by the sacrifice of Christ. Either Christ died to save sinners, or He died to make them savable. The Calvinistic view, "particular" or "limited atonement," believes that Christ died to accomplish redemption for only a part of Adam's race, the "elect." On the other hand, the most popular view, held by Arminians and Amyraldians, teaches that Christ died for every one in general and, thus, for no one in particular. It is called "universal" or "unlimited atonement."

This "general-redemption" view holds that Christ died for every person who ever lived since Adam in order to make salvation possible to any sinner who will repent and believe the gospel. In dying, Christ paid the sin debt, restoring to all sinners, as a matter of mercy, some of the spiritual ability that was lost in Adam's fall. Anyone may be saved who will exercise this restored ability to repent and believe the gospel. Once the sinner has freely exercised this option, God saves him. Thus, God's purpose in Christ's death was *not the actual saving of anyone in particular* but only making the opportunity of salvation available to *all who will repent and believe the gospel.*

On the other hand, the "limited-" or "particular-redemption" view holds that Christ, in obedience to the Father's will, went to the cross in order to redeem particular individuals (God's elect), securing their eternal salvation. In other words, God's purpose was that Christ should actually *save particular sinners* by His sacrifice.

In truth, unless one is a universalist (believing that all men will eventually be saved), no one believes in a truly "unlimited" atonement. All evangelicals maintain that the effect of the atonement is limited to believers only. The problem, therefore, is to define from Scripture what God intended for the sacrifice of Christ to accomplish.

116

Proofs and Preconceptions

Dr. Charles C. Ryrie boldly but without demonstration declares that "exegesis clearly supports the unlimited position."[187] This seemingly makes a strong argument for the position. I disagree but also admit that it is difficult for many to see the limited-atonement position in a casual reading of the Bible. This difficulty is based on two problems. First, most people read with presuppositions of what the Bible teaches. For example, one prejudgment is that the words *"all,"* *"every,"* and *"world"* in the Scriptures are all-inclusive terms, meaning every person who ever lived since Adam.[188] Therefore, for example, when Paul writes that Christ died as *"a ransom for all"* (I Timothy 2:6), it is *assumed* that Paul meant every person who ever lived. (This problem will be discussed in Chapter 12.)

Another presupposition has to do with God's declaring His love to every sinner. In dealing with John 3:16, Ryrie writes, "Now if John 3:16 is so restricted, then no limited redemptionist could tell his young children, for example, that God loves them, since he could not know at that age whether or not they belonged to the elect."[189] Ryrie's comment, frankly, is *not* exegesis and does not prove what John 3:16 teaches. (Although Arminians and Amyraldians seem to have a need to tell every sinner that God loves them, I came to believe limited atonement studying this very text. See Chapter 12.)

The second difficulty concerns the false assumption that limited atonement makes the promiscuous preaching of the gospel hypocritical, if not impossible. (This is the subject of Chapter 9.) To offer salvation to the nonelect for whom Christ did not die would make God a liar, so they say. Considerable controversy has raged over the years about what has come to be known as the "well-meant offer" of the gospel.[190] David Engelsma writes:

> Preaching is exactly the communication of doctrine and truth, that is, the announcement of that which God has done and will do in Jesus Christ. It is the official declaration of *news,* the good news of God's gracious salvation. . . . To construe preaching as "in the first moment" in the imperative mood (telling man what he must do) and not in the indicative mood (telling man what God has done and promises to do) is to produce the monstrosity that passes for gospel-preaching today.[191]

All Christians acknowledge that everyone is a sinner deserving of judgment, but they somehow see God as unjust if He does not provide an opportunity for every sinner to be saved. This "fairness" issue is quickly and vigorously raised when anyone suggests that God has chosen to save only a part of these undeserving sinners. (See Chapter 6.)

Does anyone deserve to be saved? Would not God be perfectly just to leave every sinner to his just condemnation? Would God be "unfair" to the condemned masses if He, for purposes of His own, showed mercy to only one individual, thus saving him? How, then, is God unjust in saving a great host of these undeserving sinners but not all? Even the "unlimited-atonement" position believes that only a part of Adam's race will be redeemed. But how? In one view, it is God who does the saving. In the other view, it is man, who, in a sense, saves himself by his own believing. In one view, Christ's sacrifice is God's great price paid to secure trophies of grace. In the other view, Christ's sacrifice is a commodity bartered among sinners, hoping for takers. Which view really honors God?

PROBLEMS, PROBLEMS, PROBLEMS

Let us now turn our attention to the oft-ignored problems and inconsistencies which are raised by an unlimited atonement. The question which persistently nagged me, compelling further study, was this: What did Christ actually do in His death?

I have asked people, "Do you believe that Christ actually died for you—had you specifically in mind on the cross, suffered for your individual sins?"

The answer is always, "Yes, of course!"

"Do you believe that He died for your unsaved neighbor also?" (assuming that the neighbor is nonelect).

"Yes, I do!"

"What, then, did Jesus Christ do for you, a believer, more than He did for your neighbor, an unbeliever?"

"Why, nothing."

"What is the difference between you and your neighbor if Christ died equally for you both?"

"I believed, and he did not."

"Then you must admit that it was not the death of Christ that actually saved you. Christ made it possible for you to be saved only by removing some obstacle that stood in the way of God's mercy. You must also admit that, with respect to salvation, either you have something to commend yourself to God or else your neighbor has something to discredit himself before God since Christ died equally for you both. Besides, what are you going to do with the problem of double jeopardy?"

118

The problem of double jeopardy—the sinner's having his sins paid for twice: Christ's paying for them first, and the unbelieving sinner paying for them again in hell—causes people to start staring blankly as if the discussion were getting too deep. Simply, people are naturally unwilling to examine the problems which their position creates. Sometimes their excuse is, "We are not theologians!"

> But you have no right to back out of argument. Whatever God has given us He has given *us,* and we are meant to apply our minds to it, whether it is comparatively simple, or whether it is comparatively difficult, as this is. We have no right to ignore Scripture, and if we do, we do so at our peril. Indeed it is an insult to God, who raised up men to write these very Scriptures for our instruction, for our enlightenment, and for our establishment in our most holy faith.[192]

1. Double Jeopardy

What about those who are theologians? How do they deal with this problem? Charles Ryrie states the problem accurately: "If Christ died for all, then the sins of the nonelect were paid for at the cross by the death of Christ, and will be paid for again at the judgment by the condemnation of the nonelect to the lake of fire. So in effect their sins are paid for twice. Logically, then, either the death of Christ should not include the nonelect, or the nonelect should not be condemned to the lake of fire."[193] Ryrie's solution to the problem may be summed up as effectually denying substitutionary atonement. He compares the death of Christ to the student aid funds available at a school where he once taught. Sufficient funds were available for any who might want them, but the students must apply in order to get them.[194] However, that illustration, applied to double jeopardy, denies substitutionary atonement.

Double jeopardy is a legal problem. If Christ actually paid for all the sins of all people, why would anyone have to go to hell and suffer punishment for his own sins (John 8:24)? The sin debt is paid. Sinners should no longer be liable for judgment. Justice simply will not allow a penalty to be exacted twice. George S. Bishop has written:

> If Christ died for all alike, then He did no more for those who are saved than for those who perish. . . . He paid the redemption price for many who are yet paying in their own eternal anguish the wages of sin, which is death. To say this is of course to convict God of the grossest

injustice, for it is to represent Him as receiving from the hands of Christ full atonement, and then as dashing down to perdition millions of those for whom Christ had died to atone. The story is told of Pizarro that when he had imprisoned the Peruvian Inca, that monarch, lifting his hand to the level of his head upon the wall behind him, promised to fill the apartment with silver and gold to that level, provided Pizarro would let him go free. Pizarro agreed to this, and then when the loyal subjects of the Inca, by denying themselves to the utmost, had brought together the requisite ransom, Pizarro led forth their beloved Inca, and before their smiling and expectant faces put him to excruciating death. That Pizarro, lifted and broadened to infinite proportions, is the shadow which a universal atonement projects upon God—it makes an infinite Pizarro and subverts the very substratum upon which is built His throne.[195]

Do you not see the insult to God's wisdom that comes from belief in an unlimited atonement?

2. Unbelief

The problem of double jeopardy is usually shrugged away with the obvious answer that sinners are in hell because they rejected Christ. Many universal-position people cite John 3:18 as proof that Christ died for every sinner. The sinner's unbelief, when confronted with Christ's claim on him, condemns him. John 3:18, however, does not teach that rejection of Christ is the cause of the sinner's condemnation. *"He that believeth not is condemned already* [and remains so], *because he hath not believed on the name of the only begotten Son of God."* Sinners are condemned by their position in Adam. The only escape from condemnation is to believe on Christ, who paid their ransom. However, if we say that sinners are condemned because they did not exercise faith in God's offer of pardon—that they are in unbelief—we have more problems:

(1) Unbelief is one, *but only one,* of the sins for which sinners will suffer God's wrath (Revelation 21:8; Colossians 3:5-7; Galatians 5:19-21). Therefore, if Christ suffered for *all* sins, including the sin of unbelief, we are back to the problem of double jeopardy. Why should a sinner have to suffer for the sin of not believing on Christ when Christ paid for that sin on the cross?

(2) All sinners enter this life in unbelief and struggle with that sin even after salvation. Are there different kinds or degrees of unbelief, and

120

if so, how do we distinguish between them? Is there a kind of unbelief that is ultimate and final that cannot be pardoned? Did Christ suffer the penalty for an unpardonable sin? *Either none of us is saved* because all are guilty of unbelief, or we are back to a *limited atonement* because (as some suggest) Christ did not suffer for the unpardonable sin of unbelief. Or we are faced again with the problem of double jeopardy if Christ did suffer for all forms of unbelief. There is no viable alternative.

(3) There are those who teach that when one hears the gospel and rejects it, he becomes liable for this ultimate sin of unbelief—this *unpardonable sin.* How many times must a man reject the gospel before it becomes the *final* sin of unbelief for which he is justly condemned? Does the number of times vary with different people? Are sinners warned when they have approached the limit of God's patience and are in danger of committing the sin which cannot be forgiven? If so, how are they warned?

(4) How can anyone who has never heard the gospel be guilty of rejecting Christ? How could anyone commit the unpardonable unbelief if he is ignorant of the gospel's demands for faith in Christ? What of those, who, when they do hear the gospel, neither actively accept nor reject it? Is passively ignoring the demands of the gospel as serious as actively rejecting it? Must a sinner stop *unbelieving* of his own accord in order for him to believe Christ to salvation?

These tough questions need to be answered from Scripture if one is to support the "unlimited atonement" position.

3. Did Christ Die for No One in Particular?

In order to avoid the questions raised by the view that Christ actually died in the stead of specific individual sinners and for their individual sins, the disciples of Arminius plainly stated that Christ did not specifically die for anyone. This is the only logically tenable position one can take and still hold to the view of unlimited atonement. James Arminius wrote, "The immediate effect of the death of Christ is not the remission of sins or the actual redemption of any."[196] Arminius's disciple Grenvinchovius wrote, "Christ did not properly die to save anyone."[197]

4. Hypo-Calvinism: The "Four-Point" Position

Non-Substitutionary (Substitutionary) Atonement?

Interestingly, most modern universal redemptionists, unlike true Arminians, claim also to believe in substitutionary atonement. A typical doctrinal statement reads, "We believe the Lord Jesus Christ died as a substitutionary sacrifice for the sins of all men."[198] These people do not believe in universal salvation. Neither do they truly believe in substitutionary atonement, although they say so. One cannot have his cake and eat it too. If one defines *substitution* as "putting instead of; one in the place of another," one must believe in either universalism (everyone will be saved) or limited atonement (that only the elect are saved). Universal redemptionists avoid this problem by teaching a *conditional* atonement.

Dr. Charles R. Smith, professor of theology at Grace Theological Seminary, Winona Lake, Indiana, explained what universal redemptionists really teach: "The cross was not intended to save certain individuals, rather it was intended to make all men savable."[199] Smith calls his position "forensic equivalence."[200] Under this doctrine, Christ did not actually pay for individual sins but rather suffered punishment equal to or greater than what any sinner would have suffered had he suffered for his own sins. Smith cites Dr. Alva J. McClain, late president of Grace Theological Seminary:

> Christ bore the sins "of the world" (John 1:29) . . . in the sense that He paid an adequate penalty, made an adequate provision for us all. We are not to view this as involving an individual and separable penalty for each individual. Due to the infinite value of His Person, He bore a penalty which was more than equal to the penalty that could be paid by all humans throughout eternity. Exact equivalence of punishment was unnecessary and impossible. . . . He did not pay *the* payment which we would otherwise be required to pay. . . .
>
> Though an adequate payment was made on behalf of *all*, the payment is not credited to our account until we respond in faith to the Spirit's work in our hearts in calling us to Himself.[201]

Here we see Christ's sufferings viewed as a kind of pool which contains a sufficient or equal payment for any and all who might wish to avail themselves of it. They need but simply apply for it. Any sinner who rejects Christ is unable to take from the pool and must suffer for his own sin as a consequence. This is the very thing that Dr. Ryrie explained in his illustration of student aid funds. This provisional redemption is a clear denial of substitutionary atonement.

Who Limits the Atonement?

How, then, does God save sinners? Did Christ actually die in the place of particular individuals? Or did He die for the benefit of mankind, securing an *opportunity* which must be appropriated by

122

sinners in order to be effectual? Who really limits the atonement? Charles H. Spurgeon said it well:

> We are often told that we limit the atonement of Christ, because we say that Christ has not made a satisfaction for all men, or all men would be saved. Now, our reply to this is, that, on the other hand, our opponents limit it: we do not. The Arminians say, Christ died for all men. Ask them what they mean by it. Did Christ die so as to secure the salvation of all men? They say, "No, certainly not." We ask them the next question— Did Christ die so as to secure the salvation of any man in particular? They answer, "No." They are obliged to admit this, if they are consistent. They say, "No. Christ has died that any man may be saved if"—and then follow certain conditions of salvation. Now, who is it that limits the death of Christ? Why, you. You say that Christ did not die so as infallibly to secure the salvation of anybody. We beg your pardon, when you say we limit Christ's death; we say, "No, my dear sir, it is you that do it." We say Christ so died that he infallibly secured the salvation of a multitude that no man can number, who through Christ's death not only may be saved, but are saved, must be saved and cannot by any possibility run the hazard of being anything but saved. You are welcome to your atonement; you may keep it. We will never renounce ours for the sake of it.[202]

The death of Christ is limited only by the intention of God. It is certainly not limited in its power. The non-Calvinist is forced to admit that many "for whom Christ died" will never partake of the benefits of His death. Therefore, both non-Calvinists and Calvinists actually believe in some kind of a limited atonement.

Who Makes God Unfair?

It must be asked, if God's election of only *some* sinners to salvation is a Bible fact, why would an "unlimited atonement" be necessary? On the other hand, if Christ's death was a ransom for *all* sinners, would not the election of *some* sinners be legitimately viewed as *unfair*? Would not such a ransom obligate God to provide an opportunity of salvation to everyone for whom Christ died? To fail to provide such an opportunity would degrade the work of Christ by making it both unnecessary and futile in the cases of the nonelect. The anti-Calvinist Samuel Fisk is right to claim that a four-point position is inconsistent with the whole scheme of Calvinism. He writes,

> Unconditional election means that God has already selected some from among men to be saved, and only they. And it necessarily follows that the rest will certainly not be saved. Then if Christ died for this latter group, He died in vain; His blood shed for those sure to be lost was an act of futility. Therefore the four-pointer should see that this unlimited atonement just doesn't fit in.[203]

DIRECT EFFECTS OF CHRIST'S DEATH

The Bible says that Jesus Christ, in His death, *"obtained eternal redemption for us"* (Hebrews 9:12). Christ died for sinners as their Substitute, paid the debt of their sins, redeemed them from the guilt and power of sin, and secured their salvation as a direct effect. Thus, the death of Christ purchased all the gifts of grace and faith needed for elect sinners to experience salvation. This view is called "particular redemption" or "limited atonement."

The Purpose of His Sacrifice—Did God Succeed?

Jesus Christ came to redeem sinners from their sin by the payment of a price in order to bring them to God: *"For Christ also hath once suffered for sins, the just for the unjust, that* [Gk. *hina,* introducing a purpose clause—'in order that'] *he might bring us to God, being put to death in the flesh, but quickened by the Spirit"* (I Peter 3:18). In order to bring us to God, Christ must make us acceptable to God. To do this, He makes us righteous: *"For he hath made him to be sin for us, who knew no sin; that* [again, Gk. *hina*—'in order that'] *we might be made the righteousness of God in him"* (II Corinthians 5:21). If Jesus Christ died for everyone, as the unlimited position proposes, are *all* then *"made the righteousness of God in him"*? If not, Christ failed in His purpose. He died for the purpose of making those for whom He died righteous and for the purpose of bringing them to God. Yet, according to the unlimited atonement scheme, multitudes for whom He died will never be *"made the righteousness of God in Him."* Can we really accept, therefore, the unlimited thesis? If so, we attribute impossible failure to God and cheapen Christ's sacrifice.

Whom Did Christ Redeem?

The death of Christ is said to result in a redemption—*"the redemption that is in Christ Jesus"* (Romans 3:24). This term is defined by several Greek words which indicate a "loosing," a "deliverance from bondage," a "freeing from captivity," and a "buying back." This is done with "a purchase" (Gk. *agoradzo*).

A purchase may be defined as the *exchange* of value for value. Three elements are necessary for an exchange to be made: an object to purchase, a purchaser, and a purchase price. For example, if I want a piece of land, I go to the one who owns it and, after agreeing upon a price (the value of the land), I pay the stated price and take possession of the land. This is a purchase because all three elements are in place. There is an exchange—the value of the land desired for the value of money. Fundamental contract law is based on these premises.

Let us take this concept and apply it to the unlimited-atonement view. The item of value which Christ purchased is the satisfaction of God's justice, which gives God the freedom to save anyone if that one will meet God's terms. So, what is actually purchased? Certainly not any individual sinner but rather only an *opportunity* for any sinner to redeem himself, in a sense, by his own decision.

The Bible, however, presents the work of Christ as a *redemption of sinners*. *"He hath visited and redeemed his people"* (Luke 1:68). With value greater than silver and gold (I Peter 1:18, 19), the blood of Christ was paid to God, freeing guilty sinners. *"For ye are bought with a price"* (I Corinthians 6:20). *"Feed the church of God, which he hath purchased with his own blood"* (Acts 20:28). *"Thou wast slain, and hast redeemed* [Gk. *agoradzo*, 'purchased'] *us to God by thy blood out of every kindred, and tongue, and people, and nation"* (Revelation 5:9). Christ did indeed purchase *"the church"* and *"us,"* *"his people,"* to God. The price was His blood. We have an exchange of value; an actual purchase was made.

Particular redemptionists see nothing "potential" in the results of Christ's death. The person who believes Christ died for every man must, however, view Christ's death as having only potential value. The Scriptures do not speak of "potential" life or death but of Christ's actually securing life for those for whom He died and rose again as a substitute (II Corinthians 5:14, 15). By His sacrifice, Christ *"obtained eternal redemption"* (Hebrews 9:12), not just the possibility of it if we believe. To subscribe to the latter is to so cheapen the sacrifice of Christ's blood as to, by inference, impugn God's omniscience.

A Problem Passage?

One passage which is relevant to the discussion of Christ's purchasing sinners is II Peter 2:1. It deals with *"false teachers"* who *"bring in damnable heresies, even denying the Lord that bought them."* Did Jesus Christ purchase apostates who will suffer God's wrath? This "problem" verse is best answered by George Smeaton in *The Apostles' Doctrine of the Atonement*:

> The term Lord (*despotane*) has special emphasis, denoting a Lord who rules over others with unlimited power [not *kurios*, denoting Christ as a Savior]. While ostensibly appearing to serve Christ, they in substance deny His dominion and atoning sacrifice, spreading views at variance with these fundamental doctrines. . . . The comment of Piscator and of the Dutch annotations [the theologians at Dort who first listed the "five points" of Calvinism] is much to be preferred, *viz.* that these false teachers are described according to their own profession and the judgment of charity. They gave themselves out as redeemed men, and were so accounted in the judgment of the church while they abode in her communion. This is simple and natural. The passage by no means affirms that any but the true church or the sheep of Christ are truly bought by atoning blood.[204]

Second Peter 2:1 is cited, not because it is a real problem, although it seems to be the verse on top of the verse list against limited atonement. I cite it to illustrate a point: in the debate, are we really interested in examining the Scriptures, or are we satisfied to grab at a few "proof texts"? In studying to write this chapter, I collected a number of anti-limited-atonement sources. They are remarkably similar in content and direction, as if the writers have collaborated or borrowed heavily from a common source. Several writers expressed that they have little problem with four points of Calvinism. It is always the doctrine of limited atonement, or particular redemption, that is rejected.

"Four-pointers" remind me of the fellow who lived on the Mason-Dixon Line during the Civil War. He thought he could avoid taking sides by wearing Union pants and a Confederate shirt. Such compromise only got him shot at from both sides. "Four-pointers" should seriously examine their consistency.

Questions

Do limited redemptionists make poor evangelists and missionaries? Ryrie admits that "believing in limited atonement does not necessarily dampen one's evangelistic efforts. Some great evangelists, like Spurgeon, held limited atonement. And some who hold unlimited atonement fail in their responsibility."[205] We could list a great host of evangelists and missionaries who have held this doctrine. It has not curbed their zeal.

Do limited redemptionists fail to be good students of the Scriptures? This writer has consistently found that limited redemptionists are profoundly in love with God's Word. They are diligent students who believe in careful study of the Word, welcoming correction by the Scriptures.

Do limited redemptionists fail to glorify God? This writer has discovered to his delight that, in general, limited redemptionists profoundly love the Lord their God. They long to know more about Him. They love to examine His person and character. They demonstrate sincere and hearty devotion to God.

Why is particular redemption the anathema of modern evangelicals? Hold to four points and one will find acceptance and fellowship. Hold to particular redemption and find oneself rejected and disfellowshipped.

Does the answer to these questions not lie in our basic nature to want to be in control of our own choices? One can believe in a doctrine of election and either relegate it to "paradox" or define it as God's electing sinners He foresees as choosing Him. However, one cannot hold to particular redemption and hold a view other than Jesus Christ's redeeming those individuals chosen of the Father and given to Christ.

Here is where non-Calvinism's humanism and arrogant abrogation of God's power in the world most clearly shows itself. To subscribe to the non-Calvinistic position is to view Christ as a door-to-door salesman of salvation and His sacrifice as a commodity to be hawked and bartered. Can mankind be *so* arrogant and egotistical as to place human choice over God's immutable will? I say a resounding "no!"

11

HOW DID CHRIST SAVE HIS PEOPLE?

It can easily be shown from Scripture that God the Father assigned to Jesus Christ a specific task in sending Him to earth (John 5:30; 6:37-39; 8:42; Ephesians 3:11). What that task was can also be easily demonstrated (John 6; 10; 17)—God the Father gave to Christ a people to save:

> *All that the Father giveth me shall come to me; and him that cometh to me I will in no wise cast out. For I came down from heaven, not to do mine own will, but the will of him that sent me. And this is the Father's will which hath sent me, that of all which he hath given me I should lose nothing, but should raise it up again at the last day* (John 6:36-39).

The Father and Son entered into covenant before the world began. In Isaiah 53:10 God declares that His *"pleasure"* (His will) would *"prosper"* in Christ's hand, for He would *"see his seed"* (the fruit of Christ's labors, His children). A definite transaction was in view here. Samuel Rutherford (1634) argued:

> It is a work of Christ as Mediator, and written in the commission His Father gave Him, that He should lose none, but raise him up at the last day (John iv. 39.) In Eph. v. 27, He presenteth His church to Himself, a glorious church, not having spot or wrinkle. He shall get His bride, the church, all arrayed in His Father's clothes, in at heaven's gate, and slip her hand in His Father's hand, and say, Father, see her now! I have done my part; I have not laboured in vain.[206]

How Christ saved those given Him by the Father is explained by two tasks for which Christ took human flesh to perform. First, Christ serves as a mediator and priest for them. Second, Christ actually took their punishment as a substitute in covenant union with them. Let us examine these areas.

THE PRIESTHOOD OF CHRIST

A priest is a person appointed by God to represent people and to transact with God on their behalf (Hebrews 5:1). Jesus came to earth and was *"made like unto his brethren, that he might be a merciful and faithful high priest in things pertaining to God, to make reconciliation for the sins of the people"* (Hebrews 2:17). Thus, as a priest, Christ represents *"the people"* and acts on their behalf: *"Seeing he ever liveth to make intercession for them"* (Hebrews 7:25). Only those who *"come unto God by him* [have access to God by means of His priestly intercession]" is he *"able"* to save (Hebrews 7:25).[207]

According to Hebrews 5:1, an essential part of the priest's work of intercession is to offer *"both gifts and sacrifices for sins."* Christ's superiority over the Old Testament priesthood of Aaron is seen in that Christ *"offered up himself"* (Hebrews 7:27) *"once for all"* (Hebrews 10:10). The very important teaching of the book of Hebrews is that one cannot divorce the death of Christ from His work as *"high priest over the house of God"* (Hebrews 10:21). Just as a priest represents people and intercedes to God in their behalf by offering sacrifices for sin and securing forgiveness and reconciliation for those he represents, so Christ's death was an offering to God in behalf of those whom He represented as priest and mediator.

This brings us to the question, who are the people Christ represents as a priest? Christ came *"to taste death for every man"* (Hebrews 2:9). The word *"man"* does not appear in the Greek text; so the verse actually reads, *"taste death for every one* [Gk. *pantes,* 'everyone']. *"* In order to determine just who the *"everyone"* in this phrase includes, the principle of priesthood (that a priest represents particular people) must be kept in mind.

Now, notice in the context of Hebrews 2:10 that *"many sons,"* *"the children,"* and *"the people"* are mentioned (Hebrews 2:10, 13, 14, 17). These are *the ones with whom Christ identifies* by taking their nature upon Himself (*"to be made like unto his brethren"*) in order to *represent* them as their high priest. It is for *"every one"* of these that He *"tastes death . . . to make reconciliation for the sins of the people"* (Hebrews 2:9, 17).

It should be quite evident from even a casual reading of Hebrews 2 that Christ represented a particular people—*"the children which God hath given me"* (Hebrews 2:13). This truth is confirmed by His own high priestly prayer recorded in John 17:9: *"I pray for them: I pray not for the world, but for them which thou hast given me; for they are thine."* He intercedes for *"them"* whom He represents as priest.

Would it not be strange if Christ refused to pray for those for whom He died? Yet, if Christ died for the whole world of sinners, why would He say, *"I pray not for the world"*? He did not pray for the world and He did not represent the world because He did not *die* for the world. He acted only for those whom the Father had *"given"* Him—*"the children"* (Hebrews 2:13). John Owen sums up this concept beautifully:

> "Christ being come an high priest of good things to come, by his own blood he entered in once into the holy place, having obtained eternal redemption for us," verses 11, 12. Now, what was this holy place and to what end did he enter into it? Why, he "is not entered into the holy places made with hands, which are the figures of the true; but into heaven itself, now to appear in the presence of God for us," verse 24. And what doth he there appear for? Why, to be our advocate, to plead our cause with God, for the application of the good things procured by his oblation unto all them for whom he was an offering; as the apostle tells us, "If any man sin, we have an advocate with the Father, Jesus Christ the righteous," 1 John ii. 1. Why, how comes that to pass? "He is the propitiation for our sins," verse 2. His being *hilasmas,* a propitiatory sacrifice for our sins, is the foundation of his interceding, the ground of it; and, therefore, they both belong to the same persons . . . which breaks the neck of the general ransom; for according to that, he died for millions that have no interest in his intercession, who shall have their sins laid to their charge, and perish under them.[208]

Christ became a priest for His own, and His death was as an offering made by Him for them.

THE COVENANT-HEAD OF A NEW RACE

Christ's death was a *vicarious* (substitutionary) sacrifice. Paul in Romans 5:19 summarizes the nature of our Lord's task by comparing it with Adam's disobedience: *"For as by one man's disobedience many were made sinners, so by the obedience of one shall many be made righteous."* Adam, as the representative of the human race, disobeyed God, which resulted in *all* his descendants' being made sinners subject to the wrath of God. Thus, one sin; many sinners. In this verse the word *"many"* is used as a comparative, showing how one man's action affects those, the *"many,"* he represents. But in the eighteenth verse, Paul uses *"all"* to show the actual extent or result of the actions of each representative: *"Therefore as by the offence of one judgment came upon all men to condemnation; even so by the righteousness of one the free gift came upon all men unto justification of life"* (see also I Corinthians 15:21, 22).

Because of their theological prejudice, many commentators do not see that Paul is making *exact* parallels between Adam's disobedience (with its result) and Christ's obedience (with its result). The importance cannot be overstated: Adam's action affected all of those whom he represented; Christ's action affected all of those whom He represented. Adam's disobedience rendered all his descendants sinners under the judgment of God, even before *any* of them were born. The proof of this is that *"all die,"* even infants, who cannot be responsible for personal sin. *"Even so"* (exact parallel), Paul says, *"by the righteousness of one, the free gift came upon all men unto justification of life"* (Romans 5:18).

It is at this point that the non-Calvinistic commentators start doing the "fancy two-step," trying to evade the incontrovertible conclusion Paul forces upon them. For example, the well-known Lutheran commentator R. C. H. Lenski writes, "What Christ obtained for all men, all men do not receive."[209] That statement *clearly denies* what the verse plainly states. What Christ obtained for all the people He represented, they will receive. *"The free gift came* [aorist tense, indicating an accomplished, not potential, act] *upon all men unto justification of life"* (Romans 5:18). Now, if one takes the phrase *"all men"* to mean every descendent of Adam, then this verse must be interpreted to teach universal salvation, for Christ obtained *"the free gift"* for all men.[210]

This brings up a significant point about how people "read" the Bible. In discussing the issue of Calvinism with people, one begins to understand how a person's theological bent influences his thinking. When he reads, for example, that Christ gave Himself *"a ransom for all,"* [211] he cannot read it literally as meaning every sinner who ever lived, for then he must conclude that every sinner will be saved. Therefore, most non-Calvinists read the verse in this way: "'*Who gave himself a ransom for all* [conditionally].' Christ gave Himself for every sinner," they reason, "but sinners must trust in Christ in order to have salvation. Never mind what the word *ransom* means. Christ gave Himself for the salvation of *all, conditioned* upon their acceptance of Him." This is a sloppy approach that misinterprets God's Word.

All for whom Adam acted are condemned by Adam's action. We *know* undeniably that the whole human race is affected by Adam's disobedience, for the whole race was *"in Adam."²¹²* *"Even so,"* all for whom Christ acted are affected by Christ's action. Paul uses the same line of logic in II Corinthians 5:14: *"We thus judge that if one died for* [Gk. *huper,* 'as a substitute for'] *all, all died* [as a subsequent of the action of the substitute]." All those *"in Christ"* died in Him when He died (Romans 6:6).

SUBSTITUTIONARY ATONEMENT—A PROBLEM

Christ's death was a substitutionary sacrifice made for those whom He represented.

> *For he hath made him to be sin for us* (II Corinthians 5:21).

> *Christ . . . hath given himself for us an offering and a sacrifice to God* (Ephesians 5:2).

> *For Christ also hath once suffered for sins, the just for the unjust, that he might bring us to God* (I Peter 3:18).

God demands the punishment of sin because punishment is the response of God's nature against moral evil. Therefore, if any are to be saved, Jesus Christ must fulfill the requirement for a substitutionary sacrifice. When I say *must*, I do not mean that Christ was obligated to die, for He voluntarily offered Himself. I mean that Christ is the only sacrifice that is acceptable before God. He alone can pay the infinite debt of our sins.

Christ's paying our sin debt is often compared to a penniless man's owing a million dollars and a billionaire's paying the debt for him. This illustration (or something similar) is used to teach that Jesus Christ was *surety* to pay our punishment. This may work under civil law: if Fred Z. owes money, the only requirement his creditor usually makes is that the debt be paid on time; he does not care who pays the debt.

This will *not* work, however, under criminal law. For example, if Fred Z. robs a bank, criminal law will not let Joe X. pay his debt: Fred must pay it himself. Before God, our sins are *criminal* acts, not financial debts. Christ's death as a substitution for Fred Z. is not allowable under criminal justice. In general, Old Testament legal principles are the same:

> *The soul that sinneth, it shall die. The son shall not bear the iniquity of the father, neither shall the father*

bear the iniquity of the son: the righteousness of the right-
eous shall be upon him, and the wickedness of the wicked
shall be upon him (Ezekiel 18:20; see also Psalm 49:7-9).

One must keep in mind the argument of Romans 5 discussed above if he is to understand the substitutionary nature of Christ's sacrifice. All those who are *"in Adam"* die (come under the corruption and condemnation of sin) because Adam represented the human race and acted in its behalf. One man disobeyed, and his disobedience was accepted for all his posterity. In other words, the race was in *union* with Adam.

In order to save *some* of Adam's condemned race, Jesus Christ had to be made the head of a new race. Therefore, Jesus Christ *"was made in the likeness of men"* (Philippians 2:7).

> *Forasmuch then as the children are partakers of flesh and blood, he also himself likewise took part of the same; that through death he might destroy him that had the power of death, that is, the devil. . . . Wherefore in all things it behoved him to be made like unto his brethren, that he might be a merciful and faithful high priest in things pertaining to God, to make reconciliation for the sins of the people* (Hebrews 2:14, 17).

Christ became a man, suffered, and died as a substitute for men. God's acceptance of Christ's work was demonstrated in that Christ was raised again from the dead (Romans 4:25). In this He was made *"a quickening spirit,"* regenerating some of Adam's descendants so that *"in Christ shall all be made alive"* (I Corinthians 15:22).

If it is contrary to legal principles for the innocent to pay the penalty for the guilty, how could God be just and at the same time allow His innocent Son to die for sins He did not commit? Since we *know* God did just that, we must conclude that God's accepting Christ's sacrifice was done under a principle other than divine justice. That principle was mercy.

Jesus Christ, *as one,* acted for all who would be part of His new race—His own (Matthew 1:21), His sheep (John 10:15), His church (Ephesians 5:25, 26). *"As thou hast given him power over all flesh, that he should give eternal life to as many as thou hast given him"* (John 17:2). To do this, all of those for whom He is head must be placed *in Christ* in order that in Him they may act. This is what is termed "union with Christ."

133

UNION WITH CHRIST

Obviously, all of the human race is *not* in union with Christ. So we must ask, who is in this union, and when were they placed into this union with Christ? The Scripture clearly answers these questions for us: *"According as he hath chosen us in him before the foundation of the world"* (Ephesians 1:4). Before the foundation of the world, God set His love upon *"us,"* His elect, placing us into union with Christ.

God entered into a "covenant" with His Son to carry out His purpose to redeem a people for His name (Acts 15:14-18). Christ's coming as a Redeemer is based on the promises of that "covenant." *"And this I say, that the covenant, that was confirmed before of God in Christ, the law, which was four hundred and thirty years after, cannot disannul, that it should make the promise of none effect"* (Galatians 3:17). Here Paul addresses the *"covenant . . . confirmed before of God in Christ,"* to create a union *"in Christ."* The Father and Son confirmed this union *before* the giving of the law so that it cannot be nullified by the law. It is based upon a *promise* and not upon any contingencies of the sinners who shall be part of this union. Therefore, the law, which requires that justice be served on sinners, *cannot affect the promise.*

In this union, Christ and His own become *one* so that the sins of the elect actually become Christ's and His righteousness becomes theirs (II Corinthians 5:21). Only in this way could God legally accept the substitutionary sacrifice of Christ. Our sins actually became His own, and He paid for them as His own. Our salvation, which is nothing less than Christ's imparting Himself to us in the fullness of all that He is, is ours in this union. What a marvelous saving grace!

All of this was done by His sovereign purpose and not by anything which He foresaw in the believer. *"Who hath saved us, and called us with an holy calling, not according to our works, but according to his own purpose and grace, which was given us in Christ Jesus before the world began"* (II Timothy 1:9). *"And the grace of our Lord was exceeding abundant with* [not 'because of'] *faith and love which is in Christ Jesus"* (I Timothy 1:14).

This union with Christ is one of the greatest doctrines of the Word of God. Dr. J. W. Alexander (no relation to me) called this truth "the central truth of all theology and religion."[213] The whole of the Christian life operates out of this union. Paul said, *"I am crucified with Christ: nevertheless I live; yet not I, but Christ liveth in me: and the life which I now live in the flesh I live by the faith of the Son of God, who loved me, and gave himself for me"* (Galatians 2:20).

This union is illustrated four ways in the New Testament: (1) the building of a spiritual house (I Peter 2:4, 5; Ephesians 2:20-22); (2) the union of a husband and wife (Ephesians 5:31, 32; Romans 7:4; II Corinthians 11:2); (3) the union of the vine and branches (John 15:1-10); (4) the relationship of the head and the body (I Corinthians 6:15; 12:12; Ephesians 1:22, 23).

All of the practical aspects of the Christian life come out of this union. *"At that day ye shall know that I am in my Father, and ye in me, and I in you"* (John 14:20). *"But of him are ye in Christ Jesus, who of God is made unto us wisdom, and righteousness, and sanctification, and redemption"* (I Corinthians 1:30). His life is our life, which we have by virtue of this union.

> *When Christ, who is our life, shall appear, then shall ye also appear with him in glory* (Colossians 3:4).

> *Now if we be dead with Christ, we believe that we shall also live with him* (Romans 6:8).

> *Whereby are given unto us exceeding great and precious promises: that by these ye might be partakers of the divine nature, having escaped the corruption that is in the world through lust* (II Peter 1:4).

Our redemption not only is *by* Christ but also is *in* Christ:

> *"Being justified freely by his grace through the redemption that is in Christ Jesus"* (Romans 3:24).

Our freedom from wrath and condemnation is by virtue of this union:

> *"There is therefore now no condemnation to them which are in Christ Jesus"* (Romans 8:1).

We are new creations in Him:

> *"Therefore if any man be in Christ, he is a new creature: old things are passed away; behold, all things are become new"* (II Corinthians 5:17).

We experience the love of God in Christ and find our security in Him:

> *"Who shall be able to separate us from the love of God, which is in Christ Jesus our Lord"* (Romans 8:39).

135

We have our victory in Him:

> *Now thanks be unto God, which always causeth us to triumph in Christ, and maketh manifest the savour of his knowledge by us in every place* (II Corinthians 2:14).

> *For in him dwelleth all the fulness of the Godhead bodily. And ye are complete in him, which is the head of all principality and power* (Colossians 2:9, 10).

Our spiritual unity is in Christ:

> *So we, being many, are one body in Christ, and every one members one of another* (Romans 12:5).

> *There is neither Jew nor Greek, there is neither bond nor free, there is neither male nor female: for ye are all one in Christ Jesus* (Galatians 3:28).

To sum up, the nature of Christ's death was *representative*—a substitutionary sacrifice. Christ identified with the children God gave to Him in order to become their great High Priest and to offer Himself for their sins. Christ also identified Himself with His own so that He might represent them as the head of a new race, acting for them in obedience and taking upon Himself their just punishment. These facts have found their fulfillment in the great truth of union with Christ. In the concept of union, God achieved the goal of *"bringing many sons unto glory"* (Hebrews 2:10). In identifying with them, Christ actually became one with them.

> *O the depth of the riches both of the wisdom and knowledge of God! how unsearchable are his judgments, and his ways past finding out!* (Romans 11:33).

12

WHOSOEVER WILL
AND WHOSOEVER WON'T

John 3:16 is the most popular verse in the Bible, having been learned by many a Christian at his mother's knee. This "gospel in a nutshell" is the text of countless sermons on God's great love. However, many Christians take this verse out of its context in order to prove what it does not say—that God loves every person in the whole world and that God is longing for every sinner to come to salvation. Such a view is that of one who wrote, "The loving heart of God longs to see all people saved."[214] Although this sentiment is touching, it actually reduces God's great redemptive love to an anemic sort of affection that will be frustrated by most sinners' rejecting the gospel. Does John 3:16 support this view?

John 3:16 simply states that God loved the world by giving His Son; that the motive for redemption, the love of God, involves Christ's being lifted up as a sacrifice (John 3:14); and that whoever believes will have everlasting life. This chapter seeks to disprove three notions commonly taught from John 3:16: (1) that the verse is a free offer of salvation; (2) that the verse teaches God's redemptive love is bestowed on everyone; and (3) that the word *world* includes every person who ever lived.

CHRIST CAME TO SAVE SINNERS

First, John 3:16 does not teach that a free offer of the gospel is made to everyone. It teaches only that because God gave His Son, believers (*"whosoever believeth"* or "the ones believing") will not perish. Although the gospel is to be preached generally in the hearing of everybody, Jesus Christ made it clear that He came to offer salvation to sinners only: *"I came not to call the righteous, but sinners to repentance"* (Luke 5:32). The "righteous"—those who suppose that they are righteous—do not see their need for salvation. The gospel is *only* for those who see that they are sinners.

But someone will say, "I thought everyone is a sinner." This is true, but in order to answer a call to sinners, a person must recognize that *he*, truly being a sinner, is the object of that call. The "righteous"

Jews, for example, would not recognize the Savior, for they did not see themselves as sinners. Indeed, they were angry with Jesus because it was with *sinners* that he kept company (Luke 5:30). Jesus responded to their concern, explaining that He kept company with sinners because, as it is only the sick who need a physician, so it is the sinner who needs a Savior. The Great Physician will not press His services on those who do not need them.

Spiritual Blindness

The issue is not whether one *has* a need (for everyone does) but whether one *sees* his need. The natural condition of the race is spiritual blindness (Ephesians 4:18). Only the convincing and illuminating work of the Holy Spirit can bring the sinner to see his need. Jesus promised that when the Holy Spirit came into the world, He would convince sinners that they were sinners (John 16:8). Those who are convinced of the Holy Spirit that they are sinners are called to salvation. No one will be convinced that he is a sinner without the Holy Spirit.

The Pharisees were spiritually blind, and Jesus left them in that condition. Indeed, the Word of God is very clear that God intended that they should not "see" (Matthew 13:9-18; Romans 11:8-10). *"Some of the Pharisees . . . said unto him, Are we blind also? Jesus said unto them, If ye were blind* [that is, if you understood your blindness]*, ye should have no sin* [you would be forgiven]*: but now ye say, We see; therefore your sin remaineth"* (John 9:40, 41). Had the Pharisees a proper understanding of their condition, they would have been saved. Those who are not convinced of their blindness—that they are sinners—are neither called nor offered salvation.

There is no offer of anything at all in this verse. In fact, not one of the "whosoever" verses teaches either that Christ died for every person or that everyone is offered salvation. That idea must be inferred. All that the "whosoever" verses teach is that, on the basis of Christ's death, God promises to save all who believe the gospel, nothing more. There is nothing in John 3:16 which declares that God offers salvation to every sinner.

DOES GOD LOVE EVERYBODY?

Second, the verse does not teach that God's redemptive love is bestowed on everyone who ever lived. Evangelicals generally teach that the "whosoever" verses prove universal atonement (that Christ died for everyone). They teach that if provision was not made for everyone, offering salvation to "whosoever will" would make the offer dishonest. Again, in the clear light of God's Word, this supposition does not stand up to scrutiny. Rather, redemptive love is particular (discriminatory) in nature and cannot be frustrated. In love God *accomplishes* the redemption of those whom He loves; He does not merely attempt to do so. Since not every person is redeemed, redemption is limited by God Himself.

Now, if God, for purposes of His own sovereign will, chooses not to redeem all of Adam's sinful race, can we find fault with God's love? "You may ask, 'Is God loving when he chooses not to redeem everyone?' And I reply, 'Is God loving when he sends a person to hell—even after Jesus has already paid the price for his release [which would be the natural result of the universal atonement position]?'"[215] Do we, God's creatures, dictate to God whom and how He should love? Do we undeserving sinful creatures so wish to be the determiners or modifiers of God's intention? The idea of elective, redeeming love did not originate with man but with a thrice-holy, completely righteous God. It is man's foolish and prideful opinion that judges this view of God to be unworthy of Him.[216]

"So"—What?

Most Christians, like Oliver B. Greene in his commentary, read the word *so* in John 3:16 in this way:

> That little word "so" signifies that there are not enough words in all the languages of the world to express the depth, the height, the length, or the breadth of the great love of God upon man. How much "so" means in John 3:16, the wisdom of man can never reason out and the tongue of man can never tell. Only God, in eternity, can explain how much He loved us when He "**SO** loved" that He gave Jesus to die for us.[217]

Of course, we ought to magnify God for His great redeeming love. There is no greater love. Indeed, only eternity will be sufficient to grasp the magnitude of God's love. However, the word translated *"so"* is *houto* in the Greek, an adverb meaning "thus" or "on this wise." In the Greek text *so* stands at the head of the sentence, thus reflecting its importance in the sentence. It answers to *as* in verse fourteen: *"As Moses lifted up the serpent . . . so must the Son of man be lifted up . . . so* ['in this way'] *God loved the world that He gave His only begotten Son* [as a sacrifice]. *"* Had John intended to describe how much God loved the world, he would have used *tosoutos,* "so great," or "so much" (Matthew 8:10; 15:33).

In making *so* a modifier of God's redemptive love and then extending that love to every sinner, we devalue rather than magnify that love. We depreciate it by saying that God's great redeeming love cannot redeem anyone unless *we* add something—our own believing—to it. Dr. J. I. Packer explains:

> We have limited the atonement far more drastically than Calvinism does, for whereas Calvinism asserts that Christ's death, as such, saves all whom it was meant to save, we have [in effect] denied that Christ's death [alone], as such is sufficient to save any of them. We have flattered impenitent sinners by assuring them that it is in their power to repent and believe, though God cannot make them do it. Perhaps we have also trivialized faith and repentance in order to make this assurance plausible ("it's very simple—just open your heart to the Lord . . ."). Certainly, we have effectively undermined the basic conviction of religion—that man is always in God's hands. In truth, we have lost a great deal. And it is, perhaps, no wonder that our preaching begets so little reverence and humility, and that our professed converts are so self-confident and so deficient in knowledge, and in good works which Scripture regards as the fruit of true repentance.[218]

God's Wrath and Redemptive Love

Who benefits from this redeeming love that God declares He has for the world? In order to answer this question, we need to understand the present collective status of the human race in its relationship with God. First, notice the phrase *"that whosoever believeth in Him should not perish."* Here we have a purpose clause that gives us the reason why God gave His Son. It literally reads, *"In order that all who believe should not perish."* The clause indicates that those who believe were in danger of perishing and that God's giving His Son prevents that from happening.

On the other hand, what about those who do not believe? *"He that believeth not is condemned already . . . shall not see life; but the wrath of God abideth on him"* (John 3:18, 36). The Greek indicates continuous action and demonstrates that wrath and condemnation are already in place, resting and abiding on unbelievers traveling the broad way. All who do not benefit from God's love are subject to God's wrath (Romans 1:18; 2:8; 9:22; Ephesians 2:3; 5:6; Colossians 3:6; Revelation 19:15). This passage does not say that God loves everyone and that He is offering His Son to all. This passage does not say that those who choose Christ will not perish. This passage does not say that those who refuse Christ will find God's love turned into wrath. No, all are subject to God's wrath save those upon whom He has graciously bestowed His love—the *"world"* of believers in John 3:16.

Paul told the believers at Thessalonica, *"For God hath not appointed us* [believers] *to wrath, but to obtain salvation by our Lord Jesus Christ, who died for us"* (I Thessalonians 5:9, 10). Here we see that some people are delivered from God's wrath through the death of Christ. This deliverance is the love of God in demonstration.

Therefore, the *love* of John 3:16 is a redemptive love that expresses itself in the act of redemption. This redemptive love is not demonstrated solely in an *act* of giving but in what *results* from that act of giving. This *love* is defined as "the will or intention to do good to the one so loved"; it is benevolent love. For example, I love my wife and want her to be happy with reliable transportation. Suppose that her car has suffered a mechanical breakdown. What should I do? Should I buy her some parts and tools to repair it? There would be reason to question my profession of love for her if I provide her with only the *means* of repairing the car but she is left to accomplish the *end* of it— do the actual repairs. When God says that He loves me and wants to redeem me, He will supply both the *means* and the *end*.

> *But God commendeth his love toward us, in that, while we were yet sinners, Christ died for us* [the means]. *Much more then, being now justified* [the end] *by his blood* [the means], *we shall be saved from wrath* [the end] *through him* [the means]. *For if, when we were enemies, we were reconciled to God* [the end] *by the death of his Son* [the means], *much more, being reconciled, we shall be saved* [the end] *by his life* [the means] (Romans 5:8-10).[219]

There is a need: God's chosen ones are lost, in bondage, under judgment, without payment, justly condemned, and in danger of eternal punishment. God, motivated by love, meets the need of His elect by giving His Son as a sacrifice for them. How? That is where the little word *"so"* comes in, and the result is profound!

Two Seeds

God had in eternity, by election, already determined to save some of lost mankind for His glory. In order to do this, He made a distinction between His own and the rest of mankind. This is the teaching of Genesis 3:15: *"And I will put enmity between thee* [Satan] *and the*

141

woman, and between thy seed and her seed; it shall bruise thy head, and thou shalt bruise his heel." Notice first that God said, *"I will put enmity."* Therefore, it is God who makes the distinction between the seed of the woman and the seed of the serpent, Satan.

Who are the seed of Satan? *"In this the children of God are manifest, and the children of the devil: whosoever doeth not righteousness is not of God"* (I John 3:10). Jesus told the Jews, who insisted that they were the legitimate seed of Abraham, that they would do the deeds of their real father, who was not Abraham: *"Ye are of your father the devil, and the lusts of your father ye will do"* (John 8:44). This verse applies to all unbelievers. *"Wherein in time past ye walked according to the course of this world, according to the prince of the power of the air, the spirit that now worketh in the children of disobedience"* (Ephesians 2:2).

Who is the seed of the woman? Genesis 3:15 is understood by most commentators to be the first Messianic promise. Paul tells us in Galatians 4:4-6 that the promise of Genesis 3:15 is fulfilled in Christ:

> *But when the fulness of the time was come, God sent forth his Son, made of a woman, made under the law, To redeem them that were under the law, that we might receive the adoption of sons. And because ye are sons, God hath sent forth the Spirit of his Son into your hearts, crying, Abba, Father.*

Christ's bruising (*"thou shalt bruise his heel"*) would result in the redemption of some of Adam's fallen race, making them sons of God by adoption. In other words, Christ's incarnation and sacrifice were for the purpose of making a people (children of God) who would be distinct from the seed of the serpent, Satan.

In John 17:6 Jesus Christ's high priestly prayer demonstrates that His work was to separate Adam's race into two distinct groups: *"I have manifested thy name unto the men which thou gavest me out of the world: thine they were, and thou gavest them me; and they have kept thy word."* God purposed to take out of the world a people for Himself. These people, Jesus said, were His Father's even before He redeemed them with His blood (*"thine they were"*). *"This people have I formed for myself; they shall shew forth my praise"* (Isaiah 43:21). It is a people of "universal" composition (Jews and Gentiles): *"Blessed be the Lord God of Israel; for he hath visited and redeemed his people"* (Luke 1:68).

> *Simeon hath declared how God at the first did visit the Gentiles, to take out of them a people for his name. And to this agree the words of the prophets; as it is written,*

142

After this I will return, and will build again the taber-
nacle of David, which is fallen down; and I will build
again the ruins thereof, and I will set it up: That the
residue of men might seek after the Lord, and all the
Gentiles, upon whom my name is called, saith the Lord,
who doeth all these things. Known unto God are all his
works from the beginning of the world (Acts 15:14-18).

That there is also enmity between believers and unbelievers is
quite clear: *"If ye were of the world, the world would love his own: but*
because ye are not of the world, but I have chosen you out of the world,
therefore the world hateth you" (John 15:19). *"I have given them thy*
word; and the world hath hated them, because they are not of the
world, even as I am not of the world" (John 17:14).

In order to accomplish the task of redeeming His people, Christ
must destroy the enmity they have toward God and reconcile both God
and His people. This He did on the cross:

And all things are of God, who hath reconciled us to
himself by Jesus Christ, and hath given to us the min-
istry of reconciliation; To wit, that God was in Christ,
reconciling the world unto himself, not imputing their
trespasses unto them; and hath committed unto us the
word of reconciliation (II Corinthians 5:18, 19; see also
Colossians 1:20, 21 and Romans 5:10).[220]

Ephesians 2:16 bears out the fact that God was reconciling both
Jew and Gentile into one body: *"And that he might reconcile both unto*
God in one body by the cross, having slain the enmity thereby." If
Christ reconciled us to God by the cross, then reconciliation *resulted*
from His work and is not just a potential reconciliation, needing something from the sinner to make the reconciliation effective. God's
redemptive love was working to take out of the world a people for His
name. Therefore, God's love is not bestowed upon every person who
ever lived but only upon His own.

TWO OPPOSING "WORLDS"

John 3:16 does not teach that God wants everyone who ever lived
to be saved. As we have discussed, first, the verse is not a free offer of
salvation to anyone. Second, John 3:16 is a declaration of God's discriminatory, elective love. Therefore, third, the *"world"* of John 3:16
does *not* include every person who ever lived. It cannot be the *"world"*
Jesus said He would not pray for in John 17:9.

The word *world* (*kosmos*) is used in different ways in the Scripture. (1) It is used of the creation, universe, or earth itself (Matthew 13:38; 25:34; John 1:9, 10; I John 4:9). (2) It is used of material possessions (Matthew 16:26; I John 3:17). (3) It is used of a highly organized system or lifestyle of men in rebellion to God and under the control of Satan (John 7:7; 8:23; 17:6, 9; Galatians 4:3; Ephesians 2:2; Colossians 2:8; James 4:4; I John 2:15-17). This is where we get the idea of "worldly" and "worldliness." (4) It is used of the inhabitants of earth in general, but not necessarily every individual ("representative universalism")[221] (Luke 12:30; John 1:29; 3:16; 14:22; I John 2:2). The Apostle John uses *world* this way many times to emphasize the universality of the gospel—that it was for more than just Jews. (5) *World* can also mean every one of a particular group (Jews in John 12:19; believers in John 6:33, 51; unbelievers in I John 3:1, 2; 5:19).

As we see, then, at least two of these *worlds* are set in contrast. *"Behold, what manner of love the Father hath bestowed upon us, that we should be called the sons of God: therefore the world knoweth us not, because it knew him not"* (I John 3:1). The *"world"* of this verse is clearly distinguished from God's elect (*"us"*), for *"the world knoweth us* [the elect] *not."* Obviously, this *world* is not the same *world* of John 3:16 because it is implied that the Father did *not* bestow His love on this world. The Father bestowed His love on *"us"* with the result that the *"world"* does not know us. The world's "not knowing us" is compared with its not knowing Christ and strongly suggests the enmity described in I John 2:15-17. Thus, in John 3:16 we have the *"world"* on whom God did bestow His love, and in I John 3:1 we have the *"world"* on whom He did not bestow His love.

There is an enmity (mutual hatred—Genesis 3:15; cf. Psalm 5:5) between God and the "world" of God-hating sinners: *"Ye adulterers and adulteresses, know ye not that the friendship of the world is enmity with God? whosoever therefore will be a friend of the world is the enemy of God"* (James 4:4, see also Romans 8:7). This enmity was established in the Garden when Adam willingly and deliberately chose Satan's lie over God's truth. From that point Adam's race came under the wrath of God.

Yet people today continue to stroll calmly and without concern through the wide gate and down the broad way to their ruin in eternal hell! There is little thought of the God whom they have offended. There is no understanding of God's being their enemy by virtue of their sinful offenses. Rather, they regard Him as loving and forgiving them, no matter how sinfully they live. This God, "who loves you and waits to save you if you will let Him," is not to be feared, for He is no threat to sinners. This is not the picture of God that Scripture paints.

Logical Considerations

The main support for the teaching of unlimited atonement is the number of passages in the Bible that use "universal" terms such as *"all," "every,"* and *"whole world." "And he is the propitiation for our sins: and not for ours only, but also for the sins of the whole world"* (I John 2:2). The *"whole world"* is interpreted to mean every person who ever lived since Adam. Let us note how these universal terms are used in Scripture and what principles govern their use.

How can we interpret the correct sense that *"world"* has in any given passage, especially those relating to the death of Christ? The answer is simple—by following the normal rules that govern the use of such words in their context. In both Greek and English the same grammar principle applies: the sense of a word is governed by the context of its use. For example, one might correctly say that he had a cookout and that *everyone* came. Obviously, *everyone* does not mean every single person who ever lived. The context decides the meaning of *everyone*—in this case, friends, invited guests, and relatives.

Why is it, then, that passages concerning Christ's death are not given the same consideration when defining the scope of these supposed universal terms? Rather, they are interpreted by *what one believes they teach*: they are governed by one's theological predisposition. If one believes that Christ died for every person who ever lived, he reads *"world"* as meaning every person. Since present-day teaching on these references assumes that premise, limited atonement (that Christ died only for His own) is hard for many to accept. This need not be the case if one remembers that the context of the passage usually clarifies the extent of these terms.[222]

The argument of the unlimited atonement position makes use of the following logic:

> *Major premise:* The word *world* means every person who ever lived.
> *Minor premise:* Christ died for the *world.*
> *Conclusion:* Therefore, Christ died for every person who ever lived.

If it can be shown from Scripture that the word *world* (also *all,* and *every*) are used anywhere in Scripture to mean *anything* other than "everyone who ever lived," then the major premise of the above syllogism cannot be true and the conclusion is therefore false.

"World"

As we have listed above, the word *world (kosmos)* has various uses in Scripture. John uses the word more than any other New Testament writer. Being a Jew, John writes to Jews but emphasizes the universality of the gospel.[223] John teaches that the gospel is for both Jews and Gentiles—*"the whole world"* (John 11:50-52). For example, when John said that the Lamb of God took *"away the sin of the world"* (John 1:29), he meant that the sin-bearing Lamb of God was not exclusively for Israel. Christ came to bear away the sin of the whole world of believers. He was not arguing that Christ took away the sins of every person.

The word *world* is generally more narrowly limited to a *representative group* in Scripture. Note some examples:

In Luke 2:1 *("that all the world should be taxed")* the *world* means only the citizens of the Roman Empire. Obviously, nobody outside the governing arm of Rome would enroll himself for the purpose of paying Roman taxes. Neither could Caesar tax those who were already dead.

In Romans 1:8 *("that your faith is spoken of throughout the whole world"),* *"whole world"* means all the Christian world in the Roman Empire.

In Romans 11:12 *("if the fall of them* [Israel] *be the riches of the world"),* the *"world"* obviously means something other than fallen Israel (Gentiles, as the context shows).

In John 12:19 *"world"* *("behold, the world is gone after him")* means only many people in Judea, certainly not everybody in the whole world. It did not even include all the people in Judea, for it did not include the speaker and his audience.

There are many more examples in Scripture, but these should be sufficient to demonstrate that the logic requiring that *"world"* mean every person who ever lived is false. It cannot be used to prove that Christ's dying for the world means He died for every person who ever lived since Adam.

"All"

What we have just considered with *world* can also be demonstrated with the word *all. All* is sometimes used in Scripture to include everyone who ever lived (Romans 3:23; 5:12; *etc.*), but again, the context must decide. For example, in I Corinthians 10:23 Paul wrote that *"all things were lawful"* for him. Did he mean that he could lie, cheat, steal, commit adultery and murder? Of course not! He meant he could do all things which were not already unlawful or forbidden by

146

Scripture. So, *all*, like *world*, must obviously be interpreted in the context of its use to determine who or what it includes.

One interesting verse germane to our argument is John 6:45. In this verse our Lord is quoting the prophets (Isaiah 2:3; 54:13; Jeremiah 31:33, 34; Micah 4:2): *"It is written in the prophets, And they shall be all taught of God."* Then Christ explains: *"Every man therefore that hath heard, and hath learned of the Father, cometh unto me."* Here is clear proof that *all* in Scripture can be limited by interpretation. Jesus Himself limited the use of *all* in these Old Testament passages to include only those who had *"heard and learned of the Father."* Certainly Jesus made no mistake in His interpretation.

All is also often used in Scripture to mean "every sort of." Sometimes the translators of the Authorized Version (KJV) supplied the word *"manner"* to clarify this use, such as in Matthew 4:23, where it is said that Jesus healed *"all manner of disease among the people."* He did not heal every single diseased person but all sorts of diseases in order to show that He had power over every kind of disease.

An Exposition of *"All"*

First Timothy 2:4 and 6 are often used to prove Christ's death to be universal in its scope. Actually, there are three *"all's"* in the passage. In verse one, Paul exhorts that *"intercessions . . . be made for all men."* The particular object of the intercession is seen in verse two: *"for kings, and for all that are in authority."* The reason for intercession is that *"we may lead a quiet and peaceable life in all godliness and honesty."* Obviously, Paul is interested to establish Timothy in a ministry free of conflict with authorities.

The *"all men"* of verse one is best understood as "all sorts of men," particularly the sort of men who exercise authority over people. Although the word *manner* is not found in this verse, "all manner of," or "every sort of," is the best understanding of *all men* in this verse.

To encourage this intercessory prayer, Paul presents two arguments: one from the Father (vv. 3, 4), and one from the Son (vv. 5, 6). The first is that it is the Father's will (Gk. *thelema*, "His intention") that *"all* [sorts of] *men should be saved* [Jews, Gentiles; bond, free; male, female; rich, poor; young, old; kings, slaves; *etc.*] *and come to a* [full] *knowledge of the truth"* (I Timothy 2:4). Now, if it were God's intention that *all*, in the absolute sense, should be saved, then why is not every person saved? Why has not every person an opportunity to come to the truth? God's determinative will or intention cannot be frustrated (Isaiah 46:10, 11).

If it is God's will that every person have a full knowledge of the truth, why has not every person a knowledge of the truth? Why have multitudes lived and died without ever so much as hearing the name of Jesus, let alone hearing the gospel? God certainly has the power to make universal evangelism possible.

How can we say it is God's will that every person have a knowledge of the truth if God has purposely limited Himself to feeble human efforts to propagate that truth? He knows humans miserably fail in obeying the Great Commission. Will God jeopardize the opportunity of many to hear the gospel by trusting the task to unfaithful servants? I think not.[224]

Why did the Father "hide" the gospel from some people such as the *"wise and prudent"* (Matthew 11:25)? Why did Christ "hide" the truth in parables from the Pharisees by saying that it was *"not given to them"* to know the mysteries of the kingdom (Matthew 13:11; cf. John 12:37-40)? Why did He "hide" the gospel from some *"that are lost"* by permitting Satan to blind their eyes (II Corinthians 4:3, 4)? These facts show us that Paul cannot mean that God wants every person who ever lived to come to a knowledge of the truth. *"All"* must be interpreted as something else.

Paul's second argument to exhort us to pray for all sorts of men is that Christ's mediatorial work involves bringing all sorts of people to God (I Timothy 2:6). This work requires reconciling men by the payment of a ransom. Paul is here quoting Jesus (Matthew 20:28; Mark 10:45). Jesus, however, used the word *many,* not *all* (*"to give his life a ransom for many"*). Why would Paul substitute *all* for *many?* Would that not contradict Jesus? Does Paul mean that Christ's ransom is for everyone who ever lived? Again, in order to argue that position, one must prove that *all* in this context means everyone who ever lived. The context must decide. We do know from both experience and Scripture that Christ's work purchased all kinds of men to God (Revelation 5:9) but not every person who ever lived.

Therefore, the best interpretation of the three *all*'s in I Timothy 2:1-6 is *"people of all sorts"*: *"I exhort . . . that . . . prayers . . . be made for all* [sorts of] *men. . . . God . . . will have all* [sorts of] *men to be saved. . . . Christ Jesus . . . gave himself a ransom for all* [sorts of people].*"*

However, if *all* means "every one of," the question still remains, every one of whom? The answer is found in the verse itself: *"Who gave himself a ransom for all* [either "every one of," or "all sorts of" people] *to be testified* [to be attested to] *in due time"* (I Timothy 2:6). This verse, properly read, does not say that Christ died for every person in the world but only for those who will each be revealed through the gospel at the proper time.

SUMMARY

John 3:16 does not teach that God loves everyone nor that Christ died for everyone. Those ideas must be inferred. The *"world"* in John 3:16 is to be understood as representative universalism—the "whole world" of believers, both Jews and Gentiles, distributed over the whole earth in many generations. This makes the best sense for these three reasons:

First, there is no offer of the gospel or anything else in the verse. This verse states only that God loved the world in giving His Son for them in order that all who believe should not perish.

Second, redemptive love is a love of purpose that (in God's case) infallibly secures a result on the ones He loves. God gave His Son in order to secure the actual salvation of His loved ones, not to secure only the possibility of salvation.

Third, Jesus was sent by His Father to provide salvation from sin for more than just believing Jews. Even though salvation was of the Jews, it was not exclusively for the Jews, as John points out in his gospel. Therefore, John says, *"God loved the world"*—His elect (both Jew and Gentile) but not everyone in the human race.

There is a fundamental principle here: God's love secures the salvation of His own. *"Now . . . when Jesus knew that his hour was come . . . having loved his own which were in the world, he loved them unto the end"* (John 13:1). What does this mean? The premier Puritan theologian, Dr. John Owen explained it best:

> A man may love another as his own soul, yet perhaps that love of his cannot help him. He may thereby pity him in prison, but not relieve him; bemoan him in misery, but not help him; suffer with him in trouble, but not ease him. We cannot love grace into a child, nor mercy into a friend; we cannot love them into heaven, though it may be the great desire of our soul. . . . But now the love of Christ, being the love of God, is *effectual and fruitful* in producing all the good things which he willeth unto his beloved. He loves life, grace, and holiness into us; he loves us also into covenant, loves us into heaven.[225]

To God be the glory!

13

WHY BOTHER TO EVANGELIZE?

A question frequently asked is, If God has assured that all He has elected will indeed come to salvation, why do we need to evangelize? The answer may seem simplistic: *God commanded us to do so!* Paul understood this. He said,

> *For though I preach the gospel, I have nothing to glory of: for necessity is laid upon me; yea, woe is unto me, if I preach not the gospel! For if I do this thing willingly, I have a reward: but if against my will, a dispensation of the gospel is committed unto me* (I Corinthians 9:16, 17).

A *"dispensation* [Gk. *oikonomia*, 'a stewardship'] *of the gospel"* was committed to Paul. It was a privilege and a responsibility for which he understood an accountability. Oh, that all of God's people would realize this important truth—that we must *"preach the gospel"*! Regardless of our theology, our lack of diligence in this matter is our great shame.

> *And he said unto them, Go ye into all the world, and preach* [Gk. *kerusso*, "to proclaim a message from the King"] *the gospel* [Gk. *euaggelion*, 'good news,' from which we get our word *evangelism*] *to every creature* (Mark 16:15).

> *And that repentance and remission of sins should be preached in his name among all nations, beginning at Jerusalem. And ye are witnesses of these things* (Luke 24:47, 48).

> *And the gospel must first be published among all nations* (Mark 13:10).

> *Go ye therefore, and teach all nations, baptizing them in the name of the Father, and of the Son, and of the Holy Ghost* (Matthew 28:19).

All these verses and many more plainly command us to do the work of evangelism.

Does sovereign-grace doctrine kill evangelism? Critics of unconditional election continually labor the point that predestination is incompatible with evangelism. It is true that some do ignore the responsibility of evangelism (hyper-Calvinists), but the sovereign-grace doctrine does not encourage disobedience. This important distinction does not seem to occur to those who are bent on prejudicial and ill-informed examinations of TULIP. Samuel Fisk writes in his *Calvinistic Paths Retraced*:

> Yet there are those who declare that the stricter form of Calvinism enhances true evangelism. But why concern at all over "evangelism" if men are regenerated by a direct act of God and then in consequence of that take the step of receiving Christ as Savior? In such circumstances, any so-called evangelism would be something largely out of our hands, and a thing to look back at rather than something of importance for which to plan ahead.[226]

This reasoning is slanderous, for it suggests that in order to be consistent, a Calvinist must disobey what God plainly commands in Scripture. R. L. Sumner echoes this notion: "Why get excited about evangelism and soul winning if nothing you do or don't do effects [sic; *effect* means to actually accomplish] the final outcome?"[227] Both of these critics fail to understand that as God has determined the end, He has also determined the means. What the evangelist does or does not do does *affect* (have an effect on) but does not *effect* the final outcome. Only God can do that.

The problem here is a flawed definition of evangelism. J. I. Packer has written an excellent treatment of this subject in *Evangelism and the Sovereignty of God*: "It is our widespread and persistent habit of defining evangelism in terms, not of a message delivered, but of an effect produced in our hearers."[228] The Bible clearly demonstrates that evangelism is the delivering of a message from God. We are to deliver the message, but we are to trust God with the results. If the criterion for success in evangelism is the results we get, then Paul was in error when he stated, *"I have planted, Apollos watered; but God gave the increase"* (I Corinthians 3:6).

DOES GOD'S SOVEREIGNTY IN SALVATION MAKE EVANGELISM UNNECESSARY?

No, We Are Commanded to Preach the Gospel!

Critics of sovereign grace see the doctrine of God's sovereignty in salvation as denying that sinners must choose Christ for salvation.

They see Calvinism's God as coercing sinners against their will. Therefore, if the sinner has no choice, evangelism would be an unnecessary activity, rendering null and void both the reason for evangelism and the message of evangelism.

According to these critics, men like Andrew Fuller, William Carey, George Whitefield, and Charles Spurgeon could not really have been Calvinists because they believed strongly in the importance of evangelism and missions. The evangelistic and missionary fervor of these men proves nothing of the kind! On the contrary, it proves only that they took seriously God's command to preach the gospel to every creature! Evangelism is an important part of obedience and an important tenet of Calvinism! Charles Spurgeon has written:

> The grand object of the Christian ministry is the glory of God. Whether souls are converted or not, if Jesus Christ is faithfully preached, the minister has not labored in vain, for he is a sweet savour unto God as well in them that perish as in them that are saved.
>
> [But] our great object of glorifying God is, however, to be mainly achieved by the winning of souls. We must see souls born unto God. If we do not, our cry should be that of Rachael, "give me children, or I die." If we do not win souls, we should mourn as the husbandman who sees no harvest, as the fisherman who returns to his cottage with an empty net, or the huntsman who has in vain roamed over hill and dale. . . . The ambassadors of peace should not cease to weep bitterly until sinners weep for their sins.[229]

It should be clear from previous chapters of this book that Calvinists believe in man's moral agency and responsibility. God's sovereignty and human responsibility are not contradictory. The doctrines of grace are the gospel which must be preached to sinners. Spurgeon also wrote:

> And, do not believe, dear friends, that when you go into revival meetings, or special evangelistic services, you are to leave out the doctrines of the gospel; for you ought then to proclaim the doctrines of grace rather more than less. Teach gospel doctrines clearly, affectionately, simply, and plainly, and especially those truths which have a present and practical bearing upon men's

condition and God's grace. Some enthusiasts would seem to have imbibed the notion that, as soon as a minister addresses the unconverted, he should deliberately contradict his usual doctrinal discourses, because it is supposed that there will be no conversions if he preaches the whole counsel of God. . . . This is a strange theory, and yet many endorse it. According to them, we may preach the redemption of a chosen number to God's people, but universal redemption must be our doctrine when we speak with the outside world; we are to tell believers that salvation is all of grace, but sinners are to be spoken with as if they were to save themselves. . . . We have not so learned Christ.

. . . Men need to be told that, except divine grace shall bring them out of their enmity to God, they must eternally perish; and they must be reminded of the sovereignty of God, that He is not obliged to bring them out of this state, that He would be right and just if He left them in such a condition, that they have no merit to plead before Him, and no claims upon him, but that if they are to be saved, it must be by grace, and by grace alone.[230]

No Honest Christian Dares Take Credit.

Even non-Calvinists recognize God's sovereignty in salvation. This is demonstrated in at least two ways: First and foremost, all believers give full credit to God for their salvation. Dr. J. I. Packer writes:

As you look back, you take to yourself the blame for your past blindness and indifference and obstinacy and evasiveness in the face of the gospel message; but you do not pat yourself on the back for having been at length mastered by the insistent Christ. You would never dream of dividing the credit for your salvation between God and yourself.[231]

Second, Christians pray for the lost.

I think that what you do is to pray in categorical terms that God will, quite simply and decisively, save them: that He will open the eyes of their understanding, soften their hard hearts, renew their natures, and move their wills to receive the Saviour. . . . In prayer, then (and the Christian

153

is sanest and wisest when he prays), you know that it is God who saved men; you know that what makes men turn to God is God's own gracious work of drawing them to Himself; and the content of your prayers is determined by this knowledge. Thus, by your practice of intercession, no less than by giving thanks for your conversion, you acknowledge and confess the sovereignty of God's grace. And so do all Christian people everywhere.[232]

I read somewhere about a discussion between a Calvinist and an Arminian. The Arminian asked the Calvinist, "If God has already decided who will be saved, why do you pray for the lost?" The Calvinist responded, "If you think that God must not influence the sinner's will, why do *you* pray for the lost?"

IS SOUL WINNING THE BELIEVER'S MOST IMPORTANT RESPONSIBILITY?

No, Obedience Is the Believer's Primary Duty.

The doctrines of grace do not relieve the Christian of his obligation to obey all God's commands faithfully. Obedience, not soul winning, is the first duty of every Christian: *"Behold, to obey is better than sacrifice, and to hearken than the fat of rams"* (I Samuel 15:22). Sovereign-grace doctrines do, however, relieve the believer of the burden of "getting results." He is to leave the results with God.

Dr. Rice argues:

> The hyper-Calvinistic heresy is particularly appealing to the carnal nature, unwilling to have the heart-break, the burden for soul winning, unwilling to pay the price of separation and perhaps ostracism which goes with all-out soul winning, unwilling to pay the price for the fullness of the Spirit in continual self-crucifixion and waiting on God.[233]

It may be that some would have such a warped Calvinism as Rice asserts, but serious Christians are not willingly disobedient. To blame one's disobedience on his believing a sovereign-grace gospel is a serious error based on misinformation.

The vast majority of professing Christians believe that sinners are free to choose or reject Christ; yet, it is a sad truth that most of them have never once witnessed the gospel of Christ to a lost sinner. Most Christians have never led a soul to Christ. Some estimates state that the percentage of believers who have never done more than invite someone to church or pass out a tract is close to ninety percent! In addition, the number of consistent soul winners is pitifully small. So, if the critics of sovereign grace are correct in charging that predestination provides a good excuse for lazy Christians, why are there so few who embrace the doctrines of grace? Also, if these doctrines are to blame for the lack of soul-winning zeal among those who hold them, what is to blame for soul-winning coldness in the ranks of free-willers?

No, it is not Calvinism but carnality; it is not doctrine but disobedience; it is not predestination to salvation but predilection to laziness; it is not sovereignty but selfishness that explains why people do not witness for Christ. In the parable of the talents (Matthew 25:14-30), the wicked and slothful servant blamed his failure on the sovereignty of his master. His master, however, explained that his sovereignty should have *motivated* his servant's obedience.

The Dangers of an Unbiblical Philosophy of Evangelism

The free-will gospel advocates hold a dangerously unbiblical philosophy of evangelism in thinking they need to persuade everyone they can reach to be saved. Accordingly, free-will gospel responsibility is much more than proclaiming the message as clearly and faithfully as possible: it is converting as many sinners as possible. Possibly the most serious danger is the shadow that "soul winning" casts upon God's wisdom. He knows about how miserable is the obedience of the best of Christians. How, then, could God place the eternal destiny of souls in the hands of careless, inconsistent, and often willfully disobedient Christians? On the contrary, a belief in God's sovereignty in salvation is not only Scriptural but is also the most sensible approach to the subject of evangelism.

One may observe several other dangers of this unbiblical philosophy that believes soul winning is the Christian's most important duty and that equates numbers with success.

1. This Unbiblical Philosophy of Evangelism Has Led to Covering Up Sin in the Lives of "Successful" Soul Winners.

The current evangelical philosophy of soul winning that rejects God's sovereignty in salvation often gives the false assumption that the soul winner is a spiritual person simply because he has results in soul winning. This assumption can lead one to justify unspiritual behavior. Some have gone so far as to set up an unscriptural "merit" system by which they teach that God tolerates worldliness in the soul winner's life in proportion to the number of souls he has won![234]

155

2. This Unbiblical Philosophy of Evangelism Tends to Introduce Humanistic Methods into the Work of Soul Winning.

A competitive spirit among conservative evangelicals causes soul winners to strive among themselves to see who is the most successful. This pressure of competition to produce results can tempt the soul winner to "fudge" or even outright lie in the reporting of souls (box-scoring).

It can also lead to the use of dubious sales techniques to "get decisions." For example, some years ago my wife attended a workshop in which she was instructed in gimmicks to get people to make decisions. She was taught to lead the prospect by nodding her head as she asked questions. This little trick would improve her chances of getting a "yes" to the critical question—"Will you receive Jesus now?" Faithful and diligent use of this procedure would augment her "tally of souls." She might even qualify for the silver pin and top honors in her local soul-winning club! This is no exaggeration. Where is the Holy Spirit in this "how-to-get-converts-in-thirty-seconds-guaranteed-or-your-money-back" approach? It is this foolishness that grieves the Holy Spirit. How it degrades the gospel and cheapens the work of the blessed Savior.

3. This Unbiblical Philosophy of Evangelism Encourages Carnal Motives for "Getting Saved."

The philosophy of evangelism we are critiquing also relies on appealing to the carnal interests of the unregenerate in order to accomplish a spiritual work. The gospel is reduced to an offer of "fire insurance" or "heavenly real estate." The gospel is offered as a quick fix for the problems the sinner is facing. Jesus is seen as a heavenly "happiness" promoter. Salvation is preached as if the sinner were doing God a favor by getting saved.

Biblically viewed, the gospel is the "good news" that the offended God has provided forgiveness of sins and reconciliation. This gospel requires humility and repentance on the part of the sinner, not face saving. Rather than appealing to base selfishness and greed, God changes the sinner's nature first. This change allows the sinner to receive the gospel with the proper motive of love and gratitude for the Savior.

4. This Unbiblical Philosophy of Evangelism Promotes Unhealthy Pressure to Get Results.

Some preachers will do almost anything to get people motivated to win the lost. There are churches that not only require the paid staff to go soul winning every week but also require them to get decisions down the aisle and into the baptistry every Sunday. This "produce-or-else" approach to ministry is certainly consistent with the suspect philosophy that God is depending on Christians to get as many people into heaven as possible. If there might be people who could have gone to heaven but will not because some disobedient Christian was not doing his job, there ought to be pressure put on Christians. Every member, not just the paid staff, should thereby be required to get results!

But is pressure for results God's means of encouraging faithful service? What about those faithful servants who preach the gospel in difficult places? Sadly, there have been good missionaries who lost support because they could not show results. Good men have been written off as failures because they could not keep up with the numbers game. They have been cast aside as "nobodies" because they cannot boast of larger-than-Day-of-Pentecost results. Some good men have even left the ministry over this pressure because they did not feel "cut out" to be gospel "salesmen."

5. This Unbiblical Philosophy of Evangelism Leads to Compromise and Inclusivism.

Another error in the pressure-to-get-results approach is Jesuit casuistry—the end justifies the means. Getting larger crowds in order to evangelize allows for all kinds of worldly entertainment and compromises with liberalism in the name of evangelism. Church services turn into circuses, nightclubs, and rock concerts. The *"foolishness of preaching"* (I Corinthians 1:21) is dumped in favor of the latest Hollywood spectacular. All this justifies the means to reach more people where they are. "But we are getting results!" many argue. What about obedience? Is it not the Holy Spirit using the Word of God that gets results? "Ah, but we can get a lot *more* results in the score box by using 'Willy World and the Philistine Phive' in concert, singing all their latest hits!" Just as carnal prayer can be an abomination to God (Proverbs 28:9), so also can "evangelism" attempted in the flesh without the power and leading of the Holy Spirit be an abomination to God (Titus 1:16).

6. This Unbiblical Philosophy of Evangelism Fills the Churches with Spurious Converts.

Anyone who has led folks to Christ knows that some of them never go on for the Lord. They have no further interest in baptism or becoming faithful members of the body. Getting decisions does not mean getting converts. Powerful evangelists who get quantifiable results that sustain their campaigns psychologically and financially do not always get spiritual, lasting fruit.

I have heard the speculations of several Christian leaders about the number of unconverted people who are members of Bible-believing, fundamental churches. These estimates range from fifty to eighty percent or more. It is no wonder that pastors become frustrated with Sunday-morning Christians who are never moved to be anything else. I have long since ceased to be shocked by the revelations of the depths of sin in which many seemingly faithful Christians are living. Isn't it right to question the salvation of these people? Jesus said, *"By their fruits ye shall know them"* (Matthew 7:20).

How did all these false believers get into the church? Could these false conversions be the result of a cheap gospel that sells people on how much God grieves over them because He needs them to fulfill something lacking in Himself? Could it be that these false conversions are the result of a self-focusing gospel that has a genie-god who just waits to do wonderful things for the sinner who will rub the lamp? Could it be a false gospel with its focus on the sinner's problems and how God can work a little miracle to fix them? "Surely you want salvation, don't you? It is free; it will cost you nothing. You have nothing to give up and everything to gain. Just nod your head and take my hand. I'll even pray for you because I know you mean it. It is just that easy. There, now, doesn't that *feel* better?" That certainly is not the biblical gospel.

HOW FAR DOES THE CHRISTIAN'S RESPONSIBILITY EXTEND IN EVANGELISM?

Responsibility in evangelism is much more than winning souls. The great commission of Matthew 28 calls us to *"teach* [make disciples of] *all nations."* The "discipling" involves baptizing (for submission and obedience) and teaching (for knowledge and growth in spiritual stature) converts to observe *all* the words of Christ. The Word of God sets forth the whole process of evangelism as far more than "four things God wants you to know." Evangelism is also the cooperative labor of the whole church, not the competitive enterprise of rival Christians: *"So then neither is he that planteth any thing, neither he that watereth; but God that giveth the increase"* (1 Corinthians 3:7). Each believer is to use the gifts and callings of God under the direction and power of the Holy Spirit as Paul tells us in Roman 12:

> *For I say, through the grace given unto me, to every man that is among you, not to think of himself more highly than he ought to think; but to think soberly, according as God hath dealt to every man the measure of faith. For as we have many members in one body, and*

*all members have not the same office: So we, being
many, are one body in Christ, and every one members
one of another. Having then gifts differing according to
the grace that is given to us . . . let us . . . be . . . serving
the Lord.* (Romans 12:3-11).

In my life, it was an understanding of the so-called "Calvinistic
heresy," not soul-winning pressure, that motivated obedience and dedi-
cation to Christ. Do not misunderstand me. Evangelism is *essential* to
obedience, but the Lord requires obedience to *all His commands,* not
just soul winning!

Preaching the Gospel of Love?

I was once asked how I could believe the doctrines of grace and
honestly tell people that God loved them and Christ died for them. I
replied, "I don't." Nowhere in God's Word are we ever told that God
loves everybody. In fact, we are clearly told that mankind is under the
wrath of God (John 3:36). Neither by precept nor example does the
Bible teach us to present the gospel in terms of God's loving the sinner.
Indeed, there is far too much "good news" presented in terms of how
God loves and longs to save people but precious little "bad news" presented first, showing the sinner his need for the gospel. As Arthur Pink
says, presenting Christ to those who do not see their need of a Savior is
like casting pearls before swine.[235]

There are two things that must be taken into consideration concerning any declaration of God's love. (1) How is love defined? Divine
redemptive love is set forth in the Greek word *agape. Agape* is a love
of benevolence—that which secures a benefit to the one loved. It is the
bestowing of good upon the loved one as in John 3:16. The word *"so"*
limits God's redemptive love to the *demonstration,* the giving of God's
Son, and to the *end,* the resulting salvation of believers.

There are various kinds of love. The kind of love that the Bible
declares as redemptive love (Deuteronomy 7:6-8) is a discriminating
choice. This redemptive *agape* love must never be confused with
God's love of compassion for His creation (His patience and goodness
toward all His creatures as seen in His providential government). The
Creator's compassion for His creation, even fallen sinners, manifests
itself in the fact that He is willing for the rain to fall on hardened
rebels and saints alike. He restrains evil. He tolerates sin and sinners,
postponing the judgment and punishment that sinners deserve. He
freely showers His material blessings on mankind. The Creator is
good and generously sheds that goodness upon all His creation. But this

compassion is not the benevolent unconditional redemptive love that the Father gives to His own children.

(2) Does God love everybody? There are several Scripture references that state that God does not love everybody: *"That the world may know that thou . . . hast loved them* [His own, for whom He was praying; thus implying that God did not love the world], *as thou hast loved me"* (John 17:23; cf. v. 9). *"But I know you, that ye have not the love of God in you"* (John 5:42). The only people who can claim that God loves them are believers, for they are the only ones who are the recipients of His ultimate good (Romans 5:8). *"He that hath my commandments, and keepeth them, he it is that loveth me: and he that loveth me shall be loved of my Father . . . If a man love me, he will keep my words: and my Father will love him"* (John 14:21, 23). Pink comments: "Why say, 'he that loveth Me shall be loved of My Father' if the Father loves *everybody? . . .* If He loves all men without exception, then the distinction and limitation here mentioned is quite meaningless."[236] The reader is encouraged to do his own study of the Greek word *agape* in a good concordance to see that the recipients of *agape* are God's own—His elect—not the world in general.

It is interesting to note that not once in the book of Acts is the love of God used in declaring the gospel or in appealing to sinners. Now, it is not good to build a doctrine from the book of Acts alone, but a study of the book is very valuable to see how the apostles first preached the gospel. Surely, if God's love were a great motivating factor to get sinners saved, we should find it used in the early declarations of Christ's message of salvation. We do not. We must never go beyond Scripture to say or promise anything to sinners more than God has declared in His Word. How, then, should we preach the gospel?

Preaching the Gospel of Grace

1. To Whom Should We Preach It?

We need to determine who should be the recipients of the gospel message. God gives us clear direction for this in His Word—to preach the gospel to every creature. In doing this, we are authorized to command and invite *all* people to repent and believe the gospel. It is not for us to concern ourselves about who is elect and who is not. That is God's business. We are responsible to proclaim the message of salvation and offer the promise that all who will believe may receive it: *"For whosoever shall call upon the name of the Lord shall be saved"* (Romans 10:13). *"Him that cometh to me I will in no wise cast out"* (John 6:37).

2. What Must Be Said to the Sinner?

It is not proper to encourage a person to receive salvation who sees no need for it. The term *"salvation"* reveals the idea of hope for rescue and deliverance, but what deliverance is there to one who knows no peril? Salvation means nothing to the wretch who is oblivious to his danger. What gives hope to a complacent soul?

Information about the certain judgment of the holy and just God is what a person requires, not the assurance of the love of God. A candidate for salvation is one who should be convicted of his sin and guilt, not comforted with warm feelings of God's good will. The fear of God must possess the one who understands how resolved God is to punish his sins and to avenge Himself of His injured dignity. Only when the sinner is awakened to the enormity of his fault, only when he is seized with the liability of his error, only when he is terrified with God's wrath against him, should the hope of Christ the Savior be preached to him. To such a soul is the gospel truly "good news."

People should never be referred to as "poor" victims, suggesting that, through no fault of their own, they have a problem from which they cannot extract themselves without a little help from an eager and willing God. Neither must the gospel be preached in terms of helping the despondent out of his problems and crises. Sin and guilt are the issue, not marriage problems, addictions, financial woes, wayward children, or such like. True, sin is always at the root of our problems, but salvation is not from problems. Salvation is from wrath and judgment (I Thessalonians 1:10). Sinners will by these means be brought face to face with the fact that they have offended a holy God. This offended God has sworn that sinners shall be punished in hell forever (Matthew 10:28).

When presenting the gospel, the exact content of the gospel message taken from Scripture is all that we are authorized to declare. But in declaring the gospel, the whole gospel must presented.

First, salvation cannot be obtained by sinners themselves, neither by will nor by works (Titus 3:5; John 1:12, 13). Salvation is a gift of God's will and mercy alone.

Second, salvation is through the intervention of a Savior, Christ the Lord, the only Savior of those who believe (Acts 4:12).

Third, the Saviorhood of Christ rests on the propitiation (I John 2:2) of His substitutionary death, burial, and resurrection, the fact of which must be personally believed by the sinner (I Corinthians 15:1-4). In other words, the wrath of God is appeased by the cross work of Christ, not by a sinner's act of believing.

161

Fourth, the sinner must repent of his sin and iniquity (Acts 20:21), an act that necessitates God's enablement (II Timothy 2:25, 26).

Fifth, the gospel directs the sinner to receive Christ (John 1:12), resting upon gospel facts by faith, trusting the promise of God that by Christ he will be saved (Ephesians 2:8, 9).

It takes more than a quick word and an emotional appeal to communicate the gospel to this Bible-ignorant age. Real, God-ordained, Spirit-motivated evangelism requires a knowledge of the facts of the gospel as declared in Scripture. Understanding these facts is essential to faith. To obey God in evangelism means that we must pattern our preaching and teaching on the example of the New Testament apostles. Paul referred to himself as a *"teacher of the Gentiles in faith and verity* [truth]" (I Timothy 2:7). As noted earlier in this chapter, Charles Spurgeon emphatically urged that in preaching the gospel, we must clearly emphasize the doctrines of grace.

Evangelism is the means God has chosen to bring His elect to salvation. The Bible clearly sets forth not only the message but also the method by which that message is to be presented. The results are to be left to God. Therefore, modern evangelicals must stop using humanistic means to force decisions that not only give false hope to sinners but also fill the churches with professors of Christ who have no spiritual life necessary to the life of the church. We must throw out the sentimental nonsense that passes for the gospel and attributes to God things He never said. Let us practice instead the kind of evangelism spoken of by Paul in I Thessalonians:

> *"Knowing, brethren beloved, your election of God.*
> *For our gospel came not unto you in word only, but also*
> *in power, and in the Holy Ghost, and in much assur-*
> *ance"* (I Thessalonians 1:4, 5, 9).

CONCLUSION

What passes for gospel in this age of evangelical confusion is, in my view, far removed from the true gospel of Christ, Paul, and the reformers. The "old" gospel focuses upon God. It produces believers who humbly bow in contrite submission with gratitude and joy that God has chosen to extend undeserved mercy to sinners. It recognizes that God has the sovereign prerogative to save or not to save whomever He wills. It does not see sinners as the helpless victims of sin who are deserving of God's rescue attempt. It does not view sin as merely hurtful to humans but as an offense to God. It views sinners as both unable and unwilling to repent, as the enemies of God and truth. It views the death of Christ as the actual means of saving sinners by redemption, not merely the providing of an opportunity for sinners either to believe or not believe in Christ.

The more I understand of God's great plan of redemption, the more I am disturbed with the trend of modern evangelicalism. There seems to be a focus upon "what God is supposed to be doing for me" rather than on the biblical admonition to *"know the Lord"* (Hebrews 8:11; see also John 17:3; I Chronicles 28:9; Jeremiah 24:7). To worship a god other than the true and living God, who has revealed Himself in the Word of God for us to know, is to worship the figment of one's imagination. The notion that God is an infinite teddy bear, more interested in our personal comfort and happiness than in holiness and obedience to truth, is false and idolatrous. It is no wonder that Christianity has lost its power and influence in this wicked age.

Without a doubt, the center of the contention between the old and new gospels is the place of human "free will." It is always intriguing that whenever one insists that it is God who must save us, the rejoinder is always, "But we have a choice!" Calvinism never denies that there is a choice. What Calvinism insists on is, were it not for God's work of grace in the heart, a person's choice would *always* be to reject Christ. Man cannot and will not come to salvation without divine mercy!

Perhaps God will be pleased to use this book to help seeking Christians understand God's sovereign purposes relating to salvation. It is my hope that if this study has not changed the mind of the non-Calvinistic reader, it will at least provoke him to serious study of God's Word, a worthy endeavor in and of itself and encouraged by Scripture.

Also, it is my prayer that this book will present a correct understanding of Calvinism in contrast to the popular erroneous concepts pawned off as Calvinism.

I close this book by quoting Charles Haddon Spurgeon. I do not think that the editors of the periodical in which this quotation appeared understood that Spurgeon was referring to the doctrines of Calvinism. Nevertheless, Spurgeon's words are certainly appropriate for the Calvinistic preacher of today.

> When I came to London as a young minister, I knew very well that the doctrines which I preached were by no means popular, but I for that reason brought them out with all the more emphasis.
>
> What a storm was raised! I was reading the other day a tirade of abuse which was poured upon me about twenty years ago. I must have been a horridly bad fellow according to that description. But I was pleased to observe that it was not I that was bad, but the doctrines which I preached.
>
> I teach the same truths now, and after having preached them these four and twenty years or so, what can I say of the results? Why, that no man loses anything by bringing the truth right straight out.
>
> I wish to bear this witness, not about myself, but about the truth which I have preached: Nothing has succeeded better than preaching out boldly what I have believed, and standing to it in defiance of all opposition, and never caring a snap of the fingers whether it offended or whether it pleased.[237]

APPENDIX

WAS DR. JOHN R. RICE ARMINIAN IN HIS DOCTRINE?

What position did Dr. John R. Rice take on the way of salvation? In *Predestined for Hell? No!* Rice cites Loraine Boettner's *The Reformed Doctrine of Predestination* as teaching that there are only three systems that claim to set forth a way of salvation through Christ: (1) Universalism—that all people will be saved; (2) Arminianism—that Christ died equally for every child of Adam so that anyone may be saved on condition of their receiving Christ (though not necessarily permanently); (3) Calvinism, "as taught by Calvin himself and by the Westminster Catechism involving Calvin's doctrine of predestination."[238]

Of the three, Rice argued that "the great evangelists and soul winners have usually been men who were *not* Arminian, because they believed in salvation by grace, without works. Moody, Torrey, Chapman, Truett, Billy Sunday, Bob Jones, Billy Graham, for example; *none of them have been Arminian.*"[239] Rice's objection to Arminianism hangs on what he considers two objectionable teachings of the doctrine: (1) salvation by works—"They know that the Bible clearly teaches salvation by grace and not of works"; (2) salvation on probation—"They do not believe that a saved person . . . may lose his salvation at any moment."[240] Along with the "the great evangelists and soul winners," it is safe to say that Dr. Rice did not consider himself to be Arminian.

However, discounting Universalism, Rice indignantly scoffed at Boettner's view: "Do you really believe that the only two systems of doctrine . . . are Arminianism and hyper-Calvinism?"[241] Again, "Calvinism especially appeals to those who think that hyper-Calvinism is the only answer to Arminianism."[242] This leads us to ask what position on the way of salvation did John R. Rice take? If neither Universalism, Calvinism, nor Arminianism is the correct position, is there another legitimate position?

Yet, in spite of his scoffing, Rice admitted, first, "The Arminian position does such violence to the grace of God, many would rather be Calvinists."[243] That statement certainly suggests that Rice thought Calvinism to be the only alternative to Arminianism. Second, as evidenced by his terminology, he implied that he was temperately

Calvinistic: "So says extreme Calvinism,"[244] suggesting that his Calvinism was of a moderate variety. He also consistently referred to true "five-point" Calvinism as "hyper-Calvinism" and "Calvinism gone to extremes." Third, he embraced the doctrine of the perseverance of the saints. On one hand, he called this doctrine "a great and blessed truth," but on the other, criticized its "terminology that is questionable."[245] So, then, what position on the way of salvation did Rice hold?

It has always amused me that conservative and evangelical preachers speak of their doctrinal position relative to the number of points of Calvinism that they hold. However, ask them exactly what they mean by each point and one quickly discovers that they are not Calvinists at all. Why do they not refer to themselves as, say, "four-point Arminians"? Dr. Rice did not admit to holding even one point of Calvinism without modification. Is there such a thing as a "half-point Calvinist"? Would a man who had *no* kind words for true Calvinism not rather wish to be known as an Arminian? If an animal looks like a duck, quacks like a duck, and swims like a duck, should we not conclude that it is a duck? One need only compare the statements of Dr. Rice with those of Arminianism to demonstrate that Dr. Rice was, in fact, a four-point Arminian.

The following points compare the statements of Jacobus Arminius and the Arminian remonstrants at the Synod of Dort with those of Dr. Rice. The Calvinistic view is represented by Scripture. The quotes from the Arminians are all taken from Dr. John Owen's "A Display of Arminianism," *The Works of John Owen*, volume 10. Let the reader compare the columns and judge for himself.

1.   Did Adam's sin result in condemnation for the whole race?

Calvinism says, "Yes."
   "*Wherefore, as by one man sin entered into the world, and death by sin; and so death passed upon all men, for that all have sinned*" (Romans 5:12).
   "*By one man's offence death reigned*" (Romans 5:17).
   "*Therefore as by the offence of one judgment came upon all men to condemnation*" (Romans 5:18).
   "*In Adam, all die*" (I Corinthians 15:22).
Arminianism says, "No."
   "Original sin is neither a sin properly so called which should make the posterity of Adam guilty of God's wrath, nor yet a

166

punishment of any sin on them. God neither doth nor can in justice appoint any to hell for original sin."

"It is absurd that by one man's disobedience many should be made actually disobedient."

"Infants are simply in that estate in which Adam was before the fall."

John R. Rice says, "No."

"No one ever went to hell because of Adam's sin."[246]

"It was inherent in the kind of being that God created; man must be allowed to choose. But knowing *that some men sometimes would choose wrongly*, God planned . . . to offer an atonement for the salvation of sinning men!"[247]

"Death and salvation are *potential*, for the race of sinners was not yet born when Adam sinned, but his sin *potentially* made all sinners."[248]

2. Can human "free" will frustrate the sovereign will of God?

Calvinism says, "No."

"Declaring the end from the beginning, . . . saying, My counsel shall stand, and I will do all my pleasure: . . . I have spoken it, I will also bring it to pass; I have purposed it, I will also do it" (Isaiah 46:10, 11).

"And all the inhabitants of the earth are reputed as nothing: and he doeth according to his will in the army of heaven, and among the inhabitants of the earth: and none can stay his hand, or say unto him, What doest thou?" (Daniel 4:35).

"So shall my word be . . . it shall not return unto me void, but it shall accomplish that which I please, and it shall prosper in the thing whereto I sent it" (Isaiah 55:11).

Arminianism says, "Yes."

"It is in the power of man to hinder the execution of God's will."

"We doubt nothing but many things which God willeth, or that pleaseth him to have done, do yet never come to pass."

"It may be objected that God faileth of his end: this we readily grant."

"Those things God would have us freely do ourselves; he can no more effectually work or will than by the way of wishing."

"The will of man ought to be free from all kind of internal and external necessity in its actions."

John R. Rice says, "Yes."

"Men do resist the will of God."[249]

"The Bible says many wonderful things about God, but it never says that God is an absolute, unlimited sovereign."[250]

. . . the "man-made doctrine of 'absolute sovereignty of God.'"[251]

"God is love, and love limits absolute sovereignty."[252]

"It is a matter of the will to disregard God's commands. Men do have a choice and exercise their choice. God may decide some matters for men but never moral matters. . . . God grieves when men turn away."[253]

3. Are faith and repentance God's gift to the elect?

Calvinism says, "Yes."

"For by grace are ye saved through faith; and that not of yourselves: it is the gift of God: Not of works, lest any man should boast" (Ephesians 2:8, 9).

"For who maketh thee to differ from another? and what hast thou that thou didst not receive? now if thou didst receive it, why dost thou glory, as if thou hadst not received it?" (I Corinthians 4:7).

"The faith of the operation of God" (Colossians 2:12).

"For unto you it is given in the behalf of Christ . . . to believe on him" (Philippians 1:29).

"If God peradventure will give them repentance" (II Timothy 2:25).

Arminianism says, "No."

"That God should require that of us which himself will work in us is a ridiculous action."

"There is nothing truer than that one man maketh himself to differ from another. He who believeth when God commandeth, maketh himself differ from him who will not."

"I may boast of mine own, when I obey God's grace, which it was in my power not to obey, as well as to obey."

"God would have all men to be saved, but compelled with the stubborn malice of some, he changeth his purpose, and will have them to perish."

John R. Rice says, "No."

"But in the sense of being accountable . . . men are not dead. Their minds, their consciences, their powers of choice are not dead. They are dead in trespasses and sins, and so do not have everlasting life in a spiritual sense, but they can choose."[254]

168

"Can a spiritually dead man repent? Yes, if God tells him to! [The assumption is that God does not need to give the sinner power to repent and believe]."[255]

"He made a man who could turn to God, and serve, and follow and trust Him, or who could hatefully, wickedly reject Christ and God."[256]

4. Is election conditioned on foreseen repentance and faith in the sinner?

Calvinism says, "No."

"He hath chosen us in him before the foundation of the world . . . Having predestinated us . . . according to the good pleasure of his will" (Ephesians 1:4, 5).

"God hath from the beginning chosen you to salvation" (II Thessalonians 2:13).

"The faith of God's elect" (Titus 1:1).

"Who hath saved us, and called us . . . not according to our works, but according to his own purpose and grace . . . given us in Christ before the world began" (II Timothy 1:9).

"That the purpose of God according to election might stand, not of works, but of him that calleth" (Romans 9:11).

Arminianism says, "Yes."

"God hath determined to grant the means of salvation unto all without difference; and according as He foresees men will use those means, so he determineth [elected] them."

"The sole and only cause of election is not the will of God, but the respect of our obedience."

"You say that election is the rule of giving or not giving faith; and, therefore, election is not of the faithful, but faith of the elect: but by your leave this I must deny."

"We profess roundly that faith is considered by God as a condition preceeding election, and not following as a fruit thereof."

John R. Rice says, "Yes."

"No, election is not 'unconditional.' God knows who will trust Him when they hear the gospel and chooses them to be carried through till they be 'conformed to the image of his Son.'"[257]

"Election is based on God's foreknowledge of who will trust Christ. So salvation depends upon personal faith in Christ."[258]

"The only people that God predestinates to be saved are those whom . . . God knows will . . . come to trust in Christ to be

169

saved. It is not that predestination causes people be saved. No, they are only predestinated to be saved because God knows that they will put their trust in Christ."[259]

5. Does Christ's death on the cross actually redeem anyone?

Calvinism says, "Yes."

"And you . . . hath he reconciled in the body of his flesh through death" (Colossians 1:21, 22).

"By his own blood he entered in once into the holy place, having obtained eternal redemption for us" (Hebrews 9:12).

"Thou shalt call his name JESUS: for he shall save his people from their sins" (Matthew 1:21).

"Thou wast slain, and hast redeemed us to God by thy blood" (Revelation 5:9).

"Take heed therefore unto yourselves, and to all the flock, over the which the Holy Ghost hath made you overseers, to feed the church of God, which he hath purchased with his own blood" (Acts 20:28).

Arminianism says, "No."

"The immediate and proper effect or end of the death and passion of Christ is, not an actual ablation [removal] of sin from men, not an actual remission of iniquities, justification, and redemption of any soul."

"A potential and conditionate reconciliation, not actual and absolute," is obtained by the death of Christ."

"The death and satisfaction of Christ being accomplished, it might come to pass that, none fulfilling the condition of the new covenant, none should be saved."

"Only it was a means of obtaining such a possibility of salvation."

"Why then, the efficacy of the death of Christ depends wholly upon us."

John R. Rice says, "No."

"Every poor sinner is bought by the blood of Jesus."[260]

"So all that are ever born are *potentially* made alive in Christ. . . . He is the Saviour of the world, and *potentially* the Saviour of all, *depending on their faith in Him*."[261]

"God has plainly told us that Christ atoned for the sins of the whole world, that God's tender heart longs to see all saved, that light and invitation and conviction does come to every sinner, and that the blessed invitation is given to every son and daughter of Adam to repent and trust Christ for salvation!"[262]

6. Does salvation infallibly secure persevering saints into the everlasting kingdom?

Calvinism says, "Yes."

"I give unto them eternal life; and they shall never perish, neither shall any man pluck them out of my hand. My Father, which gave them me, is greater than all; and no man is able to pluck them out of my Father's hand" (John 10:28, 29).

"Thou hast given him power over all flesh, that he should give eternal life to as many as thou hast given him. . . . [N]one of them is lost" (John 17:2, 12).

The Arminians say, "No."

"No such will can be ascribed unto God, whereby he so would have any to be saved, that from thence his salvation should be sure and infallible," said Jacobus Arminius.

Dr. Rice says, "Yes" with reservation.

"In this, all Bible believers agree if we simply mean that those who are saved have everlasting life."[263] [In other words, just as God would have all sinners to be saved but cannot effectually obtain that desire, so God would have every saint live in obedience to His will. He does, however, secure all professing believers, even though they might refuse to obey and serve Him. Dr. Rice and many other evangelicals take a strong stand on this point, but it is not the logical conclusion of the other four points. If salvation requires that man respond in faith of his own initiation, then it would be consistent that the man ought to have the right to change his mind. Arminians have already figured that out. What if a man decides it is too much trouble to be a Christian? Must he be forced to see salvation through to heaven? Would it not be cruel to force a man to go to heaven who would be miserable going there?]

Now, if it looks like an Arminian and talks like an Arminian, even though it denies being an Arminian, are we not safe to say it is an Arminian—perhaps an Arminian in denial?

There is very much more that could be said about Dr. Rice's efforts at "correcting the errors of hyper-Calvinism."[264] He consistently misrepresented the doctrine. He failed to demonstrate historical accuracy on the controversy. He never once exegeted the Scriptures to prove the points he wanted them to "plainly" teach. He ignored the multitude of texts which opposed his opinions of God and the gospel. He did very little to explain the myriad texts which "clearly" support Calvinism. He also managed to contradict himself occasionally, such as when he pontifically declared: "The Bible has no doctrine of 'reprobation,' and the Bible does not use that word, or any word like it."[265] Then two paragraphs later he writes: "God may turn him over to a *reprobate* mind."[266] The bottom line in Dr. Rice's war on Calvinism, in my opinion, is found in this revealing statement:

> *How could I feel toward God, if I should find out that* when He said, "whosoever will" He did not mean that, because He had made men so that many of them could not repent if they would? *How would I feel toward the Saviour if I found that,* though He professed to die for the sins of the whole world, He had already consigned some people to Hell with no chance to repent, no matter how much they wished to do so?[267]

This quote reveals John Rice's heart in the matter. Since when do human feelings, rather than the Word of God, determine what is truth? Rice expressed concern over how *he* would feel about a God who could do as He pleased. Ignoring his misrepresentation of the "blessed" doctrines of sovereign grace, let us suppose that God is as Dr. Rice described Him above. Who is Dr. Rice to question God? God is God. This is exactly the objection which Paul faced in Romans 9: *"Nay, but, [Dr. Rice], who art thou that thou repliest against God? Shall the thing formed say to him that formed it, Why hast thou made me thus?"* (Romans 9:20).

However, Rice was no different from the multitude of conservative and evangelical Christians who would rather create their own idea of a god who gushes with loving concern for reprobate, rebellious, wicked, God-hating sinners who can hush up the Holy Spirit, affront the Lord Jesus, and frustrate God's marvelous saving grace. They would rather have a weak and anemic savior who can be hawked and bartered to the lowest bidder. They would rather have a holy spirit begging sinners to love a savior whom they would just as soon ignore. Like all sinful humans, Dr. Rice simply did not want a God whose sovereign will disturbed Rice's sensibilities of fairness and justice. He did not want a God who could say, *"I will have mercy on whom I will have mercy"* (Romans 9:15).

GLOSSARY

Note: Many terms in this glossary have more than one application. The following uses here are limited to the Calvinistic/Arminian controversy. While English, Greek, and Bible dictionaries were consulted for accuracy of these definitions, exhaustive and complete treatments of these terms will not be found here. My purpose is mainly to define my use of these terms in this book.

Amyraldianism

The doctrine of universal grace developed by Moise Amyraut, Amyraldus, or Amyrault, of France in the seventeenth century. A theory of salvation that teaches there are two conflicting decrees: a general decree by which God wills the salvation of all men, and a specific decree by which God wills the salvation of the elect. On one hand, Amyraldianism alleges a rejection of Arminianism by insisting on a sovereign election of God, while, on the other hand, it charms Arminianism by holding forth an Arminian gospel appeal.

anti-creedal

A resistance to the use of creeds or confessions to define what one believes. Anti-creedalism is usually a reaction to those who, wittingly or unwittingly, rely on the authority of creeds at the expense of Scripture. Baptists have tended to be anti-creedal, asserting "no creed but the Bible."

antinomian

Against law. An antinomian believes that a Christian is not obligated to keep God's law.

antinomies

Seemingly contradictory facts. There can be no actual contradictions in Scripture. Those passages that seem to be in contradiction are called antinomies because they are misunderstood, not because they are contradictory.

antisectarian, -ism

The reluctance to stand firmly on any doctrine that is likely to cause a division or separation within a religious body. Various denominations are formed over the unique interpretation of some doctrinal issues. Those who value unity above all differences are usually antisectarian.

Arians

A sect believing that Jesus Christ was a created being, not God come in the flesh. They believed that God uniquely indwelled Christ at His baptism so that He became a special and unique instrument of God's purpose. The controversy surrounding this belief was settled at the Council of Nicea in favor of Athanasius's accurate interpretation of the Scripture regarding Christ's deity and humanity.

Arminianism

An unbiblical humanistic doctrine established by Jacob Hermann, who lived from 1560 to 1609, known best by the Latin form of his last name, Arminius. It is a system of the doctrine of salvation rejecting God's sovereign involvement in a person's salvation. Its five basic tenets are (1) Partial ability—Sinners can choose Christ for salvation; (2) All foreseen faith elected—Election is dependent on the sinner's being persuaded to take the gospel offer; (3) Non-discriminatory atonement—Christ's death was an atonement for the sins of every person who has lived in the world since Adam; (4) Saving grace resisted—Since grace requires the sinner's response, it can be rejected; and (5) You can lose it—Since God's saving work is contingent upon the response of the sinner, salvation is conditional upon a sinner's decision to keep saved.

atonement (see *limited atonement* and *unlimited atonement*)

The making of amends or setting things right. Sin has incurred God's wrath against mankind. Atonement is the payment of a satisfaction to the justice of God. The cross work of Christ was God's means of satisfaction, being a substitutionary or vicarious offering.

autonomy (of individuals)

Self-law; the disposition in which the creature acts as if he were free of responsibility and obligation to God and therefore free of judgment and punishment.

Biblicist

(1) A term for people who claim to believe the Bible only for all matters of faith and practice. (2) One who interprets the Bible literally.

call (see *effectual call*), **-ing**

To invite or summon. In the Calvinistic system there are two calls by which God's elect are brought to salvation. (1) The *general outward call*, implied in the Great Commission (Mark 16:15), is the preaching of the gospel to all sinners. It is called "general" because it assumes every sinner who hears it is under responsibility to obey it—to repent of sin and turn to the Savior. (2) The Holy Spirit directs an *inward effectual call* whereby the elect are brought willingly to repentance and faith in the Lord Jesus Christ. The term *"call"* in the New Testament usually refers to the effectual inward call.

Calvinism, -ist

A biblical doctrine held by the Protestant reformers as consistent with Scripture and formulated as what is known as *The Five Points of Calvinism* (in honor of the great French theologian, John Calvin). It is a system of the doctrine of salvation insisting on God's sovereign involvement in a person's salvation. Its five basic tenets are the response of the Synod of Dort to the remonstrances of the disciples of Arminius and include the following: (1) Total depravity—sinners are both unwilling and spiritually unable to respond on their own in repentance and faith to God; (2) Unconditional election—God chooses sinners to be saved wholly apart from anything He foresees in them; (3) Limited atonement—Christ's redemption is for the elect only; (4) Irresistible grace—God's Spirit works so that the elect are effectually and inwardly brought to salvation; (5) Perseverance of the saints—the evidence of one's salvation is that God preserves him in conformity to Christ and holiness.

Canons of Dordt (or Dort)

The Calvinistic statement of faith by an assembly of theologians at Dordt, Holland, that resulted from the Arminian challenge in 1617 to the orthodox position on salvation.

choosing (verb)

God's predetermination before the world began to select certain people for special purposes including salvation and service.

contingencies

Events outside one's sphere of control that may frustrate or prevent one from accomplishing a desired objective.

creed

(1) A formal statement of religious belief; a confession of faith; (2) A system of belief, principles, or opinions.

creedalism

(1) Using creeds or confessions of faith to define what one believes; (2) A reliance on creeds and confessions rather than on the Scriptures themselves to defend one's faith. There is a danger in relying on creeds rather than on Scripture.

depravity

The loss of original righteousness and love for God. Positively, it means that man's moral nature has become corrupted and that he has an irresistible bias toward evil. The depraved man can do nothing perfectly pleasing to God. He cannot, no matter how hard he tries, love God with all his heart or his neighbor as himself; nor can he change his supreme preference for himself or so radically transform his character that he can live according to God's law. Without the saving grace of God no salvation is possible.

dispensation

A stewardship or administration. *Dispensation* appears in the NT four times: I Corinthians 9:1-7; Ephesians 1:10; 3:2; Colossians 1:25. In the first two and the fourth references, it means "stewardship," "office," "commission"—involving the idea of administration. In Ephesians 1:10 *dispensation* refers to God's plan of salvation.

doctrine

"To teach." Doctrine is a principle or body of principles presented for acceptance or belief.

dogma, -tism

(1) *Theology.* A doctrine or a corpus of doctrines relating to matters such as morality and faith set forth in an authoritative manner by a church; (2) An authoritative principle, belief, or statement considered to be absolutely true.

double jeopardy

A legal situation in which a person is tried and punished twice for the same crime.

double predestination

The positive and negative sides of predestination: predestination to heaven and predestination to hell.

Downgrade controversy

The name given to the controversy within the Baptist Union of Great Britain during the 1880s and 1890s over extending fellowship to Baptists who defected from evangelical doctrine due to German Rationalism. Charles Spurgeon separated from the Baptist Union during this controversy.

dualism

The philosophy believing that evil and good eternally coexist as necessary entities in the universe.

effectual calling

The inward call directed to God's elect by the Holy Spirit whereby they are brought willingly to repentance and faith in the Lord Jesus Christ. The term *"call"* in Scripture usually refers to the effectual call.

egoism

A theory (from human self-centeredness) that one's own good either is or ought to be the sole motive operative in human choice.

election

God's eternal and immutable decree to choose from sinners those whom He will save, providing the source of their salvation (grace through Christ) and the means (regeneration by the Holy Spirit).

The sovereign decree of God to choose out (from *ek* and *lego*, "to pick out") is the basic idea in election. This concept is applied in at least five ways: to elect those who are to be saved, to elect the means of their salvation in Christ, to elect the means in the redeeming activity of the Holy Spirit, to elect the results in the implantation of Christ's righteous nature to those who are saved, and to elect the destiny of eternal fellowship with God.

Much attention has been given to the relation between God's sovereign choice in election and the foreknowledge of God since the two concepts are related in Romans 8:27-30 and I Peter 1:1, 2. Erroneous interpretations have implied that election was based on a foreknowledge by God ("prior" knowledge) of the choice that man would make. This interpretation not only contradicts the idea of sovereignty but also ignores the basic meaning of the word *foreknow.*

When election refers to salvation, its subjects are individuals. The concept of universal election is foreign to Scripture; rather, particular election only is taught (Matt. 22:14; John 15:19; Rom. 8:29; 9:13, 15, 18; I Thess. 5:9).

enablement

The gift of willingness and ability to perform something previously not possible. In salvation, (1) Calvinists believe enabling is nothing short of regeneration from spiritual death; (2) non-Calvinists see enablement as wooing or assistance for reluctant sinners to exercise their natural ability to believe the gospel.

eternal security

"Once saved, always saved"; the assurance that once someone has "trusted Christ," he is saved forever, no matter how he may live afterward. This concept is opposed to "perseverance of the saints," which stresses that once God has saved a person, He will cause the believer to live a holy life. It is God who keeps and preserves His own unto the end.

evangelical, -s, -ism
(1) Technically, one who believes and preaches salvation by grace through faith alone and not by works or by the sacraments of the church; (2) a popular definition: one who evangelizes; one who emphasizes the importance of spreading the gospel.

evangelism
The proclamation of the gospel. (1) Calvinists believe evangelism to mean the faithful preaching (witnessing, *etc.*) of the gospel; (2) Non-Calvinists often mean "winning souls"—getting people saved by convincing them of their need of Christ.

exegesis
The critical analysis or interpretation of a word or passage of the Bible.

fairness
Often confused with *justice*, *fairness* is the unbiblical idea that all people should be treated equally, especially with respect to salvation.

faith
Faith has both an active and a passive sense: in the former, meaning "fidelity," "trustworthiness"; in the latter, "trust," "reliance." An example of the first is found in Romans 3:3, where "the faith of God" means His fidelity to His promises. In the overwhelming majority of cases, it has the meaning of reliance and trust.

Active faith is to trust in the claim of something presented. Thus, in the NT sense, faith is trust in the claims of Christ with respect to His teaching and the redemptive work He accomplished at Calvary. Faith is not to be confused with a mere intellectual assent to the doctrinal teachings of Christianity, though that is obviously necessary. The reformers stressed three elements in faith: (1) knowledge of the truth, (2) assent to the facts presented, and (3) trust—radical and total commitment of oneself to Christ as Savior and Lord.

Unbelief, or lack of faith, appears everywhere in the NT as the supreme evil. Not to make a decisive response to God's offer in Christ means that the individual remains in his sin and is eternally lost.

foreknowledge (see *election*)
From "to know" in the sense of intimate knowledge—"to love." (1) Biblically, the determination, decree, or foreordaining of events

178

ahead of time according to a plan; (2) for non-Calvinists it means a belief in God's prior knowledge.

free will

The right and ability to choose without coercion, and the freedom to carry out one's desires under God's sovereign will. Calvinists do not deny that humans have free will. They deny that humans can freely act contrary to their nature. Sinners are free to sin, but they are not free to be holy. Neither do Calvinists believe that sinners are forced to be saved against their wills. God first makes sinners to be willing by changing their nature.

fundamental, -ism, -ist

(1) Original; first; holding to the original position of a group (*e.g.*, Baptists); (2) Many Christians today use the term to mean "essential" or "necessary," reducing doctrines on which groups agree to a minimum in order to fellowship.

general redemption (universal redemption)

The view that Christ died for every person who ever lived since Adam in order to make salvation possible to any sinner who will repent and believe the gospel.

glory, -ification

(1) Concerning God, it is the display of His divine attributes and perfections. (2) Concerning man, it is the manifestation of his commendable qualities, such as wisdom, righteousness, self-control, ability, *etc.* A connotation of splendor is included. Glory culminates in the changing of the bodies of the saints to the likeness of their glorified Lord (Phil. 3:21).

gospel

(1) "Good news." The English word *gospel* is derived from the Anglo-Saxon *godspell*, which meant "good tidings." The term describes the message of Christianity—that *"Christ died for our sins according to the scriptures; And that he was buried, and that he rose again the third day according to the scriptures" (I Cor. 15:3, 4).*

gospel work

The human preaching or witnessing of the gospel.

grace (see *irresistible grace*)

God's working in an individual both to will and to do of His good pleasure. Grace is the free act of God's mercy and can neither be expected nor merited by anyone.

hermeneutics

The art of finding the meaning of an author's words and phrases and of explaining them to others; Bible interpretation.

humanism

A system or way of thought or action concerned with the interests and ideals of humans.

hyper-Calvinism

(1) The correct definition is a belief that, in the preaching of the gospel, an offer of salvation should not be made in the general hearing of any audience that may contain a mix of elect and non-elect. It is not so much wrong doctrine as wrong application of doctrine. (2) Some think the definition is supralapsarianism (see *supralapsarianism*). (3) Some think it is a denial of the "well-meant offer of the gospel" (see *well-meant offer*). (4) Many Arminians define it as believing in all (or even one or two) of the five points of Calvinism.

hypo-Calvinism (hypothetical universalism) (see *Amyraldianism*)

Amyraldianism. *Hypo-Calvinism* is a term coined by David J. Engelsma for the belief that God sovereignly elected specific humans to salvation but that Christ died for all humanity, both elect and non-elect.

idol

(1) An image or a god used as an object or instrument of worship; sometimes said of any heathen deity; (2) any object of ardent or excessive devotion or admiration; anything on which humans set their affections; that to which they indulge an excessive and sinful attachment.

idolatry

(1) The worship of idols, images, or anything made by hands, or which is not God; (2) excessive attachment or veneration for anything, or that which borders on adoration for anything that is not God; (3) anything that leads to the dethronement of God from the heart, as, for example, covetousness (Eph. 5:5; Col. 3:5); (4) worship of the true God in the wrong way, as, for example, Jeroboam when he set up images to worship Jehovah.

impute, -ation

To attribute something to a person or reckon something to the account of another, such as the imputation of Adam's sin to his posterity, the imputation of the sin of man to Christ, the imputation of

Christ's righteousness to the believer (Gen. 2:3: I Pet. 2:24; Rom. 3:24; 5:15; Gal. 5:4; Titus 3:7).

infralapsarianism (see *supralapsarianism*)
Belief of any of a group of Calvinists holding that God's decree to save the elect followed and was a consequence of the decree to permit the fall of man from grace; opposed to supralapsarianism.

iniquity
Self-will; independence from God.

interdenominational, -ism (transdenominationalism)
The working together of various denominations in cooperative engagements.

interpolation
The altering, enlarging, or corrupting of a book or manuscript by putting in new words, subject matter, *etc.*

irresistible grace
The work of God's Spirit whereby the elect are effectually and inwardly called to participate in the salvation which God offers through the gospel. It might be better termed *effectual inward calling.*

justice
(1) The quality of being right; (2) treating someone in the manner he deserves to be treated.

justification
That judicial act of God by which, on the basis of the meritorious work of Christ imputed to the sinner and received by him through faith, He declares the sinner absolved from his sin, released from its penalty, and restored to acceptance with God.

legalism
Belief that one's good deeds can earn God's favor either for salvation, sanctification, or service.

liberalism
A nineteenth-century Protestant movement (still practiced today) that favored free intellectual inquiry, stressed the ethical and humanitarian content of Christianity, and de-emphasized theology.

limited atonement (see *atonement*)
The biblical tenet that Christ's atonement was designed and intended for the elect only, ensuring the salvation of all for whom He died. Calvinists believe that the atonement was the *actual* and not merely a *potential* work of redemption.

love, God's

(1) God's faithful oversight of His creation, including fallen creatures, as seen in, for example, His causing it to rain on the just and unjust; (2) redemptive love (*agape*) is a love of purpose that (in God's case) infallibly secures a benefit for the ones He loves, His elect.

mercy

(1) Forbearance from inflicting punishment upon an adversary or a law-breaker; (2) the compassion which causes one to help the weak, the sick, or the poor. Showing mercy is one of the cardinal virtues of a true Christian (James 2:1-13) and is a part of the "fruit of the Spirit" (Gal. 5:22, 23).

modernism (see *liberalism*)

monergism, -gistic

The doctrine that regeneration is the work of the Holy Spirit alone, and that the human will, having no inclination to holiness, is incapable of assisting or cooperating.

neo-evangelicalism, -ist

A term given to a strain of contemporary theology that purports to avoid the dangers of both fundamentalism and neo-orthodoxy. The name itself originated with Harold J. Ockenga in an address at Fuller Theological Seminary in 1947. Its basic thrust may be summarized as (1) a friendly attitude toward modern science; (2) an increased emphasis on scholarship; (3) a more definite recognition of social responsibility; (4) a reopening of the subject of biblical inspiration; and (5) a willingness to enter into dialogue with theological liberalism and modern science with its evolutionary conclusions. Also called "the new neutralism."

neo-orthodoxy (crisis theology; Barthianism)

"New orthodoxy." A reaction, based on existential philosophy, to the unbelief of liberalism. Neo-orthodoxy was a theological movement that sought to return to orthodoxy. However, the return was not to the truth of Scripture. Neo-orthodoxy took biblical terms and dressed them with old modernistic definitions. The chief proponents of the movement were theologians Karl Barth (1886-1968) in Europe and Reinhold Neibuhr (1892-1971) in America.

new birth

Regeneration. The beginning of spiritual life in a believer (John 3:3, 5, 6; II Cor. 5:17; I Pet. 1:23).

nonelect

The bulk of mankind; those who have not been chosen unto salvation.

original sin

The condition of self-efficiency into which Adam, through his disobedience, plunged the human race. Original sin is the *"iniquity"* that has cursed all of Adam's descendants (Rom. 5:12).

particular redemption (see *limited atonement*)

Pelagianism

The belief, first set forth by Pelagius, a fifth-century British monk, teaching that men are born innocent and that they sin by following the example of Adam; therefore, Adam's fall was only a bad example to his posterity.

perseverance of the saints

The evidence of saving grace demonstrating obedience to the will of God and growing conformity of the child of God to Christ and holiness. *Perseverance* stresses the responsibility of the believer to live a holy and godly life by the grace and power of God.

predestination

The determination of God that events will occur as He planned them.

prevenient grace

(1) Some Calvinists use the term to mean God's beneficence toward the human race in general, providing sunshine on both the just and unjust, not immediately punishing sin, and allowing the general population to experience the fruits of the gospel—a strong moral society, prosperity, and peace; (2) the theory set forth by John Wesley and commonly accepted today that although Adam's fall did totally corrupt the race, moral ability was restored to all the race by Christ's death in order to enable lost sinners freely to chose or reject salvation.

proof texting

The practice of proving points with selected verses rather than exegeting the Scriptures, insisting on their contextual relationship. Proof texting makes Scripture texts say what the argument wishes them to say rather than taking the argument from the text. This practice often relies on the mere sound of words.

propitiation

The appeasing of the wrath of God, satisfying His justice and holiness in order to forgive sin and reconcile sinners (II Cor. 5:18-19).

183

Propitiation does not make God merciful; it makes divine forgiveness possible by requiring the death of a substitute to redeem the guilty (Rom. 3:25; I John 2:2; 4:10).

redemption

A loosing or ransom; from the secular market-place concept, "to buy back." The NT use covers both the idea of deliverance and the price of that deliverance or ransom (Rom. 3:24) In I Corinthians 6:20 redemption is viewed as being *"bought with a price."* Redemption involves the sinner's deliverance from the enslavement of sin and release to freedom in Christ (Rom. 6:4). Redemption carries the dual emphasis *from* and *to*. Redemption is from the penalty of the law, from sin, from Satan, and from all evil. Redemption is to a new freedom from sin, a new relationship to God, and a new life in Christ.

Redemption rests in Christ's satisfaction of the requirements for ransom. He took our sinful nature upon Himself in order that He might satisfy the demands of the Law by assuming our guilt. He redeemed us in order that He might deliver us from the bondage of sin (I Pet. 3:18).

reformed

A term used to distinguish Protestant churches, especially those that are Calvinistic.

representative universalism

The use of terms such as *world* or *all* to serve as an example or a type for a particular classification; *e.g.*, *world* in John 3:16 is to be understood as the "whole world" of believers, both Jews and Gentiles, distributed over the whole earth in many generations, not everyone who ever lived.

remonstrants, -ces

Arminius's followers who sued the church of Holland with five reprimands or protests ("remonstrances").

reprobation

The state of being judicially rejected; to be given up by God; to be excluded from grace and salvation; to be left to continue on one's course of willful sin and ruin. *Reprobate* is the Bible term for the nonelect.

responsibility

The condition or quality of being expected or obligated to account for something or to someone. Every person has a responsibility to repent and believe the gospel.

sanctification

Separation; setting apart. The NT uses the word in two ways: (1) to separate from the world and consecrate to God. Thus, the elect are said to be chosen through the sanctification of the Spirit (II Thess. 2:13; I Pet. 1:2). (2) Sanctification is the progressive work of Holy Spirit whereby the believer is brought into conformity to the image of Christ—becoming holy. Sanctification begins at regeneration and is completed when believers are glorified.

sectarian, -ism

Nonconformity; holding particular beliefs and practices. It has become a negative characteristic, usually applying to one who is different from the accepted standard.

secularization

To leave the influence of the Bible or religion and turn to a standard of living characterized wholly by worldly standards.

semi-Pelagian

Rejecting the view of Pelagius that mankind has not been morally corrupted by the fall of Adam, semi-Pelagianism, however, believes that Adam's fall did not totally corrupt the race. Pelagianism believes that people are spiritually healthy although exposed to Adam's "germs," from which they must take precaution. Semi-Pelagianism sees people as sick with Adam's germs but able to seek a "cure." Calvinism sees people as dead from Adam's germs and unable to seek a cure. James Arminius was a semi-Pelagian.

sin (see also *original sin*)

Anything in the creature which does not express, or which is contrary to, the holy character of the Creator. Sin is also the transgression of God's character and commandments. Sinners are corrupt, hostile to God, and guilty before Him (Rom. 5:12ff.). The essence of sin is living independently of God, expressing enmity against God, resulting in alienation, wrath, and judgment. The solution to the problem of sin is found in the redemption provided by Christ (Rom. 3:21-8:39).

sinner

One who sins. Every person born since Adam is a sinner.

Socinianism

A sixteenth-century Italian sect holding Unitarian views, including denial of the divinity of Jesus.

sovereign, -ty
> Supreme authority, independent and unlimited. No one except God is truly sovereign.

sublapsarianism (see *infralapsarianism*)

substitution
> To put instead of. Substitutionary atonement means that Christ died, taking the punishment of sinners in their stead. Thus, whatever satisfaction of justice Christ earned in His sacrifice belongs to those for whom He died because He died "for them."

supralapsarian, -ism
> Belief that God's decree to elect some of mankind to salvation preceded the decree to permit the fall of man. It is opposed to infralapsarianism.

synergistic
> A "working together." In theology, synergism is a doctrine that denies that God is the sole agent in effecting regeneration, teaching that humans must cooperate with divine grace in their salvation.

theology
> (1) The study of the nature of God and religious truth; rational inquiry into religious questions; (2) a system or school of opinions concerning God and religious questions; (3) a course of specialized religious study usually at a college or seminary.

total depravity (see *depravity*)

traducianism, -ist
> The belief that God created Adam *"a living soul,"* and all other souls, including Eve, have come from Adam.

transdenominationalism (see *interdenominationalism*)

unconditional election (see *election*)

universal redemption (see *general redemption*)

universalist, -ism
> One who believes that all will be saved.

unlimited atonement (see *general redemption*)

vicarious (see *substitute*)

well-meant offer
> The teaching that God desires the salvation of all men, even reprobates, although He has purposed to save only the elect. God desires

some things (*e.g.*, that every person be saved) that He has not been pleased actually to bring to pass

world

In Scripture *world* has the idea of an orderly arrangement (*kosmos*). It has various uses: (1) creation, universe, or earth itself (Matt. 13:38; 25:34; John 1:9, 10; I John 4:9); (2) material possessions (Matt. 16:26; I John 3:17); (3) the lifestyle of men in rebellion to God and under the control of Satan (John 7:7; 8:23; 17:6, 9; Gal. 4:3; Eph. 2:2; Col. 2:8; James 4:4; I John 2:15-17); (4) the inhabitants of earth in general but not necessarily individuals ("representative universalism") (Luke 12:30; John 1:29; 3:16; 14:22; I John 2:2); and (5) everyone of a particular group (Jews in John 12:19; believers in John 6:33, 51; unbelievers in I John 3:1, 2; 5:19).

BIBLIOGRAPHY

Alexander, David, and Pat Alexander, eds. *Eerdmans' Handbook to the Bible*. Grand Rapids, Mich.: William B. Eerdmans Publishing Co., 1973.

Arminius, James. "The Works of James Arminius," *The Master Christian Library,* version 5. Albany, Ore.: Ages Software, 1997.

"Articles of Faith of the Gospel Standard Strict Baptist Churches." Harpenden, Herts, Engl.: Gospel Standard Trust Publications, 1998.

Bishop, George S. *The Doctrines of Grace*. Grand Rapids, Mich.: Baker Book House, 1977.

Boettner, Loraine. *The Reformed Doctrine of Predestination*. Phillipsburg, N. J.: Presbyterian and Reformed Publishing Company, 1932.

Bookman, Doug. "God's Sovereign Pleasure." *Masterpiece*, 3, 4, (July/August 1990), 23-25.

Booth, Abraham. *The Reign of Grace*. Grand Rapids, Mich.: Wm. B. Eerdmans Publishing Company, 1949.

Branson, Bruce. "Arminian, Calvinist, or Biblicist?" Hartley, Ia.: Central Baptist Church, n. d.

Bridges, Jerry. *Trusting God Even When Life Hurts*. Colorado Springs, Colo.: NavPress, 1988.

Brown, Colin, ed. *Dictionary of New Testament Theology*. Grand Rapids, Mich.: Zondervan Publishing House, 1986.

Bruce, F. F. *Tyndale New Testament Commentaries, The Epistle of Paul to the Romans*. Grand Rapids, Mich.: Wm. B. Eerdmans Publishing Company, 1963.

Bryant, T. Alton, ed. *The New Compact Bible Dictionary*. Grand Rapids, Mich.: Zondervan Publishing House, 1967.

Calvin, John. *Calvin's Commentaries*, Vol. XXII. Grand Rapids, Mich.: Baker Book House, 1989.

----------. *Institutes of the Christian Religion*. Philadelphia: Westminster Press, 1960.

Chantry, Walter. *Today's Gospel: Authentic or Synthetic?* Carlisle, Penn.: Banner of Truth Trust, 1970.

Clark, Gordon. *Ephesians.* Jefferson, Md.: The Trinity Foundation, 1985.

----------. *Essays on Ethics and Politics.* Jefferson, Maryland: The Trinity Foundation, 1992.

----------. *God and Evil.* Hobbs, N. Mex.: The Trinity Foundation, 1996.

----------. *Three Types of Religious Philosophy.* Jefferson, Maryland: The Trinity Foundation, 1989.

Cole, C. D. "The Bible Doctrine of Election." Lexington, Ky.: Bryan Station Baptist Church, n. d.

Coles, Elisha, *God's Sovereignty.* (1678 rpt.). Edmonton, Alberta: Still Waters Revival Books, n. d.

Dallimore, Arnold. *George Whitefield.* Edinburgh: The Banner of Truth Trust, 1989.

Davidson, A. B. *Hebrews.* Edinburgh: T. & T. Clark, 1959.

Davis, J. D. *Illustrated Davis Dictionary of the Bible.* Nashville, Tenn., Royal Publishers, Inc., 1973.

Ella, George M. *John Gill and the Cause of God and Truth.* Durham, England: Go Publications, 1995.

Engelsma, David J. *Hyper-Calvinism and the Call of the Gospel.* Grand Rapids, Mich.: Reformed Free Publishing Association, 1994.

Fisk, Samuel. *Calvinistic Paths Retraced.* Murfressboro, Tenn.: The Biblical Evangelist, 1985.

Fuller, A. G. *The Principal Works and Remains of Rev. Andrew Fuller.* London, England: Bell and Daldy, 1864.

Gerstner, John H. *Wrongly Dividing the Word of Truth.* Brentwood, Tenn.: Wolgemuth and Hyatt, 1991.

Gill, John. *Body of Divinity* (1839 rpt.). Atlanta, Georgia: Turner Lassetter, 1965.

----------. *The Cause of God and Truth* (1855 rpt.). Paris, Arkansas: The Baptist Standard Bearer, Inc., 1992.

----------. *Exposition of the Old and New Testaments,* 9 vol. (1810 rpt.). Paris, Arkansas: The Baptist Standard Bearer, Inc., 1989.

----------. *Sermons and Tracts,* 6 vol. (1814 rpt.). Choteau, Mont.: Old Paths Gospel Press, 1997.

----------. *The Doctrines of God's Everlasting Love to His Elect, and Their Eternal Union with Christ.* (1732 rpt.). Paris, Arkansas: The Baptist Standard Bearer, Inc., 1987.

Good, Kenneth. *Are Baptists Calvinists?* Rochester, N. Y.: Backus Book Publishers, 1988.

----------. *Are Baptists Reformed?* Lorain, Ohio: Regular Baptist Heritage Fellowship, 1986.

----------. *God's Gracious Purpose as Seen in the Gospel of John.* Rochester, N. Y.: Backus Book Publishers, 1979.

Greene, Oliver B. *The Gospel According to John,* Vol. I. Greenville, S. C.: The Gospel Hour, Inc., 1966.

Hastings, James, ed. *A Dictionary of the Bible,* 5 vol. New York: Charles Scribner's Sons, 1923.

Hiscox, Edward T. *The New Directory for Baptist Churches.* Grand Rapids, Mich.: Kregel Publications, 1970.

Hoeksema, Herman. *Whosoever Will.* Grand Rapids, Mich.: Reformed Free Publishing Association, 1945.

Horne, Charles M. *The Doctrine of Salvation.* Chicago: Moody Press, 1984.

Horton, Michael. *Putting Amazing Back into Grace.* Grand Rapids, Mich.: Baker Books, 1994.

Kennedy, John. *Hyper Evangelism.* Edmonton, Alberta: Still Waters Revival Books, n.d.

Leach, T. W. "The Anabaptists, Their History, Hymns and Theology," *The Flaming Torch,* V. 32, Number 3, July, 1991.

Lenski, R. C. H. *The Interpretation of St. Matthew's Gospel.* Minneapolis, Minn.: Augsburg Publishing House, 1943.

----------. *The Interpretation of St. Paul's Epistles.* Minneapolis, Minn.: Augsburg Publishing Co., 1937.

Lloyd-Jones, D. Martin. *Romans: An Exposition of Chapter Nine, God's Sovereign Purpose.* Grand Rapids, Mich.: Zondervan Publishing House, 1991.

Loetscher, Lefferts A. *Twentieth Century Encyclopedia of Religious Knowledge,* 2 vol. Grand Rapids, Mich.: Baker Book House, 1955.

Long, Gary. *Definite Atonement.* Rochester, N. Y.: Backus Book Publishers, 1977.

Luther, Martin. *The Bondage of the Will* (James I. Packer and O. R. Johnston, transl.). Grand Rapids, Mich.: Fleming H. Revell, 1957.

Manton, Thomas. *A Commentary on Jude* (1658 rpt.). Carlisle, Pa.: The Banner of Truth Trust, 1989.

McClain, Alva J. *Romans: The Gospel of God's Grace.* Chicago: Moody Press, 1973.

McLachlan, Douglas R. *Reclaiming Authentic Fundamentalism.* Independence, Mo.: American Association of Christian Schools, 1993.

Murray, Iain. *The Forgotten Spurgeon.* Carlisle, Pa.: The Banner of Truth Trust, 1992.

Murray, John, and Ned Stonehouse. *The Free Offer of the Gospel.* Phillipsburg, N.J.: Presbyterian and Reformed, 1979.

New American Standard Bible. LaHabra, Calif.: The Lockman Foundation, 1971.

Newell, William R. *Romans Verse by Verse.* Iowa Falls, Ia.: World Bible Publishers, 1987.

Orchard, G. H. *A Concise History of the Baptists* (originally published in England in the 1800s) (Lexington, Ky.: Ashland Avenue Baptist Church, 1956).

Owen, John. "A Display of Arminianism" (1850-1853 rpt.), *The Works of John Owen*, Vol. 10. London: Banner of Truth Trust, 1987.

----------. "Communion with God" (1850-1853 rpt.), *The Works of John Owen*, V. 2. Edinburgh: The Banner of Truth Trust, 1965.

----------. J. H. Appleby, ed. *Life By His Death.* London: Grace Publications Trust, 1992.

----------.. "The Death of Death" (1850-1853 rpt.), *The Works of John Owen*, Vol. 10. London: Banner of Truth Trust, 1987.

Packer, J. I. *A Quest for Godliness.* Wheaton, Ill.: Crossway Books, 1990.

----------. *Evangelism and the Sovereignty of God.* Downers Grove, Ill.: InterVarsity Press, 1961.

Peterson, Jim. *Living Proof.* Colorado Springs, Colo.: NavPress, 1992.

"Philadelphia Confession of Faith." Marshalltown, Del.: The National Foundation for Christian Education, n d.

Pierce, Larry, ed. Online Bible CD ROM Version 7. Winterbourne, Ontario: Timnathserah, Inc., 1997, Topic Reference #26072.

Pink, A. W. *The Sovereignty of God.* Carlisle, Pa.: Banner of Truth Trust, 1988.

----------. *The Satisfaction of Christ.* Grand Rapids, Mich.: Zondervan Publishing House, 1955.

Piper, John. *The Pleasures of God.* Portland, Oregon: Multnomah Press, 1992.

Rice, John R. *False Doctrines.* Murfreesboro, Tenn.: Sword of the Lord Publishers, 1970.

----------. *Predestined to Hell? No!* Murfreesboro, Tenn.: Sword of the Lord Publishers, 1958.

Robertson, A. T. *Word Pictures in the New Testament.* Nashville, Tenn.: Broadman Press, 1931.

Rupp, Gordon, and Philip S. Wateson, eds. *Luther and Erasmus: Free Will and Salvation.* Philadelphia, Pa.: Westminster Press, 1969.

Rutherford, Samuel. *Communion Sermons.* Edinburgh, Scotland: James A. Dickson, 1986.

Ryrie, Charles C. *Basic Theology.* Wheaton, Ill.: Victor Books, 1986.

Salmond, S. D. F. "The Epistle to the Ephesians," *The Expositor's Greek Testament*, III, W. Robertson Nicolle, ed. Grand Rapids, Mich.: Wm. B. Eerdmans Publishing Co., 1961.

Scofield, C. I. *The Scofield Reference Bible.* New York: Oxford University Press, 1945.

Schreiner, Thomas R., and Bruce A. Ware, eds. *The Grace of God, The Bondage of the Will,* 2 vol. Grand Rapids, Mich,: Baker Book House, 1995.

Sheehan, R. J. *C. H. Spurgeon and the Modern Church.* London: Grace Publications, 1985.

Smeaton, George. *Christ's Doctrine of the Atonement* (1870 rpt.). Carlisle, Pa.: Banner of Truth Trust, 1991.

----------. *The Apostles' Doctrine of the Atonement* (1870 rpt.). Carlisle, Pa.: Banner of Truth Trust, 1991.

Smith, Charles R. "Did Christ Die Only For the Elect?" Winona Lake, Indiana: BMH Books, 1975.

Spencer, Duane Edward. *TULIP—The Five Points of Calvinism in the Light of Scripture.* Grand Rapids, Mich.: Baker Book House, 1979.

Sproul, R. C. *Chosen By God.* Wheaton, Ill.: Tyndale Publishing House, 1986.

----------. *Essential Truths of the Christian Life.* Wheaton, Ill.: Tyndale House Publishers, Inc., 1992.

Spurgeon, Charles. H. *Lectures to My Students.* Grand Rapids, Mich.: Zondervan Publishing House, 1954.

----------. *Spurgeon's Sovereign Grace Sermons.* Edmonton, Alberta: Still Waters Revival Books, 1990.

----------. *"The People's Christ" and Other Sermons.* London: Hodder and Stoughton, 1903.

----------. *The Soul-Winner.* Grand Rapids, Mich.: Associated Publishers and Authors, Inc., 1971.

Strong, Augustus H. *Systematic Theology.* Valley Forge, Pa.: The Judson Press, 1907.

Sumner, Robert L. "An Examination of *TULIP*: The Five Points of Calvinism." Murfreesboro, Tenn.: Biblical Evangelism Press, 1972.

Talbot, Kenneth G., and W. Gary Crampton. *Calvinism, Hyper-Calvinism, and Arminianism.* Edmonton, Alberta: Still Waters Revival Books, 1990.

Tenney, Merrill C., ed. *The Zondervan Pictorial Bible Dictionary.* Grand Rapids, Mich.: Zondervan Publishing House, 1967.

Thayer, Joseph Henry. *A Greek-English Lexicon of the New Testament.* New York: Harper and Brothers, 1887.

"The First London Confession of Faith, 1646 Edition." Rochester, N. Y.: Backus Book Publishers, 1981.

"The London Baptist Confession of Faith of 1689 and Keach's Catechism." Choteau, Mont.: Gospel Mission, n. d.

Theissen, Henry C. *Introductory Lectures in Systematic Theology.* Grand Rapids, Mich.: Wm. B. Eerdmans Publishing Co., 1949.

Vine, W. E. *Expository Dictionary of Old and New Testament Words.* Old Tappan, N. J.: Fleming H. Revell Co., 1981.

Waldron, Samuel E. *Baptist Roots in America.* Boonton, N. J.: Simpson Publishing Co., 1991.

Webster, Noah. *New Twentieth-Century Dictionary*, Second edition. Cleveland, Ohio: The World Publishing Co., 1967.

Williams, Colin. *John Wesley's Theology Today*. Nashville, Tenn.: Abingdon Press, 1960.

Wilson, William. *Old Testament Word Studies*. Grand Rapids, Mich.: Kregel Publications, 1978.

Zanchius, Gerome. *Absolute Predestination* (1532 rpt.). Lichfield, Mich,: Maranatha Bible Society, n. d.

NOTES

[1] Jim Peterson, citing Jeremy Rifkin with Ted Howard, *The Emerging Order* (New York: G. P. Putnam's Sons, 1979), p. 95, *Living Proof* (Colorado Springs, Colorado: NavPress, 1992), p. 18.

[2] *Ibid.* p. 19.

[3] Note that I said "one's beliefs." I do not imply that one should question the Scriptures. The Bible is the Word of God, and it alone must be our standard of faith. Our beliefs must come from Scripture, not from opinions. The tendency of humans is to hold opinions as Bible truth, especially if we can quote a verse to "prove it."

[4] For the sake of clarification in this book, *evangelical* describes those who believe and preach salvation by grace through faith alone and not by works or the sacraments of the church.

[5] Duane Edward Spencer, *TULIP—The Five Points of Calvinism in the Light of Scripture* (Grand Rapids, Mich.: Baker Book House, 1979), p. 5.

[6] I am, without apology, a fundamentalist; in fact, a fundamental Baptist. But in what sense am I a fundamental Baptist? The dictionary gives two basic concepts for the adjective *fundamental*: (1) original; first. (2) essential; necessary. Interdenominationalists use the term *fundamental* to mean "essential"—reducing doctrines necessary for fellowship to a minimum in order to promote the broadest fellowship. However, if Baptists mean the same thing, the phrase *fundamental Baptist* is a contradiction in terms. The term *Baptist* is purposely designed to define the boundaries of fellowship in a church by declaring those doctrines which would exclude, say, a Methodist. I use the adjective *fundamental* in the sense of "original or first"—holding to biblical Baptist heritage in opposition to modernism and liberalism.

[7] J. I. Packer, *A Quest for Godliness* (Wheaton, Ill.: Crossway Books, 1990), p. 126. Sadly, since writing *A Quest for Godliness*, Dr. Packer seems willing "discuss" the doctrine of justification by faith alone with the Roman Catholics. Although at this writing these discussions have not led

to negotiations, this trend among evangelicals is alarming because it may eventually lead to apostasy from truth and a return to the bondage of Rome.

[8] John Wesley's "prevenient grace" is discussed in Chapter 7 of this book. Both Finney (1792-1875) and Moody (1837-1899) were opposed to the study of theology. Moody is quoted as saying, "It makes no difference how you get a man to God, provided you get him there... My theology? I was not aware I had any." Finney believed that revival "is a purely philosophical result of the right use of the constituted means—as much so as any other effect produced by the application of means." On this premise, he instituted the invitation system with its "anxious bench." These devices to procure "revival" were labeled "new methods." They were sharply opposed by many because they used carnal means to secure a supposed spiritual end. Moody continued this emphasis and added "heart-warming" music in order to create an "atmosphere" for preaching. Most modern hymnals reflect the kind of gospel music used in his meetings with its strong emphasis on personal experience. See Iain Murray's examination of American evangelicalism (1750-1858), *Revival and Revivalism*, (Edinburgh: The Banner of Truth Trust, 1994), 455 pages, and John Kennedy's *Hyper Evangelism* (Edmonton Alberta: Still Waters Revival Books, n.d.), 33 pages. John Kennedy wrote *Hyper Evangelism* to evaluate and warn against Moody's campaigns in England and Scotland. He was a close friend of Charles H. Spurgeon.

[9] The typical attitude today is seen in the response of one Christian who was asked how he would interpret a particular verse of Scripture. He simply shrugged his shoulders and replied, "I'll just wait and ask the Lord about it when I get to heaven."

[10] John Kennedy, *Hyper Evangelism* (Edmonton Alberta: Still Waters Revival Books, n.d.), p. 2.

[11] John R. Rice, *Predestined for Hell? No!* (Wheaton, Ill.: Sword of the Lord Foundation, 1958), p. 6.

[12] I define *theology* as the science of assembling biblical truth into an orderly system—a skeleton on which to flesh out one's understanding of, relationship to, and service for God.

[13] The Arians believed that Jesus Christ was a created being, not God come in the flesh. They believed that God uniquely indwelled Christ at His baptism so that He became a special and unique instrument of God's

purpose. Athanasius, however, challenged this concept. The debate was settled at the Council of Nicea in favor of Athanasius's accurate interpretation of the Scripture regarding Christ's deity and humanity.

[14] R. C. Sproul, *Chosen By God* (Wheaton, Ill.: Tyndale House Publishers, 1986), p. 103.

[15] Of course, I understand the eschatological implications of this verse with reference to the time of the Great Tribulation (Matthew 24:21). However, I believe that the reference itself is a statement of principle which has various applications including future implications. The statement is in the context of persecution and teaches that believers who endure persecution unto the end of it shall be saved—shall evidence the saving grace of God. As in the parable of the sower (Matthew 13:20, 21), merely receiving the Word with joy does not mean salvation. The professor shows his lack of grace in the trial. Perseverance is the mark of a genuine believer.

[16] Some complain that the term *perseverance of the saints* is unscriptural terminology and implies the necessity of the believer to secure his own salvation by "holding on" to the end (see note 15 above). The Westminster Confession of Faith and the Baptist Philadelphia Confession of Faith state, "Those whom God hath accepted in the Beloved, effectually called and sanctified by his Spirit, and given the precious faith of His elect unto, can neither totally nor finally fall from the state of grace; but shall certainly persevere therein to the end and be eternally saved." Such a concept is Scriptural, for the apostle wrote to the Hebrews, *"And we desire that every one of you do shew the same diligence* [perseverance] *to the full assurance of hope unto the end"* (Hebrews 6:11).

[17] In the interest of consistency, I have developed an acrostic for our free-will (Arminian) brethren, although I am not certain that they will be pleased with the "flower" of my labors:

P artial ability
A ll foreseen faith elected
N on-discriminating atonement
S aving grace resisted
Y ou can lose it

[18] It should be noted that there have been and still are many Arminians who believe in eternal security.

[19] John Owen, "A Display of Arminianism," *The Works of John Owen*, X (London: Banner of Truth Trust, 1987), p. 14.

[20] Iain Murray, *The Forgotten Spurgeon* (Carlisle, Pa.: The Banner of Truth Trust, 1992), footnote, pp. 61, 62. Murray writes: "The error of Arminianism is not that it holds the Biblical doctrine of responsibility but that it *equates* this doctrine with an unbiblical doctrine of 'free-will' and preaches the two things as though they were synonymous. But man's will is always exercised in harmony with his nature and, as his nature is at enmity to God, so is his will. Man being fallen, his will *cannot* be neutral or 'free' to act contrary to his nature."

[21] Charles H. Spurgeon, "God's Will and Man's Will," *Spurgeon's Sovereign Grace Sermons* (Edmonton, Alberta: Still Waters Revival Books, 1990), p. 2.

[22] John R. Rice, *Predestined for Hell? No!*, p. 9.

[23] *Ibid.*, p. 5. Rice repeatedly emphasized that a sovereign-grace gospel means that God arbitrarily picks a few sinners to be saved, some of whom may not have had any desire to be saved. On the other hand, God turns a cold heart and a deaf ear to multitudes of "poor sinners" who may be seeking God and longing to have an opportunity to be saved. The cover of my copy of his book shows a hand (presumably God's) bearing a sword pointed in the back of a reluctant sinner, driving the poor man to the precipice of hell. However, not once in the book does Rice quote one honest Calvinist to support this fallacious concept of predestination. Driven by unreasonable passions, people often let their feelings replace sensible scholarship. God does predestine sinners to hell, but He did not force them to be sinners. He gives them what they justly deserve. No sinner deserves to go to heaven.

[24] *Ibid.* (emphasis added).

[25] A true "five-pointer" may fail to evangelize. This failure would make him guilty of disobedience, not of extreme doctrine. Many Arminians are also guilty of disobedience in the matter of soul winning. Should we label them "hyper-Arminians"?

[26] Article 33 of the Articles of Faith of the Gospel Standard Strict Baptist Churches, *Articles of Faith* (Harpenden, Herts, England: Gospel Standard Trust Publications, 1998), p. 40. Please note also that I do not find hyper-Calvinism offensive. Spurgeon regarded hyper-Calvinists as brethren. He argued that they were not wrong in doctrine, but only in practice.

[27] John Murray and Ned Stonehouse, *The Free Offer of the Gospel* (Phillipsburg, N.J.: Presbyterian and Reformed, 1979), p. 26.

[28] John H. Gerstner, *Wrongly Dividing the Word of Truth* (Brentwood, Tenn.: Wolgemuth and Hyatt, 1991), pp. 128-130 (emphasis Gerstner's).

[29] John R. Rice, *False Doctrines* (Murfreesboro, Tenn.: Sword of the Lord Publishers, 1970), p. 274. Evidencing antagonism (revealed in his writings), Dr. Rice seems to use the term *hyper-Calvinism* primarily in an aggravating sense to provoke his readers to take up his hostility toward Calvinism. His failure to define Calvinism properly coupled with his appreciation of Charles Spurgeon makes his defense of Spurgeon's Calvinism both amusing and confusing.

[30] John R. Rice, *Predestined for Hell? No!,* p. 22.

[31] Kenneth G. Talbot and W. Gary Crampton, *Calvinism, Hyper-Calvinism, and Arminianism* (Edmonton, Alberta: Still Waters Revival Books, 1990), pp. 76, 77.

[32] Charles H. Spurgeon, "Christ Crucified," *"The People's Christ" and Other Sermons* (London: Hodder and Stoughton, 1903), p. 166.

[33] The *Sword of the Lord* is still in publication. Dr. Shelton Smith is now the editor.

[34] I say "confusing" in the judgment of charity. Dr. Rice edited Spurgeon's sermons to remove references to sovereign-grace points.

[35] Charles Spurgeon cited by Spencer, pp. 56, 57.

[36] Rice, *False Doctrines*, p. 281.

[37] A word of clarification is in order. The Bible clearly commands that the gospel is to be preached generally in the hearing of every sinner. With that preaching comes the call to repent and believe the gospel. This call is an invitation extended to whoever will, offering—presenting—to them the promises of the gospel. This does not mean that God is offering salvation to every sinner. While all ears hear the message, only the elect "hear" the message. The promises of the gospel are made only to "whoever will come"—the elect. Herman Hoeksema, whom Dr. Rice cites in his book, has written about the proper and Scriptural use of the phrase "whosoever will." See *Whosoever Will* (Grand Rapids, Mich.: Reformed Free Publishing Association, 1945).

[38] Rice, *Predestined for Hell? No!,* pp. 102, 103.

[39] Iain Murray, p. 58.

[40] Cited by R. J. Sheehan, *C. H. Spurgeon and the Modern Church* (London: Grace Publications, 1985), p. 117. In all fairness, it should be noted that some of John R. Rice's confusion about Spurgeon may have come from Spurgeon's own tendency to equate his sovereign-grace gospel with the Arminian gospel of his day. He was not averse to cooperating with non-Calvinists in order to stand against modernism in the Downgrade controversy. He invited D. L. Moody into his pulpit and praised his work. His great burden for reaching the lost makes many of his sermons little different from the Arminian pleadings of Moody. These trends are disappointing. Truth demands a constant and careful vigil. As Dr. Gordon Clark observed, "Careful thought, clean-cut definitions, and consistency to the end are the prerequisites of progress." Gordon Clark, *God and Evil* (Hobbs, N. Mex.: The Trinity Foundation, 1996), p. 7.

[41] Charles H. Spurgeon, "Election," *Spurgeon's Sovereign Grace Sermons*, p. 171.

[42] The idea for the following comparison comes from a tract "Arminian, Calvinist, or Biblicist?" authored and published by Pastor Bruce Branson, Central Baptist Church, Hartley, Iowa.

[43] George Smeaton, *The Apostles' Doctrine of the Atonement,* (Carlisle, Pa: The Banner of Truth Trust, 1991), p. 540.

[44] Arthur Pink, *The Sovereignty of God,* (Grand Rapids, Mich.: Baker Book House, 1992), p. 200.

[45] David J. Englesma, *Hyper-Calvinism and the Call of the Gospel,* (Grand Rapids, Mich.: Reformed Free Publishing Association, 1994), p. 7. He writes:

> The well-meant offer, on the contrary, is not Reformed. It conflicts with basic Reformed truths, notably the truth of predestination. It betrays embarrassment with certain essential doctrines of Calvinism, particularly reprobation. The well-meant offer is, to coin a term, "hypo-Calvinism," that is, a teaching that *falls below* true Calvinism and that works the apostasy from Calvinism of the churches that try to hold the well-meant offer in tension with the "Five Points of Calvinism."

[46] Rice, *Predestined for Hell? No!*, p. 6.

[47] Augustus H. Strong, *Systematic Theology* (Valley Forge, Pa.: The Judson Press, 1907), p. 778.

[48] James Arminius, "The Works of James Arminius," *The Master Christian Library,* version 5, (Albany, Oregon, Ages Software, 1997), p. 7.

[49] Gratefully, I can now report that some of John Owen's works and other Puritan classics are obtainable in simplified form. These books are available from Evangelical Press, 12 Woller Street, Darlington, County Durham, DL1 1RQ, England; and from Banner of Truth Trust, P. O. Box 621, Carlisle, PA 17013.

[50] Rice, *Predestined for Hell? No!,* p. 5.

[51] *Ibid.,* p. 14. To be sectarian is to hold particular beliefs and practices. It has become a negative characteristic, usually applying to one who is different from the accepted standard. Baptists have always been regarded as sectarian because of their refusal to be associated with the Church of Rome.

[52] *Ibid.*

[53] Charles H. Spurgeon, "God's Will, Man's Will," *Spurgeon's Sovereign Grace Sermons,* pp. 2, 3.

[54] Rice, *Predestined for Hell? No!,* p. 18.

[55] *Ibid.*

[56] Some Baptists do not want to be associated with Calvinistic doctrine in order to avoid association with their former persecutors.

[57] T. W. Leach, "The Anabaptists, Their History, Hymns and Theology," *The Flaming Torch,* V. 32, Number 3, July, 1991, p. 14.

[58] *Ibid.*

[59] Cited by G. H. Orchard, *A Concise History of the Baptists* (originally published in England in the 1800s) (Lexington, Ky.: Ashland Avenue Baptist Church, 1956), pp. 295, 296.

[60] *Ibid.*

[61] Strong, p. 47. Some Baptists today would like to divorce themselves from John Gill by calling him a hyper-Calvinist. This godly saint has been lied about and slandered for years. Gill has been called a hyper-Calvinist for all but the right reasons. I know of no real evidence that he was a hyper-Calvinist. Gill wrote two outstanding volumes that ought to be studied by every Baptist preacher: *Body of Practical*

Divinity and *The Cause of God and Truth.* Some who reluctantly admit that Calvinism is Baptist doctrine will, however, insist that Baptists today follow the more "moderate"(?) Calvinism of Andrew Fuller. Fuller's moderation was nothing less than a soft-pedaling of the truth, a compromise with Arminianism; however, he maintained that he was a Calvinistic Particular Baptist like Gill. He referred to himself as a "strict" Calvinist. A. G. Fuller, *The Principal Works and Remains of the Rev. Andrew Fuller* (London: Bell and Daldy, 1864).

[62] Samuel E. Waldron, *Baptist Roots in America* (Boonton, N.J.: Simpson Publishing Company, 1991), p. 14.

[63] Edward T. Hiscox, *The New Directory for Baptist Churches* (Grand Rapids, Mich.: Kregel Publications, 1970), p. 537, footnote.

[64] *The Philadelphia Confession of Faith* (Marshalltown, Del.: The National Foundation for Christian Education, no date), pp. 20, 29, 30.

[65] Hiscox, pp. 545, 550.

[66] "Separate" Baptists were so called because they separated from the American Puritans over the issues of infant baptism, church polity, and church/state relationships.

[67] Waldron, p. 17. The seven factors Waldron lists are: (1) *The American, Democratic Ethos* (which promotes individualism and human rights and tends to ignore man's spiritual and moral depravity); (2) *Revivalism* (which promoted a doctrinal looseness that was exploited by the Arminians); (3) *Methodism* (which also flourished on the frontier to compete with Baptist expansion); (4) *Inclusivism* (the tendency to ignore differences for the purpose of mutual cooperation); (5) *Hyper-Calvinism* (the natural inclination to laziness in evangelism and the tendency to extremism); (6) *Modernism* (which gave conservatives of both Calvinistic and Arminian persuasion a common enemy against which to unite); (7) *The Fundamentalist Movement* (the transdenominationalism with its united front against liberalism; the popularity of dispensationalism and prophecy, developed mostly by non-Calvinists; the Keswick "deeper life" movement, which sprang out of Wesleyan Perfectionism; and the "easy-believism" of contemporary evangelism).

[68] *Ibid.*, pp. 16, 17.

[69] Marcus Dods as cited by Waldron, p. 17.

[70] *Ibid.*, p. 17.

[71] One compelling reason why I believe the truthfulness of the position regarding the sovereign-grace gospel is because it is so offensive to the tendencies of carnal flesh. It cuts across our sinful natures like a whip. It will not let proud humans take any credit for their salvation. For this simple and profound reason people resist it and hate it. They have called it a philosophy of man (although no proud human would ever think to invent such a system). They have ridiculed it by focusing on the foolish and disobedient behavior of some of its so-called adherents. But in spite of all of this, those who are willing to understand it find the power of God in the sovereign-grace gospel.

[72] John Calvin, *Institutes of the Christian Religion,* V. 2, Book 3, Chapter 21 (Philadelphia: Westminster Press, 1960), p. 926.

[73] *Ibid.*, p. 944.

[74] It is my experience that those who use the cliché that "Calvinism tears up churches" really do not understand the facts. It is usually those who hate Calvinism, who, with their stubborn, divisive spirit, "tear up" churches, causing trouble by resisting and opposing God-ordained leadership. However, in those cases where the fault for dissension lies with the Calvinist, it may be his personal prideful and destructive behavior rather than his doctrine that causes problems.

[75] John Piper, *The Pleasures of God* (Portland, Oregon: Multnomah Press, 1992), p. 19.

[76] *Ibid.*

[77] See Chapter 3 for Calvinism's historical development.

[78] Rice, *Predestined for Hell? No!,* p. 5.

[79] *Ibid.* (emphasis mine).

[80] Gordon H. Clark has written a valuable book explaining the three types of religious philosophy. The reader is encouraged to pursue *Three Types of Religious Philosophy* (Jefferson, Maryland: The Trinity Foundation, 1989).

[81] Many critics of the doctrines of grace use the fact that Christ loved this young man to argue for a universal love of God to sinners that can be frustrated by the sinner's refusing that love. It is assumed that because the man went away clutching his riches over Christ, he remained unsaved. That is an assumption from silence. God is in no

rush to claim His own. The work of conviction often takes time. Many believers of the past have written about the long and difficult struggles that they had with conviction and "closing" with Jesus. These testimonies seem foreign to this "four-things-God-wants-you-to-know-and-do-it-right-now-before-it's-too-late" generation of soul winners. The fact that Jesus loved him indicates that the rich young Pharisee was probably one of God's elect. We have not heard the "rest of the story."

[82] Charles H. Spurgeon, *Metropolitan Tabernacle Pulpit*, VII, p. 85, as cited by A. W. Pink, *The Sovereignty of God*, p. 4.

[83] It is interesting to hear many Christians try to explain the tragedies of life and the comfort it is to them to realize God's sovereign purposes in those tragedies. Yet, they will contradict themselves over and over in taking that sovereignty away from God when appealing to the lost to trust Him for salvation.

[84] Rice, *Predestined for Hell? No!*, p. 79.

[85] Jerry Bridges, *Trusting God Even When Life Hurts* (Colorado Springs, Colo.: NavPress, 1988), p. 18.

[86] Dr. Rice uses the term "hyper-Calvinist" to mean one who believes more than one point of Calvinism. He refers to Dr. Lewis Sperry Chafer as a "hyper-Calvinist" (*Predestined for Hell? No!*, p. 98). Chafer was an Amyraldian (see Glossary) "four-point" Calvinist. In fact, Rice takes issue with all five points of Calvinism in *Predestined for Hell? No!* He *might* be called a "half-point" Calvinist (believing in eternal security). This kind of "scholarship" certainly confuses the issue. (See Appendix, "Was John R. Rice an Arminian?")

[87] Rice, *Predestined for Hell? No!*, p. 80. Curiously, the grammar check on my computer caught the phrase "absolute sovereignty" with the message that it contained a redundancy. *Absolute* means the same thing as *sovereign*. How could God not be absolutely sovereign?

[88] *Ibid.*

[89] Gordon H. Clark, "Egoism," *Essays on Ethics and Politics* (Jefferson, Maryland: Trinity Foundation, 1992), p. 48.

[90] Dr. John Piper has documented this very tendency in evangelical circles in his excellent book *The Pleasures of God*, pp. 169-177, 179-183, notes 4, 10, and 13.

[91] Gordon Rupp and Philip S. Wateson, eds., *Luther and Erasmus: Free Will and Salvation,* (Philadelphia, Pa.: Westminster Press, 1969), p. 47.

[92] Martin Luther, translated by James I. Packer and O. R. Johnston, *The Bondage of the Will* (Grand Rapids, Mich.: Fleming H. Revell, 1957), p. 319.

[93] Gordon H. Clark, "Concerning Free Will," *Essays on Ethics and Politics*, p. 25.

[94] *Ibid.* The Roman Catholic Council of Trent (1563) decreed that if anyone "shall affirm, that man's free-will, moved and excited by God, does not, by consenting, co-operate with God . . . for the attainment of justification; if moreover, anyone shall say, the human will cannot refuse complying, if it pleases . . . let such a one be accursed." Cited from Arthur Pink, *The Sovereignty of God* (Grand Rapids, Mich., Baker Book House, 1992), p. 139.

[95] Luther, p. 319.

[96] *Ibid.*, p. 79.

[97] *Ibid.*, pp. 80, 82.

[98] Douglas R. McLachlan, *Reclaiming Authentic Fundamentalism* (Independence, Mo.: American Association of Christian Schools, 1993), p. 61. By saying that "anyone who thinks he has all the answers on this matter simply has not yet heard all the questions," is not Dr. McLachlan brushing off anyone who might disagree with him? This is a subtle accusation of pride—thinking one has all the answers. His statement makes one hesitate to offer a rebuttal. Concerning this effort to evade the problem of the compatability of God's sovereignty and human responsibility, Arthur Pink writes:

> A certain class of theologians, in their anxiety to maintain man's responsibility, have magnified it beyond all due proportions, until God's sovereignty has been lost sight of, and in not a few instances flatly denied. Others have acknowledged that the Scriptures present *both* the sovereignty of God and the responsibility of man, but affirm that in our present finite condition and with our limited knowledge it is *impossible* to reconcile the two truths, though it is the bounden duty of the believer to

receive both. The present writer [Pink] believes that it has been too readily *assumed* that the Scriptures themselves do not reveal the several points which show the conciliation of God's sovereignty and man's responsibility. . . . God has been pleased to reveal many things out of His Word during the last century which were hidden from earlier students. Who then dare affirm that there is not too much to be learned yet respecting our present inquiry! (Arthur Pink, *The Sovereignty of God,* p. 144).

[99] *Ibid.*, p. 61.

[100] *Ibid.*

[101] Piper, p. 19.

[102] Rice, *Predestined for Hell? No!,* p. 64. (Yes, Dr. Rice favorably quoted this in his book.)

[103] Chapter 13 deals more with evangelism.

[104] Rice, *Predestined for Hell? No!,* p. 28 (emphasis Rice's).

[105] *Ibid.,* p. 29.

[106] For an excellent biblical discussion of Romans 9, see D. Martin Lloyd-Jones, *Romans: An Exposition of Chapter Nine, God's Sovereign Purpose* (Grand Rapids, Mich.: Zondervan Publishing House, 1991).

[107] Alva J. McClain, *Romans: The Gospel of God's Grace* (Chicago: Moody Press, 1973), p. 175.

[108] Although the main emphasis of Romans 9 is God's sovereign will, verses 23-31 clearly refer to salvation, despite Dr. Rice's denial.

[109] I wrote a tract (never published) mocking Calvinism entitled "God's Not So Simple Supralapsarian Plan of Salvation." Curiously, Abraham Booth, another Baptist preacher (1734-1806), was also at first an ardent detractor of Calvinism, preaching the doctrines of the Arminian General Baptists. He, too, demonstrated his opposition to Calvinistic truths by writing a poem, "On Absolute Predestination," which he published. What he wrote concerning the poem after God graciously revealed to him his error echoes my thoughts exactly:

> "Which poem, if considered in a critical light, is
> despicable; if in a theological view, detestable: as
> it is an impotent attack on the honour of Divine
> grace, in regard to its glorious freeness; and a

bold opposition to the sovereignty of God. So I now consider it, and as such I here renounce it." Abraham Booth, *The Reign of Grace* (Grand Rapids, Mich.: Wm. B. Eerdmans Publishing Company, 1949), p. 38.

[110] My wife now also believes the doctrines of grace. She has found that they honor God and demonstrate His glorious majesty far more than the man-centered doctrines which we used to hold.

[111] The great eighteenth-century revivalist, George Whitefield, wrote a letter dated August 25, 1740, to admonish John Wesley about his opposition to the doctrines of grace:

> "Perhaps the doctrines of election and final perseverance hath been abused (and what doctrine has not,) but notwithstanding, it is the children's bread and ought not, in my opinion to be withheld from them, supposing it is always mentioned with proper cautions against the abuse.
>
> I cannot bear the thought of opposing you: but how can I avoid it, if you go about (as your brother Charles once said) to drive John Calvin out of Bristol. Alas, I never read anything that Calvin wrote; my doctrines I had from Christ and His apostles; I was taught them of God. . . ." Arnold Dallimore, *George Whitefield*, I, (Edinburgh: The Banner of Truth Trust, 1989), pp. 773, 774.

I identify with George Whitefield. I, too, came to these doctrines through the Word of God, not the writings of Calvin or any other Calvinists.

[112] Samuel Fisk, *Calvinistic Pathways Retraced* (Murfreesboro, Tenn.: Biblical Evangelist Press, 1985), cover note about the author.

[113] *Ibid.*, p. 57. Fisk agrees with James Arminius, who wrote: "It [faith] is a gift which is not bestowed according to an absolute will of saving some particular men; for it is a condition required in the object to be saved, and it is in fact a condition before it is the means for obtaining salvation" (James Arminius, "Certain Articles to Be Diligently Examined and Weighed," *The Master Christian Library*, version 5, (Albany, Ore.: Ages Software, 1997), p. 500).

[114] In the argument over "faith" in salvation, Fisk speaks of faith's being the only *condition* of salvation while many Calvinists stress that faith is not a *condition* but only the *means*. This is quibbling over semantics.

God requires faith on the part of the sinner in order to *experience* salvation. From the gospel perspective, we ought to be able to agree that faith is a condition, the only condition, of *experiencing* salvation.

Could it be that some Calvinists are also guilty of confusing concepts? They also argue that since election is *unconditional,* faith, therefore, cannot be a *condition* of salvation. Well, faith is certainly not a condition of *election.* Actually, faith is both a condition and a means of salvation.

[115] Fisk, p. 90.

[116] *Ibid.*

[117] James Arminius, "Certain Articles to Be Diligently Examined and Weighed," p. 497.

[118] The *New American Standard Version* seems to interpret the passage this way because it translates the verb *"willing"* (Gk. *boulomia*) in this verse as *"wishing." "Wishing"* implies that, while God may desire to save every sinner, He cannot do so because salvation is dependent upon something over which God has little or no control—the sinner's will.

[119] John Gerstner has an excellent discussion of "reading into" Scripture in his book *Wrongly Dividing the Word of Truth,* pp. 127-131.

[120] See Thayer's Greek Lexicon. D. Müller in an article on *boulomai* in *The New International Dictionary of New Testament Theology,* III, pp. 1017, 1018, states concerning the theological significance of the word, "It is always a case of irrefragable [dogged] determination." Again, "God's promise has not been made questionable by the long lapse of history; his will is the salvation of all [that He will save] (2 Peter 3:9). We have been born of this saving will (Jas. 1:18), and because God himself is the unalterable One (cf. Jas. 1:17), his gracious will cannot be overthrown."

Boulomai can be translated as "wishing" but only with respect to the ability of the one who wills to bring his desire to pass. Finite beings may will with a strong determination something that can never be realized because they lack the power to make it happen. That is no limitation to God. What He wills He does. *"I have purposed it, I will also do it"* (Isaiah 46:11).

[121] Doug Bookman, "God's Sovereign Pleasure," *Masterpiece,* 3:4 (July/August 1990), 24.

[122] John Piper, p. 123.

[123] Arno C. Gaebelein, cited by Robert Sumner, *An Examination of TULIP* (Murfreesboro, Tenn.: Biblical Evangelist Press, 1972), p. 3.

[124] Rice, *Predestined for Hell? No!*, p. 19.

[125] Luther, p. 80.

[126] Most Christians do not really understand what they believe. Some, who would vigorously object to the designation, demonstrate in practice that they actually are Arminians. They own that they believe in election, but they reject effectual redemption. Why? It is because they do not believe in a truly unconditional election. Election is the core of the position. Only the elect will come to Christ. Why, then, would it be necessary for Christ to die for any but the elect? God knew from the foundation of the world who would receive His gift and who would not. What would Christ accomplish by dying for the sins of those who must pay for their own sins in hell? The argument used is that Christ's dying for everyone who ever lived makes all men savable. Apparently, we need to make sure that the non-elect are covered just in case some might want to get saved anyway? "Consistency, thou art a jewel."

[127] Henry C. Theissen, *Introductory Lectures in Systematic Theology* (Grand Rapids, Mich.: Wm. B. Eerdmans, 1949), p. 344.

[128] *Ibid.*, p. 345.

[129] *Ibid.*, pp. 344, 345.

[130] Colin Williams, *John Wesley's Theology Today* (Nashville, Tenn.: Abingdon Press, 1960), p. 41.

[131] *Ibid.*, p. 44.

[132] The term "prevenient grace" has also been used by some Calvinists. Unlike Wesley's definition, their idea refers to God's beneficence toward the human race in general, providing sunshine on both the just and unjust, not immediately punishing sin, and allowing the general population to experience the fruits of the gospel—a strong moral society, prosperity, and peace.

[133] Williams, p. 75.

[134] *Ibid.*, p. 46.

[135] Theissen, p. 268.

[136] *Ibid.*

[137] *Ibid.*, p. 345.

[138] *Ibid.* (emphasis mine).

[139] *Ibid.*, p. 347.

[140] Thomas Manton, *A Commentary on Jude*, (Carlisle, Pa.: The Banner of Truth Trust, 1989), p. 130.

[141] The justice of God is the question Paul deals with in Romans 3:21-26. Christ's propitiation is *"set forth"* or "declared" to demonstrate the justice of God's seemingly unrighteous acts of remitting sins in the past without exacting a proper payment to satisfy His own wrath.

[142] Spurgeon, "Election," *Spurgeon's Sovereign Grace Sermons*, p. 167.

[143] Theissen, p. 347.

[144] Fisk, pp. 91, 92.

[145] Colin Brown, ed., *Dictionary of New Testament Theology*, I (Grand Rapids, Mich.: Zondervan Publishing House, 1986), pp. 534, 535.

[146] W. E. Vine, *Expository Dictionary of Old and New Testament Words* (Old Tappan, N. J.: Fleming H. Revell Co., 1981), p. 189.

[147] This phrase, *"from the beginning,"* has no article in the Greek and is used in an idiomatic sense of a point in the distant past not specifically identified. Lenski states that "the sense is the same as *'before the foundation of the world'* (Eph. 1:4)" (R. C. H. Lenski, *The Interpretation of St. Paul's Epistles* (Minneapolis, Minn.: Augsburg Publishing Co., 1937), p. 439). Note: Lenski is a Lutheran. He is, in my opinion, an honest and thorough Greek scholar, but he is by no means a Calvinist.

[148] Theologians speak of the "decrees" of God and make a great deal over the order of the decrees (which decrees came first, and so on). There is no question that God planned all the details of salvation before the earth was created or mankind fell into sin. First Peter 1:20 and Acts 2:23 make that obvious. When God says that He planned this all in terms of counsels and order, He expresses it for our finite minds to understand. We must, however, keep in mind that God is eternal and unchangeable. The triune God did not sit around in heaven thinking up ideas, discussing them, finally settling upon the best approach, and

then working out the details. God has *never* had a good idea. If there is anything that He does not *eternally* know, He is not all-knowing (omniscient) and unchanging (immutable) and therefore cannot be God. However, the humanism of one's theology does show up here in the "order" of the decrees—(1) to create, (2) to predestinate certain of the human race, (3) to permit the fall. If one believes the order just given, he is a supralapsarian (from the Latin *supra*, "before" and *lapsis*, "fall—before the fall, referring to the decree to elect before the decree to permit the fall). If one believes that the decree to permit the fall came before the decree to elect, he is an infralapsarian (from *infra*, "after"—after the fall) or sublapsarian. In my opinion, supralapsarianism gives all the glory to God. Furthermore, supralapsarianism is *not* hyper-Calvinism, as many erroneously teach.

[149] William R. Newell, *Romans Verse by Verse* (Iowa Falls, Ia.: World Bible Publishers, 1987), p. 364.

[150] A. T. Robertson, *Word Pictures in the New Testament*, IV (Nashville, Tenn.: Broadman Press, 1931), p. 525. Dr. Robertson could not be accused of ignorance in Greek. His failure to cite the compatibility of the neuter demonstrative pronoun with a feminine noun can be attributed only to his theological bias.

[151] S. D. F. Salmond, "The Epistle to the Ephesians," *The Expositor's Greek Testament*, III, W. Robertson Nicolle, ed., (Grand Rapids, Mich.: Wm. B. Eerdmans Publishing Co., 1961), p. 289.

[152] Gordon H. Clark, *Ephesians* (Jefferson, Md.: The Trinity Foundation, 1985), p. 73. See also S. D. F. Salmond, "The Epistle to the Ephesians," *The Expositor's Greek Testament*, III, W. Robertson Nicolle, ed., (Grand Rapids, Mich.: Wm. B. Eerdmans Publishing Co., 1961), p. 289. "But to what does the *touto* [that] refer? To the *pisteos* [faith] say some (Chrys., Theod., Jer., Bez., Beng., Bishl, Moule, *etc.*). The neut. *touto* would not be irreconcilable with that. The formula *kai touto* [and that] indeed might rather favour it, as it often adds to the idea to which it is attached."

[153] R. C. H. Lenski, *The Interpretation of St. Paul's Epistles* (Minneapolis, Minn.: Augsburg Publishing Co., 1937), pp. 422, 423.

[154] Newell, p. 365.

[155] Spurgeon, "Election," *Spurgeon's Sovereign Grace Sermons*, p. 177.

[156] Robert L. Sumner, "An Examination of *TULIP*" (Murfreesboro, Tenn.: Biblical Evangelism Press, 1972), p. 7.

[157] The best way to make the truth odious is to pervert it and get people emotionally disturbed over it. Why do you think Dr. Sumner uses a "baby" in his argument? Let us consider the *facts* of Scripture without emotional distortions.

[158] R. C. Sproul, *Essential Truths of the Christian Life* (Wheaton, Ill.: Tyndale House Publishers, Inc., 1992), p. 161.

[159] *Ibid.*, p. 165.

[160] Lloyd-Jones, p. 175.

[161] Owen, "A Display of Arminianism," *The Works of John Owen*, X, p. 82.

[162] Rice, *Predestined for Hell? No!*, pp. 47, 48.

[163] *Ibid.* (emphasis mine).

[164] Both Calvinists and non-Calvinists speak of God's *enabling* sinners to believe the gospel but differ in understanding the degree of that enabling. Non-Calvinists, knowing the depravity of sinners, will seek to protect "free will" by insisting that God enables sinners enough either to "freely" accept or reject salvation. Calvinists, on the other hand, see enabling as nothing short of regeneration from spiritual death—creating in sinners a heart for obedience. Because both use the same term, we need to take care in determining one's definition of the term *enablement*.

[165] God did not use these methods because He hoped that they might work but rather to demonstrate that they would not work. Those who use these same methods have not learned from Israel's example.

[166] Paul argues in Romans 9-11 that God's plan never was to save all the nation of Israel until the end of the age (Romans 11:25-29) but, rather, to leave them in the hardness of unbelief in order to bring salvation to "the whole world" through Christ. However, there has always been a remnant *"according to the election of grace"* (Romans 11:1-5). All the Old Testament saints were able to believe God and obey His will, as many examples, such as Abraham, Joseph, and David, reveal (see Luke 1:5, 6).

[167] Sumner, p. 4.

[168] *Ibid.*, p. 5.

[169] *Ibid.* (emphasis Summer's).

[170] *Ibid.*, pp. 5, 6. Dr. Sumner is typical of many who read into the Bible what they want it to say. He creates Calvinistic straw men and then has a wonderful time beating them to pieces. He, John R. Rice, and evangelists like them necessarily hate Calvinism. John Rice seemed particularly offended by the writing of Dr. Herman Hoeksema (see *Predestined for Hell? No!*, pp. 96, 97). I can understand why. Listen to Dr. Hoeksema: "All the more preemptory it is to inquire into the meaning of coming to Jesus because of the abominable travesty of it that is presented by many a modern self-styled evangelist and revivalist. And it is high time that the Church, that is the custodian of the gospel, and to whom alone is given the commission to preach the Word, should raise her voice aloud in protest against the widely practiced evil of hawking Jesus, and of presenting Him as the cheapest article on the religious market, that may either be procured or rejected by the sinner at will. . . . Oh, indeed, they admit that salvation is of grace, and some of these hawkers of salvation even prattle of sovereign grace; but this grace is, nevertheless, presented as enervated and paralyzed if the sinner refuses its saving operation!" (I say a hearty "Amen!") Herman Hoeksema, *Whosoever Will* (Grand Rapids, Mich.: Reformed Free Publishing Association, 1945), pp. 108, 109.

[171] *Ibid.*, p. 4 (emphasis Sumner's). Does the Word of God teach that every totally depraved sinner is helped sufficiently by God to believe the gospel if he wants to? Where, other than John 1:9, is that a possibility in Scripture? Saying so does not make it so. By the way, John 1:9 does not teach that either.

[172] Rice, *Predestined for Hell? No!*, p. 48. This title reveals a nice sentiment, but how can Rice actually believe that God's invitation and enablement "reach every sinner" when multitudes have lived and died without ever hearing the gospel and nearly two thirds of the world's population living today has never even heard of Christ, let alone His invitation to salvation?

[173] *Ibid.*, p. 92.

[174] Sin is the transgression of God's character and commandments. Sin is "God-belittling" because it robs Him of His rightful claim to our lives. Some modern evangelicals see the problem of sin only in its

effect on the sinner—how it hurts and how it leaves life void. Salvation is seen as God's fix for this little problem—restoring people to happiness and giving them purpose for living. The Bible, on the other hand, views sin as enmity against God, which causes alienation and results in wrath and judgment. Salvation is deliverance from both sin and wrath. As a Savior, Christ saves His people both from their sins (Matthew 1:21) and from God's wrath (I Thessalonians 5:9, 10).

[175] Rice, *Predestined for Hell? No!*, p. 53.

[176] Newell, p. 370. I would qualify Newell's statement to read that "the door is open to all *who will*, absolutely all *who will.*" Gospel invitations are not open to those who will not believe. Jesus said that He had not come to call those who thought they were righteous but only those who knew that they were sinners (Luke 5:32).

[177] The reference in Matthew 20:16 is called into question because of a lack of textual support. While some debate arises over whether it is an interpolation from chapter 22:14, the fact is there is no question of its authenticity as the words of Christ in the latter text. I agree with Lenski (R. C. H. Lenski, *The Interpretation of St. Matthew's Gospel*, Minneapolis, Minn.: Augsburg Publishing House, 1943, p. 780) that although the textual support for 20:16 is not conclusive, it is "by no means insignificant." The question which has yet to be explained is how did this phrase get into 20:16 from 22:14? My view of the divine preservation of Scripture forces me to accept the text as valid. Those who reject it also want to strip it of its meaning in 22:14.

[178] William Tyndale wrote:

> Why doth God open one man's eyes and not another's? Paul (Rom. ix) forbiddeth to ask why; for it is too deep for man's capacity. God we see is honoured thereby, and His mercy set out the more seen in the vessels of mercy. But the popish can suffer God to have no secret, hid to Himself. They have searched to come to the bottom of His bottomless wisdom: and because they cannot attain to that secret, and be too proud to let it alone, and to grant themselves ignorant, with the apostle, that knew no other than God's glory in the elect; they go and set up free-will with the heathen philosophers, and say that a man's free-will is the cause why God chooseth one and not another, contrary unto all the scripture.

William Tyndale, *An Answer to Sir Thomas More's Dialogue,* cited in Iain Murray, *The Forgotten Spurgeon,* footnote pp. 8, 9.

[179] Does one's faith prompt the new birth, or does the new birth make faith possible? Does it matter? In the view of this author, any work of God's grace which depends upon the sinner's faith makes grace a reward of debt (Romans 11:5-7). It also clearly ignores the plain facts of Scripture and experience. John tells us that believers are given the authority to become the children of God (John 1:12). These believers, John continues, are they *"which were born, not of blood*[s] [plural—not sons of God by genealogical descent], *nor of the will of the flesh* [not sons of God because parents willed to bring a child into the world through procreation], *nor of the will of man* [not sons because someone decided that he wanted to be a son], *but of God* [sons because God willed it so]" (John 1:13). How can one deny this plain verse? In John 3 Jesus clearly told Nicodemus that he must be born again; yet Jesus did not explain to Nicodemus any steps which Nicodemus must take. Rather, Nicodemus, failing to understand the spiritual nature of the assertion, nevertheless shows understanding of the process—entering the womb and being born! No one ever willed his own physical birth. No one ever called the prospective baby into conference about his will in the matter. There is not one Bible reference to the new birth that indicates how sinners are to accomplish this process. First Peter 1:3 shows us that the Father *"hath begotten us again unto a lively* [living] *hope."*

[180] Newell, p. 370.

[181] I am always amused by the ignorance of individuals who speak or write against Calvinism in that they assume that John Calvin is the author of the "five points." Careful research into the facts ought to be the first step in arguing against another person's position.

[182] Strong, pp. 777, 778. Strong cites James Richards, *Lectures in Theology,* p. 302. The supposed quote from Calvin reads:

> Christ suffered for the sins of the whole world, and in the goodness of God is offered unto all men without distinction, his blood being shed not for a part of the world only, but for the whole human race; for although in the world nothing is found worthy of the favor of God, yet he holds out the propitiation to the whole world, since without

217

exception he summons all to faith of Christ, which
is nothing else than the door unto hope.

I will admit that this quote seems to teach universal redemption. However, understanding what Calvin taught about election, it is difficult for me to believe that he changed his mind about all he wrote in his *Institutes of the Christian Religion.* Also, if Calvin is stressing the fact that the gospel is not limited to the Jews but is to be preached in all the world and to all men without distinction, it does not clearly deny limited atonement.

[183] Rice, *Predestined for Hell? No!*, pp. 12, 13.

[184] Calvin, *Calvin's Commentaries*, p. 173 (emphasis mine).

[185] Dr. John Owen was a seventeenth-century British separatist Puritan theologian. Charles H. Spurgeon said of Owen: "It is unnecessary to say that he is the prince of divines. To master his works is to be a profound theologian."

[186] H. J. Appleby has prepared a simplified version of this book entitled *Life by His Death* (London: Grace Publications Trust, 1992), 87 pages.

[187] Charles C. Ryrie, *Basic Theology* (Wheaton, Ill.: Victor Books, 1986), p. 322. Ryrie does give the limited-atonement viewpoint on II Peter 2:1; I John 2:2; and I Timothy 4:6, 10. He then lists three other texts (Hebrews 2:9; John 3:16; and Acts 17:30) without giving the limited view. Although he states that exegesis settles the argument, he does not demonstrate the *exegesis* of a single passage. We can throw individual verses at each other forever. Both sides have fully established their arguments on the verses.

I have examined all the arguments and find that the weight of evidence supports the limited view. The same evidence, however, does not faze a person whose mind is fixed upon the unlimited view. The debate can be answered only by examining the whole purpose of God in the salvation of mankind.

[188] Ryrie, in commenting on I John 2:2 concedes, "To be sure, the word "world" does not always mean all people (see John 12:19)." However, he argues, "Furthermore, the only other occurrence of the phrase "the whole world" in John's writings is in 1 John 5:19, and there it undebatably includes everybody" (*Basic Theology*, p. 321). It does? *"And we know we are of God, and the whole world lieth in wickedness."* Who are *"we"* in the passage? Is not John making a contrast—*"we"* believers contrasted with the *"world"* of unbelievers? John is not

including those who are *"of God"* in the *"whole world"* of this verse unless we are to conclude that even believers are lying in wickedness.

[189] *Ibid.*

[190] See David J. Engelsma, *Hyper-Calvinism and the Call of the Gospel.* Engelsma defends the Christian Reformed Church and Herman Hoeksema from the charge of hyper-Calvinism because they take the stand that preaching the gospel to every creature does not require that Christ die for every sinner nor that a genuine offer of salvation is made to the nonelect by that preaching.

[191] Engelsma, pp. 32, 33.

[192] D. Martin Lloyd-Jones, p. 128.

[193] Ryrie, pp. 322, 323.

[194] *Ibid.*

[195] George S. Bishop, *The Doctrines of Grace* (Grand Rapids, Mich.: Baker Book House, 1977), pp. 159, 160.

[196] Owen, "A Display of Arminianism," *The Works of John Owen*, X, p. 99.

[197] *Ibid.*

[198] This statement is typical of many churches, schools, and mission agencies that profess to believe in four points of Calvinism.

[199] Charles R. Smith, "Did Christ Die Only For the Elect?" (Winona Lake, Indiana: BMH Books, 1975), p. 12.

[200] *Ibid.*, p. 13.

[201] *Ibid.*, pp. 13, 14 (emphasis Smith's).

[202] Charles H. Spurgeon cited by J. I. Packer in *A Quest for Godliness*, p. 345.

[203] Fisk, p. 35. Samuel Fisk himself does not believe in the points of Calvinism as he has described them. He does not believe that election is to salvation. He believes Christ died for all men and rejects "perseverance of saints" in favor of eternal security.

I have found that those who claim to be Calvinistic but hold to less than all five points are usually ignorant of true Calvinism. They hold an election that is based on God's *foreseeing* the believer's faith, not *determining* it. They hold an effectual calling that can be declined by the sinner. They hold a view of man's sin that is less than total depravity. They are really Arminians who think that, because they believe in eternal security or in salvation by grace, they are Calvinists.

[204] George Smeaton, *The Apostles' Doctrine of the Atonement* (Carlisle, Penn.: The Banner of Truth Trust, 1991), pp. 446, 447.

[205] Ryrie, p. 322.

[206] Samuel Rutherford, *Communion Sermons* (Edinburgh, Scotland: James A Dickson, 1986, reprinted from the second edition, Glasgow: Glass and Co., 1877), p. 105. The quote continues:

> Let them be confounded who take this glory from Jesus, and give it over to that weather-cock, free will. For, here is an argument that hell will not answer. The Father promised Christ a seed (Isaiah liii. 10). And a willing people (Psalm cx. 3). And the ends of the earth (Psalm ii. 8) to serve Him as a reward of His sufferings. Now, shall God crack His credit to His Son, and shall Christ do His work and get the wind for His pains, except free will say, amen? There is a bairn's bargain. No, it is a part of Christ's wages, that men's free will shall come with cap in hand, and bow before Him. He shall have a willing people.

[207] When the Scripture says *"able,"* it does not mean that Christ could not save because He had no power but that He could not because He had no authority. Christ came not to do His own will but the will of His Father (John 5:30).

[208] Owen, "The Death of Death" (1850-1853 rpt.), *The Works of John Owen,* Vol. 10 (London: Banner of Truth Trust, 1987), pp. 176, 177.

[209] R. C. H. Lenski, *The Interpretation of St. Paul's Epistle to the Romans,* p. 383.

[210] One could conveniently supply the word *potential* as Dr. John Rice did (see Chapter 8). Either *"all men"* refers to every son of Adam (thus requiring a universal salvation or an altering of the text), or *"all men"* refers to every one of the sons of God in Christ. Take your pick.

[211] A ransom is the price or payment made for our redemption. "This word is derived from the Fr. *rancon*; Lat. *redemptio.* The debt is repre-

sented not as cancelled but as fully paid. The slave or captive is not liberated by a mere gratuitous favour, but a ransom price has been paid, in consideration of which he is set free. The original owner receives back his alienated and lost possession because he has bought it back 'with a price.' This price or ransom (Gr. *lutron*) is always said to be Christ, his blood, his death. He secures our redemption by the payment of a ransom." Online Bible CD ROM Version 7 (Winterbourne, Ontario: Timnathserah, Inc., 1997), Topic Reference #26072.

[212] Here we encounter the doctrine of the imputation of sin. Although it is not my purpose to discuss imputation here, the reader is encouraged to study the various views of imputation. I personally hold what is called the Traducian theory set forth by Augustine. To summarize, this view holds that we received both our bodies and souls through the natural generation of the species. Our sinful nature is inherited from our fathers. Some theologians, on the other hand, believe that God creates every soul immediately at or before birth. This view is not directly supported in Scripture.

Traducianists, however, believe that God created Adam *"a living soul,"* and all other souls, including Eve, have come from Adam. *"And so it is written, The first man Adam was made a living soul; the last Adam was made a quickening spirit"* (I Corinthians 15:45). This view is supported in Paul's teaching about the superiority of the Melchisedekian priesthood over the Levitical priesthood. The law authorized the Levites to collect tithes, but when Abraham paid tithes to Melchisedek, Paul argues that Levi paid tithes, being in the loins of Abraham (Hebrews 7:5-10). Thus, the Traducianists' view has clear Scriptural support.

[213] Cited in Strong, p. 795.

[214] Rice, *Predestined for Hell? No!*, p. 48.

[215] Michael Horton, *Putting Amazing Back into Grace* (Grand Rapids, Mich.: Baker Books, 1994), p. 143.

[216] There are various kinds of love. I do not deny that God loves all His creatures. I deny that God's redemptive love is universal, as many claim John 3:16 teaches. God's redemptive love is reserved for His elect. Compare Deuteronomy 7:6-11 and I John 3:1-3.

[217] Oliver B. Greene, *The Gospel According to John*, I (Greenville, So. Car.: The Gospel Hour, Inc., 1966), p. 165.

[218] J. I. Packer, *A Quest for Godliness*, pp. 137, 138.

[219] Note that all the phrases which speak of God's saving us are passive phrases. We contribute nothing in an active sense to our salvation. It is all of God's grace.

[220] Is *"the world"* in II Corinthians 5:18, 19 everyone of the human race in the broadest possible sense? If so, then it follows logically that the verse teaches that everyone of the human race in the broadest possible sense is saved. Since we know that most of the race is not saved, we must conclude that *world* must not mean every person who ever lived. The *world* here must be limited to believers, both Jew and Gentile, scattered throughout all the world and every generation. Further proof of this is seen in the phrase, *"not imputing their trespasses unto them."* Obviously, not everyone in the world has had his sins remitted. Thus, *world* here can refer only to those to whom trespasses are not imputed.

[221] See F. F. Bruce, *Tyndale New Testament Commentaries, The Epistle of Paul to the Romans* (Grand Rapids, Mich.: Wm. B. Eerdmans Publishing Co., 1963), footnote #1, p. 223.

[222] For example, Hebrews 2:9 states that Christ tasted *"death for every man* [Gk. *pantes*—every one].*"* In commenting on this reference, the late professor of Hebrew at New College, Edinburgh, A. B. Davidson, has written:

> The words *for, i.e.* in behalf of, *every one* have no bearing whatever on the technical question of the extent of the atonement; they are general words, indicating that the Son's death was for the benefit of the "man" or mankind spoken of in vers. 6-8, just as they are taken up again in the "many sons" of ver. 10; comp. the similar words of ver. 15 with the limitation of ver. 17. . . . The Son's tasting death was in behalf of every one, the meaning of which must be ascertained from the contents of vers. 10-18, and from the context, vers. 5-9, which speaks of the Son as He is Head of the new dispensation.

A. B. Davidson, *Hebrews* (Edinburgh: T. & T. Clark, 1959), p. 59.

[223] This is the commonly accepted understanding of the purpose of John's Gospel.

[224] It is important to emphasize again that I believe in evangelism and missions. God clearly commands all His children to be involved in taking His gospel to every person (Mark 16:15).

[225] John Owen, *Communion with God, The Works of John Owen,* V. 2 (Edinburgh: The Banner of Truth, 1965), p. 63.

[226] Fisk, p. 17.

[227] Sumner, p. 7. Does Dr. Sumner believe that the preacher actually saves the sinner or has he confused the terms *effect* and *affect?*

[228] J. I. Packer, *Evangelism and the Sovereignty of God* (Downers Grove, Ill.: InterVarsity Press, 1961), p 37.

[229] Charles. H. Spurgeon, *Lectures to My Students* (Grand Rapids, Mich.: Zondervan Publishing House, 1954), pp. 336, 337.

[230] Charles H. Spurgeon, *The Soul-Winner* (Grand Rapids, Mich.: Associated Publishers and Authors, Inc., 1971), pp. 3, 4.

[231] J. I. Packer, *Evangelism and the Sovereignty of God,* pp. 12, 13.

[232] *Ibid.,* p. 15.

[233] Rice, *Predestined for Hell? No!,* p. 6.

[234] This may sound incredible; however, I heard that teaching with my own ears from a man who later was involved in a scandal that put his moral integrity in serious question.

[235] Pink, *The Sovereignty of God,* p. 201.

[236] *Ibid.,* pp. 201, 202.

[237] Charles H. Spurgeon quoted in *The Sword of the Lord,* Vol. LIX, No. 12, June 4, 1993, p. 5.

[238] Rice, *Predestined for Hell? No!,* pp. 15, 16. It should be noted that Dr. John R. Rice was not trained in theology. He had a literary doctorate (Litt.D.) and an honorary doctorate (D.D.). He was an English teacher before entering the ministry.

[239] *Ibid.* (emphasis added).

[240] *Ibid.,* p. 6.

[241] *Ibid.* Dr. Rice defines "hyper-Calvinism" as the belief in Calvin's doctrine of predestination.

[242] *Ibid.,* p. 6.

[243] *Ibid.*

[244] *Ibid.*, p. 11.

[245] *Ibid.*, p. 25.

[246] *Ibid.*, p. 48.

[247] *Ibid.*, p. 75 (emphasis added).

[248] *Ibid.*, p. 48 (emphasis added).

[249] *Ibid.*, p. 73.

[250] *Ibid.*, p. 79.

[251] *Ibid.*, p. 67.

[252] *Ibid.*, p. 80.

[253] *Ibid.*

[254] *Ibid.*, p.53.

[255] *Ibid.*

[256] *Ibid.*, p. 76.

[257] Rice, *False Doctrines*, p. 287.

[258] *Ibid.*, pp. 287, 288.

[259] Rice, *Predestined for Hell? No!*, p. 91.

[260] *Ibid.*, p. 71. *Propitiation* means that Jesus Christ turned the wrath of God away from sinners because He satisfied God's justice against those sins. If Jesus Christ died for every "poor sinner," then no sinner is subject to God's wrath (John 3:36 *et al*).

[261] *Ibid.*, pp. 47, 48 (emphasis added).

[262] *Ibid.*, p. 39.

[263] Rice, *False Doctrines*, p. 283.

[264] Rice, *Predestined for Hell? No!*, cover blurb.

[265] *Ibid.*, p. 24.

[266] *Ibid.*

[267] *Ibid.*, p. 58 (emphasis added)

SCRIPTURE INDEX

This index represents important texts quoted in this book. Those marked with an asterisk (*) are expounded exhaustively or only slightly. Many more Scriptures quoted or referred to in the text are not listed here.

INDEX

A

Amyraldianism (See also *hypothetic universalism*), 29, 115, 173, 180
anti-creedalism, 38, 173
antinomies, 59, 173
Arians, 11, 174, 198
Arminianism, 5, 9, 15, 18, 24, 26, 29, 30, 31, 32, 38, 39, 45, 75, 115,
    116, 165, 166, 167, 168, 169, 170, 173, 174, 192, 194, 199, 200,
    201, 204, 214, 219
    five points of Arminianism, 30, 31
Arminians, 5, 15, 26, 28, 29, 31, 38, 68, 111, 116, 117, 121, 123, 166,
    171, 180, 199, 200, 204, 211, 220
Arminius, Jacobus, 9, 14, 31, 68, 74, 76, 93, 94, 121, 166, 171, 174,
    175, 184, 185, 189, 203, 209, 210
atonement, substitutionary (See also *limited atonement*), 14, 83, 119,
    121, 122, 130, 132, 133, 134, 136, 161, 174, 186

B

Baptist, 3, 21, 23, 25, 32, 33, 34, 35, 36, 37, 38, 39, 73, 75, 99, 173, 176,
    179, 189, 190, 191, 192, 194, 197, 199, 200, 202, 203, 204, 208
Baptists
    Free Will Baptist, 35
    General Baptist, 35, 208
    Particular Baptist, 35, 204
    pre-Reformation Baptists, 34
    Regular (not General Association of Regular Baptist Churches),
        35, 36, 37, 191
Biblicism, 26, 27, 28

C

Calvin, John, 4, 24, 30, 31, 32, 34, 35, 39, 62, 115, 116, 165, 175, 189,
    205, 209, 217, 218, 223
Calvinism, 4, 5, 18, 20, 21, 22, 23, 24, 25, 26, 28, 29, 30, 32, 33, 34,
    35, 38, 39, 40, 42, 45, 47, 50, 55, 58, 63, 66, 106, 111, 112, 115,
    121, 124, 126, 127, 131, 140, 151, 152, 154, 155, 163, 164, 165,
    166, 167, 168, 169, 170, 171, 172, 175, 180, 185, 190, 194, 197,
    200, 201, 202, 204, 205, 206, 208, 213, 215, 217, 219, 223
    five points of Calvinism (See also *TULIP*), 30, 33, 175, 180, 194,
        197, 202, 206
    hypo-Calvinism (See also *Amyraldianism*), 29, 121, 180, 202

Calvinists, 4, 5, 22, 24, 25, 26, 29, 30, 31, 34, 35, 48, 74, 80, 102, 106, 111, 123, 131, 151, 152, 153, 165, 166, 177, 178, 179, 181, 183, 191, 200, 202, 204, 209, 210, 211, 214, 220

Clark, Gordon, 25, 49, 51, 52

confessions
    Belgic, 31
    London, 35, 194
    New Hampshire, 36
    Philadelphia, 35, 36, 37, 192, 199, 204
    Waldensian, 34
    Westminster, 38, 199

creeds
    Nicene Creed, 11

D

Dort (or Dordt), Canons or Synod of, 11, 28, 31, 32, 126, 166, 175

double jeopardy, 118, 119, 120, 121, 176

double predestination, 75, 90, 176

E

effectual inward calling (See also *irresistible grace; Calvinism, five points of*), 13, 181

egoism, 49, 177, 206

election, 14, 15, 18, 19, 20, 21, 24, 25, 27, 29, 37, 39, 46, 47, 55, 56, 58, 61, 62, 65, 66, 67, 68, 71, 73, 74, 76, 77, 78, 79, 80, 81, 83, 84, 86, 87, 88, 89, 90, 92, 98, 108, 111, 112, 123, 127, 141, 162, 169, 173, 174, 177, 178, 186, 190, 202, 209, 210, 211, 212, 213, 214, 218, 219, 220
    conditional (See also *election, unconditional*), 76
    unconditional (See also *Calvinism, five points of; election, conditional*), 12, 66, 67, 73, 76, 77, 78, 79, 80, 83, 88, 89, 98, 124, 151, 175, 186, 211

empiricism, 8

enablement, divine, 68, 92, 99, 113, 162, 177, 214, 215

Erasmus, Desiderius, 8, 31, 51, 52, 193, 207

eternal security (See also *perseverance of the saints*), 5, 13, 15, 177, 199, 206, 219, 220

evangelicalism, 8, 66, 163, 182, 198
    evangelicals, 5, 15, 20, 22, 26, 51, 74, 93, 106, 116, 127, 138, 156, 162, 171, 198, 215

evangelism, 21, 24, 55, 148, 150, 151, 152, 155, 156, 157, 158, 159, 162, 178, 191, 192, 194, 198, 204, 208, 214, 222, 223

F

faith, 9, 12, 13, 15, 17, 21, 26, 28, 30, 34, 35, 37, 38, 39, 41, 44, 57, 66, 67, 68, 71, 73, 74, 75, 76, 77, 79, 83, 84, 85, 86, 87, 90, 92, 105, 108, 109, 110, 111, 119, 120, 121, 122, 124, 134, 140, 146, 158, 162, 168, 169, 170, 171, 174, 175, 176, 177, 178, 181, 189, 192, 194, 197, 199, 200, 204, 209, 210, 213, 217, 218, 220

Finney, Charles, 9, 198

Fisk, Samuel, 66, 67, 80, 124, 151, 190, 209, 210, 212, 219, 223

foreknowledge, 57, 67, 74, 76, 79, 80, 81, 82, 83, 169, 177, 178

free will, 4, 5, 16, 20, 26, 27, 28, 31, 32, 35, 36, 38, 42, 44, 45, 47, 51, 52, 53, 55, 56, 59, 66, 69, 70, 73, 75, 76, 99, 110, 163, 179, 193, 207, 214, 220

Fuller, Andrew, 35, 152, 182, 190, 204

fundamentalism, 4, 39, 55, 182, 192, 207

    fundamentalists, 26, 39

G

Gill, John, 24, 35, 190, 203, 204

gospel, 4, 7, 8, 9, 10, 11, 12, 13, 14, 15, 16, 19, 20, 21, 22, 23, 25, 27, 28, 29, 30, 32, 33, 34, 40, 41, 42, 44, 45, 58, 64, 65, 67, 68, 74, 75, 76, 77, 78, 80, 83, 86, 89, 97, 98, 99, 103, 104, 106, 107, 108, 109, 110, 111, 112, 113, 116, 117, 121, 137, 138, 144, 146, 148, 149, 150, 151, 152, 153, 154, 155, 156, 157, 158, 159, 160, 161, 162, 163, 169, 171, 173, 174, 177, 178, 179, 180, 181, 183, 184, 189, 190, 191, 192, 194, 198, 200, 201, 202, 205, 208, 210, 211, 214, 215, 216, 218, 219, 221, 222

    new, 8, 42, 45, 163

    old, 9, 11

grace

    prevenient (See also *Wesley, John*), 9, 14, 74, 75, 183, 198, 211

    sovereign, 4, 5, 11, 12, 26, 27, 28, 32, 33, 41, 42, 44, 65, 69, 151, 155, 172, 194, 200, 202, 203, 212, 213, 215

H

humanism (See also *Erasmus*), 8, 9, 39, 40, 41, 66, 67, 75, 76, 127, 180, 213

humanists, 41

hyper-Calvinism, 18, 20, 21, 22, 23, 24, 25, 26, 33, 58, 165, 166, 171, 180, 190, 194, 200, 201, 202, 204, 213, 219, 223

hypothetic universalism (See *Calvinism, hypo-Calvinism*), 28

I

idolatry, 49, 180
inability (See also *total depravity*), 12, 68, 75, 98, 99, 106
interdenominationalism (See also *evangelicalism*), 186
irresistible grace (See also *Calvinism, five points of*), 13, 22, 30, 66, 67, 111, 175, 179, 181

L

limited atonement, 12, 13, 22, 35, 66, 116, 117, 121, 122, 123, 124, 126, 145, 174, 175, 181, 183, 218
Luther, Martin, 17, 31, 34, 35, 51, 52, 53, 73, 192, 193, 207, 211

M

McClain, Alva J., 122
McLachlan, Douglas, 55
monergism, 55, 182
Moody, D. L., 9, 165, 191, 192, 198, 202, 208

N

nonelect (See also *reprobation*), 90, 91, 106, 112, 117, 118, 119, 123, 183, 184, 219

O

Owen, John, 16, 24, 32, 116, 130, 149, 166, 192, 199, 203, 214, 218, 219, 220, 223

P

Pelagianism, 9, 14, 31, 74, 88, 183, 185
Pelagius, 31, 183, 185
perseverance of the saints (See also *Calvinism, five points of*), 13, 14, 166, 175, 178, 183, 199
predestination, 19, 23, 24, 39, 46, 57, 74, 75, 88, 89, 90, 92, 99, 151, 155, 165, 170, 176, 183, 189, 195, 200, 202, 208, 223
providence, 37, 44, 53, 54, 55

R

Reformation, the, 7, 9, 11, 41, 42, 51, 52
    the reformers, 33, 34, 35, 50, 75, 86, 90, 163, 178
regeneration, 8, 13, 26, 69, 76, 80, 86, 92, 100, 103, 110, 111, 112, 113, 177, 182, 185, 186, 214

repentance, 12, 67, 68, 69, 70, 71, 91, 105, 106, 107, 108, 110, 113, 137, 140, 150, 156, 168, 169, 175, 177

reprobation, 88, 90, 92, 172, 184, 202

Rice, John R., 4, 23, 24, 25, 33, 42, 61, 62, 93, 94, 95, 99, 100, 115, 154, 165, 166, 167, 168, 169, 170, 171, 172, 193, 198, 200, 201, 202, 203, 205, 206, 208, 211, 214, 215, 216, 218, 220, 221, 223, 224

Roman Catholics, 197, 207

Ryrie, Charles C., 117, 119, 122, 126, 193, 218, 219, 220

S

sectarianism, 10, 32, 33, 38

Smith, Charles R., 122

sovereignty, of God, 22, 34, 41, 48, 54, 69, 76, 151, 153, 154, 168, 192, 193, 202, 206, 207, 208, 209, 223

Sproul, R. C., 11, 89, 199, 214

Spurgeon, Charles Haddon, 18, 23, 24, 25, 33, 44, 57, 59, 78, 82, 123, 126, 152, 162, 164, 176, 192, 193, 194, 198, 200, 201, 202, 203, 206, 212, 213, 217, 218, 219, 223

Sumner, Robert L., 88, 89, 98, 99, 100, 151, 194, 211, 214, 215, 223

synergism (See also *monergism*), 55, 56, 186

T

Theissen, Henry C., 73, 74, 75, 76, 77, 78, 99, 194, 211, 212

total depravity (See also *Calvinism, five points of*), 12, 14, 66, 67, 74, 175, 186, 220

TULIP (See also *Calvinism, five points of*), 11, 12, 13, 14, 22, 23, 32, 151, 194, 197, 211, 214

U

universalism, 28, 116, 122, 144, 149, 165, 180, 184, 187

W

Warfield, Benjamin, 61, 62

well-meant offer, 21, 22, 117, 180, 186, 202

Wesley, John, 9, 14, 74, 75, 76, 183, 195, 198, 209, 211